1.00

D0364534

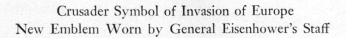

Crusader Symbol of Invasion of Europe
New Emblem Worn by General Eisenhower's Staff

U. S. Army Official Photo

General Dwight D. Eisenhower, Supreme Commander of the Allied Forces

★ ★ ★ ★
Eisenhower
Man and Soldier

MICHIGAN STATE

BY FRANCIS TREVELYAN MILLER

★ ★ ★ ★

RETURN
Cadillac ~~~~~ Public Library

THE JOHN C. WINSTON COMPANY
PHILADELPHIA
TORONTO

MICHIGAN STATE
LIBRARY

A WARTIME BOOK

THIS COMPLETE EDITION IS PRODUCED
IN FULL COMPLIANCE WITH THE GOVERN-
MENT'S REGULATIONS FOR CONSERVING
PAPER AND OTHER ESSENTIAL MATERIALS

Copyright, 1944, by

Ann Woodward Miller

Copyright in Great Britain and in
The British Dominions and Possessions

Copyright in the Philippines

Made in the United States of America

921
E362m
c. 19

Preface

THIS FIRST BIOGRAPHY of General Dwight David Eisenhower is the result of exhaustive research into original sources by a large staff of investigators. We have analyzed the Eisenhower family records, official War Department records, West Point records—visited and talked with his relatives and neighbors, his fellow officers and friends.

These include visits to General Eisenhower's birthplace in Texas, to his family home in Kansas, to his father's birthplace in Pennsylvania, and his mother's birthplace in Virginia.

We feel that this original research performs a service to our country and the world at large in presenting the *human* Eisenhower, the personality and character of the man and soldier who is one of the foremost figures in modern times. It has been our endeavor to present him in the proportions of history with as true perspective as possible with a contemporary subject, to do the pioneering for future historians and biographers.

Our purpose has been to answer these questions: Who is this Eisenhower? Where did he come from? What are his antecedents? What are his characteristics, his habits and customs of mind and conduct? Who are his family? Who are his friends? What do his neighbors say about him? How did he rise so rapidly from a comparatively unknown soldier to the command of the greatest military forces in history?

As a matter of historical record we desire to give credit to those who have cooperated in our effort to build a standard, authoritative work for homes, libraries and schools.

Director of Research: Ann Woodward Miller; research at West Point and in Pennsylvania, Charles Kingsley Fankhauser; research in Kansas, Dr. Charles Moreau Harger, L.H.D., Litt. D., intimate friend of the Eisenhower Family, and Kenneth S. Davis; military research, Werner Loeb; research in London, England, Henry Feinstein.

iii

We are further indebted for advice and records to Lt. Colonel Douglas Parmentier, chief Publications Branch, War Department; Colonel Stanley J. Grogan, deputy director Bureau of Public Relations, War Department; Colonel A. Gibson, librarian, Army War College; Warren O. Smith, War College Library.

Lt. Colonel W. J. Morton, librarian, United States Military Academy at West Point; Colonel Meade Wildrick, officer public relations at West Point; W. J. Wakefield, assistant chief clerk at West Point; Colonel T. D. Stamps, Colonel O. J. Gatchell, professors at United States Military Academy; Claude J. Harris, national historian, and Ed. J. Price, national adjutant, World War Tank Corps Association.

H. Bailey Carroll, Texas State Historical Association; Jessica C. Ferguson, genealogist, State Library and Museum of Pennsylvania; Mrs. J. A. Johnston, Virginia Historical Society; Helen M. McFarland, librarian, Kansas State Historical Society; Lucretia E. Garretson, librarian-genealogist, Iowa State Department of History and Archives; Edna L. Jacobsen, head manuscripts and history, New York State Library.

Harry Burnett, clerk Circuit Court of Augusta County, Virginia; and Mrs. Bessie Burnett; John D. Crowle, Jr., president Staunton Chamber of Commerce; Mr. John W. Wine, authority on the Stovers of Virginia; William O. Harwell, general manager Denison Chamber of Commerce, Texas.

Ross K. Cook, former genealogist-general National Society Sons of American Revolution, and genealogist of Eisenhower family; Ira P. Bromberger, former Treasurer, Dauphin County, Pennsylvania, owner of old Eisenhower Homestead at Elizabethville; E. K. Miller, managing editor of *Elizabethville Echo*; Paul A. Bear, friend of Eisenhowers in Dauphin County.

Governor Coke Stevenson, of Texas; Governor Andrew F. Schoeppel, of Kansas; Governor Edward Martin, of Pennsylvania; Governor Colgate W. Darden, Jr., of Virginia, and all members of the Eisenhower family, his friends and neighbors, whose recollections, reminiscences, and anecdotes are recorded in this volume.

Aug 18 '44 /2.00

Contents

CONTENTS

EXECUTIVE DEPARTMENT
AUSTIN, TEXAS

A TRIBUTE TO GENERAL DWIGHT D. EISENHOWER:

The State of Texas takes keen pride in the fact that it has given to the Nation and to the world one of its great sons as Commander of the Allied Forces on the European front in World War II.

General Dwight D. Eisenhower was born in Denison (Grayson County), Texas, on October 14, 1890.

Texans who know him feel assured that in this world crisis, when the very existence of our Nation and human freedom throughout the world are at stake, the future is in safe hands.

Texas, the largest State geographically in the Union and an empire within itself in natural resources, has given history such notable leaders as Stephen F. Austin, Sam Houston, William Barrett Travis, and other patriots who adopted Texas and her cause.

The State which is the birthplace of General Eisenhower is larger than Germany or France and more than twice as large as Italy. It is far larger than any of the nations which General Eisenhower and his great armies are liberating.

Texas has made an outstanding contribution in fighting manpower in the present war. To date, a total exceeding 568,000 Texas men and women are serving in various branches of our Armed Services.

I take this opportunity to extend around the world our greetings from Texas to our great General and to all of Our Boys fighting under his valiant leadership.

Coke Stevenson

COKE STEVENSON
GOVERNOR

The first Eisenhowers to come to America made their home in this Commonwealth, where the Declaration of Independence and the Constitution of the United States were later to be written.

A generation before the Nation was established the ancestors of General Dwight D. Eisenhower came from the troubled Old World to settle in the Keystone State. Here his father was born and, like many another Pennsylvanian, went forth to join in the settlement and development of the Great West. The Eisenhowers were Pennsylvanians from 1741, establishing their home near York and later at Elizabethville, where the birthplace of the General's father still stands.

It seems to me significant that General Eisenhower, leading our Allied Forces to liberate Europe, is the descendant of men who found in Pennsylvania a refuge from religious and monarchical tyranny. The State where the Liberty Bell first, "proclaimed liberty throughout the land," looks with pride upon this son of Pennsylvanians.

We have full faith that under his leadership the millions of Americans, both from Pennsylvania and other States, will press forward to victory against our foes.

Here where the first flag of freedom was made-- where the first capital of our Nation was established--we bid God-speed to General Eisenhower and every man following this flag.

EDWARD MARTIN
Governor of Pennsylvania

COMMONWEALTH OF VIRGINIA
GOVERNOR'S OFFICE
RICHMOND

COLGATE W. DARDEN, JR.
GOVERNOR

Virginia takes great pride in the
fact that General Eisenhower's mother, Ida
Elizabeth Stover, was born at Mount Sidney, Virginia,
and General MacArthur's mother, Mary Pinkney Hardy,
was born in Berkley, Virginia. Through her distinguished daughters, Virginia is represented by
the two great Generals who now command in widely
separated theatres of World War II.

General Dwight D. Eisenhower in Europe
and General Douglas MacArthur in the Pacific are
defending the cause for which Virginia has stood
throughout the years. They are waging war in
the defense of individual liberty and against
tyranny and oppression. They stand with the great
figures of another day in their gallant crusade.
Virginia salutes them both. They are great sons
of a great Nation and worthy grandsons of an
illustrious Commonwealth.

The story of Kansas, from the early days of the buffalo herds, the Indian and the Explorer, down through the years to the present dark days of World War II, has been a stirring exposition of leadership, of pioneering, and of rugged individualism. It has been a tale of faith and devotion to a belief in the right of things, in the truth of man's destiny, replete with shining examples of heroism, bravery and personal sacrifice of the individual for the welfare of the many.

General "Ike" Eisenhower, the Kansas boy who was destined to wear the four stars of his nation's military rank and who now bears the tremendous responsibility of directing the lives and fates of millions of our youth, is a typical product of the state's leadership.

In him, the strong qualities of courage, vision, wisdom and inspiration have their roots in the pioneer stock which conquered the Kansas plains and prairies and which inspired its offspring to seek its destiny in the light of Divine wisdom and truth.

The nation drew heavily upon Kansas for military leadership during the last World War. Her World War officers included seven generals, including John J. "Black Jack" Pershing, who is claimed by LaCygne, Kansas. These general officers comprise one of the greatest lists of military leaders from one state in the history of our country.

It is fitting that General Eisenhower should have been selected for the gigantic role in world history which he has been called upon to play.

It is fitting that he is a native of Kansas, that he is a product of Kansas courage, intelligence and determination. It is well that in his veins flows the blood of men who believed in God, who sought the truth in living, and whose creed was based upon the Golden Rule of the Bible, rather than upon a false code of personal selfishness and personal gain.

The Abilene farm lad who has grown into one of Kansas' greatest sons is well fitted for the obligation before him. It is well for those whose destinies are in his hands that he is the kind of a man he is; a man who looks to Right for guidance and who has the courage to do what is right despite obstacles and adversity which may beset him.

Kansas is proud of "Ike" Eisenhower. Her sons trust him. The fathers and mothers of those sons also trust him. The entire nation is back of him in his momentous task. Kansas knows that he will not fail. The fathers and mothers know that he will not fail. The sons of Kansas will not fail him.

Andrew F. Schoeppel
Governor of Kansas

Story of the Eisenhowers in war and peace

GENERAL DWIGHT DAVID EISENHOWER, Commander in Chief of the Allied Forces on land, sea, and air in World War II, is the personification of democracy against dictatorship. He is the typical American from the typical American home town who started at the bottom and has worked himself up on his own merits to become one of the most powerful figures in the world today.

The General summed up his own life in a few words at the start of the Second Front: *"Democracy? Look what it has done for me—took me off a Kansas farm—gave me the best education in the world—gave me a chance to make a career for myself."*

As he stood erect, strong, soldierly in his headquarters directing the greatest invasion in history, there was a symbolic insignia on his shoulder—the shield of the modern crusader. This emblem epitomizes at a glance everything he is fighting for: its black background represents the darkness of Nazi oppression. Over it is the sword of the ancient crusaders, flames rising from the hilt and leaping up the blade. This represents avenging justice by which the power of the enemies of democracy will be broken. Above the sword is a rainbow emblematic of hope, containing all the colors of the national flags of the Allies. And above these is an heraldic chief of azure (blue), emblematic of

1

the peace and tranquillity which will be restored to the enslaved peoples.

This is the objective of the United Nations in World War II —the symbol worn by General Eisenhower and all the officers and enlisted men on his staff, American and British, during the great invasion.

General Eisenhower's forefathers came to the New World to escape wars and religious persecutions in the Old World. More than two centuries after they had found peace and security in America, he returned to the Old World to help liberate it from the oppressions and injustices which his own ancestors had fled.

The Eisenhowers have been in America over two hundred years. Theirs is one of the old pioneer families in the settlement and building of the nation. The name was originally spelled Eisenhauer, meaning "hewers of iron." From the contractions, Eisen, meaning iron, and "Ike" as the General is familiarly known, is created the historical cognomen, "IRON IKE."

According to tradition the first Eisenhowers lived on the banks of the Rhine, under the despotic rule of the count palatines, which began in A.D. 945 during the reign of Otto the Great, who later became Emperor of the Holy Roman Empire.

Through the centuries wars raged about them. During the Middle Ages the Palatinate passed from one ruler to another until it fell into the hands of the Kings of Bavaria. For two hundred and fifty years it was subjected to feudal conflicts for power—partitions and divisions—intrigues and bitter strife.

George the Rich was in power in Palatinate Germany when America was discovered. Martin Luther, whose cause was soon to be espoused by the Eisenhowers, was then only nine years old. Great crises were ahead, with long struggles for the spiritual and political domination of the world.

It was shortly after the Thirty Years' War (1618–1648) that the Eisenhowers fled to Switzerland (or, according to another family tradition, to Holland), then as now a refuge for the oppressed. At this same time religious refugees were fleeing to America, where the principles of freedom and the right to worship God "according to one's conscience" were being established.

The Old World was drenched in blood. Religious passions swept the nations. Germany, where the Reformation had set in, was in the midst of the conflict. The war, which began with an invasion of Bohemia by Ferdinand of Austria to claim the throne, spread like a conflagration.

The Hapsburgs, under Tilly and Wallenstein, fought to establish their supremacy over the north of Germany and the Baltics. King Christian of Denmark, and Gustavus Adolphus of Sweden, alarmed by impending dangers, came to the rescue of Germany. Tilly was mortally wounded; Gustavus was killed.

The war evolved from a struggle for religious control into a mighty conflict for political supremacy between the Hapsburgs of Austria aided by Spain, and France aided by Sweden. England remained neutral. At the end of the thirty years the Hapsburgs were defeated. Their hopes of converting Germany into a consolidated Hapsburg empire were destroyed.

The Peace of Westphalia, in 1648, ended the conflict. It was in this treaty, among its many provisions, that Swiss independence was recognized; Holland received its independence; Alsace was given to France; the German States were granted their religious and political rights.

Whether or not any of the Eisenhowers in the Palatinate were engaged in this war is not known, but the refugees who had fled either to Holland or Switzerland escaped the carnage. The Swiss, however, were to find themselves in the social and economical revolution known as the Peasant War, the towns against the farmers, when the burghers imposed heavy taxes against the country people.

The spirit of freedom was brewing in America. The first

"Toleration Act" was passed in Maryland; Roger Williams founded Rhode Island upon the basis of complete religious tolerance, a "shelter for persons distressed in conscience"; William Penn, a Quaker whose life was dedicated to peace and Christian brotherhood, founded Pennsylvania. This was the haven to which the Eisenhowers were to come.

Tides of immigration brought shiploads of pioneers to this new land of promise. Aboard these vessels were many Welsh Quakers bound for Penn's Woods. Dutch, Swedes, Finns, began to arrive. Germans, led by Pastorius, agent for the Frankfort Land Company, settled on the six thousand acres granted to them. Mennonites welcomed Penn's offer of "an asylum across the seas where they might worship God without further molestation." Religious freedom was guaranteed to all "who shall profess and acknowledge one Almighty God."

Over the sea came French Huguenots, Scotch-Irish, Hollanders, Swiss, English, German separatists, Schwenkfelders, Moravians, Dunkards, Mennonites. They set up their sawmills and tanneries; they tilled the soil and reaped their crops of grain and foodstuffs; they erected flour mills and mined minerals from the earth. They engaged in iron mining, built furnaces and forges.

One day (and here the records conflict, one stating 1732, the other 1741) a sailing vessel came into the harbor at Philadelphia, after a long voyage across the Atlantic. Among the passengers was a young man twenty-five years of age—John Peter Eisenhower, from Switzerland, great-great-great-great-grandfather of General Dwight David Eisenhower. The General is the sixth generation of Eisenhowers in America. According to family tradition, John Peter Eisenhower settled in the valley of the Susquehanna River, "probably near York."

As John Peter Eisenhower landed in the New World he found himself in the city of "brotherly love." He left behind him an almost endless chain of wars. When he was born in 1716,

Charles XII of Sweden was invading Norway. During his childhood and youth Hungary and Turkey were at war; the War of the Polish Succession was fought; the War of the Austrian Succession started.

Here in America he was to find a nation in its birth throes. He had come here a generation before the American Revolution. In their succeeding generations the Eisenhowers were to live through every great event in the building of the nation, the explorations and expansion of the thirteen original colonies to forty-eight States spreading over a continent, the development of the world's most powerful democracy. And their days of peace were to be intermittently broken by wars.

General David Dwight Eisenhower was born in Denison, Texas, on October 14, 1890, son of David Jacob Eisenhower, born in Elizabethville, Pennsylvania, on September 23, 1863, and Ida Elizabeth Stover, born at Mount Sidney, near Staunton, Virginia, on May 1, 1862. His father was the son of Jacob F. Eisenhower, born September 19, 1826, and Rebecca Mather, born March 20, 1825. Jacob F. was the son of Frederick Eisenhower, born about 1787, and Elizabeth Millerin, born about 1786. He in turn was the son of Frederick Eisenhower, born October 6, 1753. And Frederick was the son of John Peter Eisenhower, who came to this country between 1732 and 1741.

We will now take a journey to Elizabethville, Pennsylvania, meet the Eisenhower kin, examine their records, and visit the "God's Acre" where many Eisenhowers rest in peace.

· 2 ·

First Eisenhowers in America—old home in Pennsylvania

OUR FIRST PILGRIMAGE to Eisenhower landmarks in America takes us to a quaint little village, nestling peacefully in Lykens Valley, Dauphin County, in the heart of Pennsylvania.

Elizabethville, as serenely romantic as its name, is the old home of General Dwight Eisenhower's father and grandfather. As we walk along the old brick sidewalks, under spreading shade trees, passing sturdy brick houses with green lawns and flower gardens, it is difficult to believe that some three thousand miles away a grandson of this village is leading one of the world's greatest fighting forces in the world's greatest war.

Here, in this pastoral quiet, live some 1,300 people, the kind of folk who are the backbone of the nation. Upon them, and those in thousands of like communities throughout the country, we must depend for the strength and character of our nation's future. Honest, thoughtful, considerate of the rights of others, sympathetic and firm in their religious principles, these home towns are the soul of America.

Elizabethville, named by its founder, John Bender, in honor of his wife, Elizabeth, is surrounded by fertile farms, operated by hard-working, thrifty farmers who raise general crops—

6

corn, wheat, oats, rye, hay, potatoes, fruit, chickens and beef cattle.

Strangers seldom come to Elizabethville; it is away from the passenger railroad service. The nearest towns are Millersburg, nine miles to the west on the Susquehanna River, and Lykens, six miles to the east, occupying 67 acres purchased for $19.90 before the discovery of anthracite in the near-by Short Mountains. Just beyond is Williamstown, a mountain-locked coal town on a site once offered for five thousand shingles and subsequently traded for a span of horses. Twenty-five miles to the south is Harrisburg, capital of the great Commonwealth of Pennsylvania.

As we pass down the village streets in Elizabethville, we see many flags bearing stars in the windows of these old homes. Their sons—more than 127 of them—are far away on the battlefronts of World War II, fighting with the armies of liberation, on fighting planes and bombers dropping death and destruction from the clouds, or on battleships, destroyers and submarines in Uncle Sam's mighty fleet. Some of these boys are with General Eisenhower on the Second Front or with General MacArthur fighting in the island jungles of the Pacific. And Elizabethville sent seventy sons to fight for their country in World War I.

We come to an old-style red-brick house, surrounded by shrubbery and trees. This is the Eisenhower homestead in which the General's father was born. Built by the General's grandfather in 1854 (the year Lincoln challenged Douglas to debate the issues confronting the nation), it is now a landmark in Elizabethville.

Grandfather Jacob F. Eisenhower was a preacher-farmer, pastor in the Brethren in Christ Church, a religious sect which, like the Dunkards, believe in the simple life, plain living, and frugality. He and his wife Rebecca purchased one hundred acres and built this homestead.

The exact purchase price of the land, as recorded on deeds at the Dauphin County Courthouse, was $3,698.46¾. This three-quarters of a cent is testimony to the rigorous honesty of these good folk. The price was figured by acres and perches to the exact fraction of a penny. How the three-quarters of a cent was paid is not known, but probably something having the exact value of three-quarters of a penny was given to the owner, even though it might be nothing more than an egg.

Pastor Eisenhower erected a nine-room house on the property and sold it twenty-four years later for $8,500. With this money, paid in cash, the family removed to Kansas. Jacob and his wife Rebecca entered into an agreement with David Kolva, a blacksmith in Elizabethville, by which the Eisenhowers traded four acres of land for "shoeing his wagon."

Entering the old homestead, now owned and occupied by Ira P. Romberger, former treasurer of Dauphin County, we meet a most hospitable host. He and his charming wife tell us the story of the Eisenhower House.

"General Eisenhower's grandfather built this house for two purposes," says Mr. Romberger, "as a home and a meeting house. On the first floor the Brethren in Christ, frequently but not wholly accurately called the Dunkards, held their religious services and love feasts. They gathered here in their severe garb and worshipped God. This was done for humility and to follow the example set by Christ when he washed the feet of His disciples as recorded in the thirteenth chapter of St. John. There are still Dunkards in Dauphin County who knew Grandfather Eisenhower and came to this house to worship with him.

"Once a year they held a love feast in the big room. They came from far and wide, from fifty to seventy-five miles, and stayed two days, preaching, praying, eating and sleeping. When the house was filled they went to the barn to sleep.

"On the third floor is the attic, which the Eisenhowers kept open for strangers and travelers who passed this way. If a vagrant or a beggar knocked at the door, he was welcomed by Pastor Eisenhower and invited in. He never turned anybody away. He was always kind to them, fed them, and slept them in the attic, where he also repaired the children's shoes."

Mr. Romberger, while preserving the old homestead, has made alterations necessary for modern living. The entrance opens into a hallway with a Colonial stairway to the second floor. On the first floor is a large living-room, library, dining-room, breakfast room and kitchen, with washroom and toilet. Upstairs there are four bedrooms and two bathrooms. When the Eisenhowers lived here they heated the old living-room with a stove—of course there never was heat upstairs. They got their water from the never-failing spring in the backyard.

"The Eisenhowers of the old days knew nothing about modern comforts," Mr. Romberger remarks. "Bathrooms and heating systems were unknown to them. During their simple lives they would have considered them as unnecessary luxuries, probably never intended by God."

The old Eisenhower farm, too, has been transformed. Magnificent spreading pine trees line both sides of the driveway. Beautiful maple trees stand like sentinels guarding the old home. The barn and outbuildings stand about two hundred yards from the house. Here the Eisenhowers stored their crops.

General Eisenhower's father, as we shall see, left this homestead and joined the pioneers on the trails to the Great West. Ten years before he died he came back to visit his birthplace in Elizabethville. Here he sat down in the living-room and recalled his boyhood days after being away for more than a half century. While he related his memories of the meetings in the big room, he remarked, "Those were great days! Their teachings still remain in the family. Two of my brothers have been pastors in Kansas."

He walked about the old home town to see if he could find "anybody I know." Great was his pride when he recognized and called by name three boyhood friends grown old.

There are "twenty or thirty" kin of the Eisenhowers still living around Elizabethville. With humility and meekness they take justified pride in their famous kinsman. For some years they have held Eisenhower reunions. In 1941 they gathered at the Heidelberg Grove in York County; on another year the Eisenhower clan met in the park at Elizabethville.

On Sunday, after church services, we visited with his kinfolk "back home." At the home of Mrs. Emma Keefer, in Millersburg, we met second cousin Homer C. Bechtel; also Mrs. Oliver Bechtel. There were fourteen in the little group, six of them Dunkards, or as they prefer to call themselves, Brethren in Christ. All plainly dressed, they reminded one of a little gathering of Swiss or Holland Dutch. We met another second cousin, Ira Bechtel, who lives across the street from the old Eisenhower homestead.

"We must straighten out the Eisenhower genealogy," remarked Paul A. Bear, of Mt. Wolf, York County. "The traditions in some branches say the Eisenhowers came to America from Switzerland, and others say it was from Holland. But the Eisenhowers are here, and that's the thing of most importance."

Mr. Romberger had a transcript from Jacob F. Eisenhower's old family Bible. On it were inscribed the names of more than twenty of his loved ones. Their dates spanned the lifetime of the nation.

We visited the little Keefer Cemetery, near Free Grace Church, between Elizabethville and Millersburg. Here, on simple, moss-covered tombstones we found inscribed the names of Eisenhowers from the year 1789, when George Washington became first President of the United States. Under the green grass mounds lay Barbary, John D., Anny, John H., Samuel F., Peter A., Lydia A., Emma J., Clinton, Elizabeth, Leah Jane.

Among them were four sons and two daughters of Jacob and Rebecca Eisenhower, grandparents of General Eisenhower, who lie a thousand miles away in Belle Spring Cemetery near Abilene, Kansas. Here in Elizabethville lie the wife and son and daughter of Frederick Eisenhower, great-grandfather of General Eisenhower, who rests in Belle Spring in faraway Kansas.

> Beneath those rugged elms, that yew-tree's shade,
> Where heaves the turf in many a moldering heap,
> Each in his narrow cell for ever laid,
> The rude forefathers of the hamlet sleep. . . .

Villagers of Elizabethville, folk who knew General Eisenhower's father and grandfather, told us many stories. Philip Eberly, in his eighty-third year, said, "I knew the Eisenhower's well. The General's grandfather was a great soul. There were four boys and three girls in the family. I played with them when I was a boy. They had one hundred hives of bees, maybe more, on their farm. And they had a vineyard and sold grapes—but they did *not* make any wine."

The venerable gentleman recalled his childhood. "I went to meetings in the Eisenhower home. They were all good people, so kind and always ready to help others. Just the kind of people you would like to have for neighbors. They never quarreled, never got into any trouble—no! no!—just fine Christians.

"Amanda was the sixteen-year-old girl—just my age. We used to hide eggs for Easter. She was a grand little girl, loyal and true. She's living now out in Kansas and writes letters about her happy childhood days in Elizabethville. I saw them when they left here for Kansas in 1878. I can see them now waving good-by as the train pulled out. We had trains here then, but about eighteen years ago they stopped carrying passengers."

Edward Paul, septuagenarian, said, "I was only four years old when the Eisenhowers went to Kansas. I lived in the old home for a while. I remember the family, how I played with the children. I was too young to get much of an impression, but they remain in memory as wonderful people."

Mrs. Kate Romberger holds fond recollections. "I was the girlhood friend of Amanda," she says. "We were inseparable companions. She was a lovely girl, so gentle and thoughtful, like all the Eisenhowers. I loved them all and missed them so when they went away."

One of the second cousins of the Eisenhowers, James E. Lentz, called on us. "I can't tell you much," he said. "My cousins left Elizabethville before I was born. Of course, I know the family traditions and the dispute whether we came here from Switzerland or Holland. Wherever it was, it looks as if General Eisenhower has gone back to liberate them. He's a great man and we're proud to be his kin."

The story of the spelling of the name—whether Eisenhower, Eisenhour, or Eisenhaur—is told by Hugh Oscar Eisenhower, of Gastonia, North Carolina, in a letter to Mr. Paul Bear, who corresponds with Eisenhowers throughout the country, including the General's wife and brothers.

"Some good-looking schoolteacher, named Miss Coffin, persuaded my grandfather to change the spelling to Eisenhower, and he wished all of us would spell it that way thereafter.

"There was an Eisenhower with General George Washington at the surrender of Cornwallis, on October 19, 1781," Mr. Bear informed us. "It was George Eisenhaur, or Isenhour, progenitor of the Carolina Eisenhowers. He first came to Pennsylvania and later moved to North Carolina, settling on land granted to him by the King of England near Taylorville, in Alexander County.

"The only other Revolutionary records I have is one of Frederick Eisenhaur who enlisted April 15, 1776, as a private in

Captain Peter Grubb Jr's. company of Miles Regiment at Lancaster, Pennsylvania.

"There were many Eisenhowers in the Civil War. My grandfather, Solomon Eisenhower, was with Company A, Fourth Minnesota Volunteer Infantry; he was from York County, Pennsylvania. Two of my great-uncles, brothers from York County, were in the Civil War: William H. Eisenhower, member of the '100-Day Men of Ohio,' and Benjamin Eisenhower. B. F. Eisenhower and Valentine Eisenhower, brothers, from Dauphin County, fought in the Civil War.

"Franklin and Samuel Eisenhower were both in Company F, 92nd Regiment, Ninth Cavalry, enlisting from Lancaster, Pennsylvania. Valentine E. Eisenhower and I. J. Eisenhower were first sergeants in Company A, 210th Regiment, Pennsylvania Volunteer Infantry, both from Dauphin County. William M. Eisenhower was a first lieutenant and James Eisenhower a sergeant in Company B, 128th Regiment, both from Berks County, Pennsylvania."

Elizabethville, with only 1,300 people, has its weekly newspaper, "The Elizabethville Echo," which holds the community together in common interests. It records what is going on in the schools, churches, and homes of the village, keeping them informed on what "our boys" are doing on the war fronts. It recently published a "Roll of Honor," three columns long, of the names of residents of Elizabethville and other neighboring communities serving in the nation's armed forces.

We stopped to visit its friendly editor, Eugene K. Miller, and found a keenly intelligent and well-informed journalist on national and world events as well as local.

"We are, of course, honored by the fact that General Eisenhower is the grandson of Elizabethville," he said. "This makes our home town a landmark." He talked about the background of the Eisenhower family in Dauphin County. Elizabethville was at one time two settlements, the eastern section first called "Cross Roads" and later "Washington Square," and the western section known as "Benderschtettle," the English equivalent is "Bender Town."

"My father, Milton A. Miller, and Clement B. Stroup were boyhood friends of General Eisenhower's father, David Eisenhower. He was only fifteen years old when he went with his family to Kansas. David and his sister Amanda competed with my father in 'spelling bees.' And there were singing circles and strawberry festivals, corn-husking parties and sleigh rides."

When Jacob Eisenhower was a boy there were three little old-fashioned schoolhouses in Elizabethville and nearby communities, and six schools conducted in private homes; also a seminary. When Jacob was eight years old there was great excitement in the village. A railroad, sixteen miles long, passed through the town from Lykens to Millersburg, with cars drawn by mule or horse over flat, strap rails. This was the fourth railroad in the nation to haul hard coal.

Religion is the dominating force in Elizabethville today, as it was in the days of the early Eisenhowers. There are four churches in the village: Lutheran, Reformed, United Brethren in Christ, and Evangelical; two banks, a mutual fire insurance company, and seven industries—the Swab Wagon Company, a shirt manufacturing company, a dress manufacturer, a flour mill, blacksmith shops, and a weekly newspaper.

As we leave the old Eisenhower homestead, we can almost imagine that we can see Jacob Eisenhower and his wife Rebecca (grandparents of General Dwight D. Eisenhower), with little David (who became the General's father) and Amanda, and all the other little Eisenhowers, turning back on that day in 1878 to give a farewell glance, starting the long journey to Kansas.

· 3 ·

Letters from "Amanda" to the folk "back home"

SITTING IN HER "little gray home in the west," sixty-four years after the Eisenhowers left Elizabethville, Pennsylvania, is a gentle lady with snow-white hair—Amanda, the sixteen-year-old Amanda, now eighty three—the sister of the fifteen-year-old David who grew up to become the father of General Dwight Eisenhower.

General Eisenhower often speaks of his Aunt Amanda, whose keen mind, amazing memory, sense of humor, love of humanity, and remarkable vitality are fast becoming folklore in the family. The little belle of Elizabethville is now a venerated patriarch in Abilene, Kansas. Nearly a half century ago she married "a boy from back home," C. O. Musser, from a Pennsylvania Dutch family in Lancaster County.

Aunt Amanda is an "armchair general" herself, and follows the movements of her illustrious nephew like a strategist. Now the first in rank of years of all the Eisenhowers, she conducts a wide correspondence with kith and kin. We are privileged here to present some of her letters. The first in this collection were written in legible and steady hand to Mr. Ira P. Romberger, who preserved the old Eisenhower homestead in Elizabethville.

15

These letters give a clear insight into the Eisenhower character; they are a home-loving, peace-loving family. Writing from her home in Abilene, Kansas, on January 22, 1943, when General Eisenhower was in North Africa with President Roosevelt and Prime Minister Churchill at the Casablanca Conference, she says:

What a thrill I got this morning when I received three letters all from dear old Pennsylvania, my birthplace. I am especially happy to write to you since you occupy the old house which my father built. I never knew any other home while living in Pennsylvania. I was in my sixteenth year when we left there, and I distinctly remember when we were on the train for the West how I wept as if my heart would break to leave all my old schoolmates and go I knew not where. . . . Only myself and my three brothers younger than I were born in the old brick house which stands there.

How I would love to go through it with you and show you which was my room and all the other things which come popping into my memory. The long room (unless it was changed) was built to hold meetings in. . . .

Yes, sir, David J. Eisenhower, the father of General Dwight Eisenhower, was born in that house. I well remember when my youngest brother was born; he was a twin but the one Clinton died very young and is buried in what was known as the Keefer Cemetery; it is close to the Horace Grace Church. There are others of our family buried there. It certainly was lovely of you to invite us to be guests at your house, when coming East, but at our age I think our traveling days are about over. We have made a good many trips back home, but since Mr. Musser's people live in Lancaster County, and near Harrisburg, we usually put in most of our time there.

The last time we called at the old home, where Mr. Isaiah Speck then lived, was about ten years ago, but he not being home, Mrs. didn't know us. We didn't get to see the house inside, but I walked around the house, hoping to get a drink out of the old spring, but it all was changed. I saw a ladder standing at a cherry tree with ripe big red ones. I ventured up the ladder and had a taste.

Now, in getting back to the old farm, I do remember very

distinctly when Mr. Jeremiah Speck came and bought the farm, and I think paid *cash* for the same. I want you to look at the deed from my father to Mr. Speck and see the mark X my mother made. It was a custom in those days. The wife would get the sum of one dollar for her service of signing the deed.

We left there in 1878, and the ones who were then babies are now the old people, and the Eisenhowers are forgotten. . . . My brother David J. was buried almost a year ago. I miss him so much. Since I am the only one here, Abraham lives in California and Ira lives in Topeka, Kansas, I want to give you a little information about Dwight's family.

Dwight has a wife and one son, who is in school at West Point; looks as if he were going in his father's footsteps. He is a brilliant chap. The mother is living in Abilene, Kansas. She keeps a maid, for she is not able to stay alone.

We have a friend or two living in Millersburg, Pennsylvania. One is Robert Kopenhaven who worked at the Belle Springs Creamery Company when my husband was butter maker and my brother David also worked there. . . . Should you ever come this way look us up. We live on a farm, but do not farm. We are supposed to be retired, but there are always so many things which need attention. . . . With best wishes to you and yours,

Mrs. Amanda Eisenhower Musser.

Here is a letter written on January 29, 1943, when General Eisenhower's American forces, with the British under General Montgomery, were attacking Tunis and Bizerte and driving the Nazi fox, Rommel, before them:

Greeting. This letter writing is getting immensely interesting to me at least. If I could only express myself better, but just remember you are corresponding with an old lady who has had only a common country school education.

Now did I have another thrill when you said "Milton Miller"—we were schoolmates. One outstanding incident comes to my mind. In those days we used to have spelling schools and Milton Miller and Clem Stroup were our champion spellers. If they first chose Miller the other side *always* chose Stroup. You didn't say if he is still living—if so give him my kindest regards; if not, bestow it upon his son. His father and mine used to have things in common; he had some office but I don't recall what it was. . . .

Wouldn't it be interesting if everyone kept a diary. Our oldest daughter does that and many times she turns to it for information. Did I know Philip Eberley? Yes! And all the rest, Mr. and Mrs. and his brother Dan. They lived in my father's house in the corner of the farm. . . . Philip spent much time with my brother and come near Easter time these boys amused themselves by gathering the hen fruit and hiding it somewhere in the barn, so there would be plenty for Easter. There is more to it but I must not put it on paper for sometimes other people get to read our letters. . . .

Give my regards to Philip. I try to think of all of them, but when one doesn't know if they are alive or have gone to their long home, one kind of forgets about them. . . . Here is another thing to prove that I lived in the old brick house: Up in the attic there was a small room, in it my shoes, also a bed which we called The Beddle Man's Bed. If you aren't Dutch enough to know what it means ask Mr. Paul. Perhaps there are no tramps any more, at least they don't come around here like they used to. My father also was a preacher in the Brethren in Christ Church, also my two youngest brothers are preachers. Are there any of the Speck family living yet? I must bring my epistle to a close or it will find its way into the waste basket. Any more questions? I shall be happy to answer as far as possible.

Amanda Eisenhower Musser.

When General Eisenhower's air forces were bombing Sardinia and the Italian islands in the Mediterranean, and he was organizing his army for the terrific battle at Kasserine Pass, Aunt Amanda in one sentence mentions the war on March 17, 1943:

We received a letter from a Mr. Peifer from Harrisburg and he gave a history of the Eisenhowers from as far back as 1777. All these letters and papers and pictures are appreciated by us. Our family consists of two girls, married. One grandchild, a son who was called into the army about a year ago. We are hoping and praying this cruel war will soon come to a close. . . .

Mrs. C. O. Musser.

General Eisenhower's forces had won the battle for Kasserine Pass, and were battering their way toward the capture of Tunis, slowly but surely driving the Axis out of North Africa, when Aunt Amanda mentioned it in the paragraph at the end of this letter on March 16, 1943:

Greetings—Received the generous package of most beautiful pictures [of the Eisenhower homestead]. I have looked them over and over and all that looks natural of the old home is the front. Of course it all looks beautiful. I would love to take a peep into the inside but I know that is about perfect. For one can usually judge by the outside. But the man on the front porch almost hidden by the snow-covered cedar trees, he looks a bit lonesome. There certainly should be some fair maiden who would love to share a beautiful mansion like you possess. Of course if you prefer to have it that way that is your own choosing.

My youngest daughter admired the pictures so much. That kind of house is according to her ideas. So I let her have one of the smaller ones. We called there when she was three years old, so of course she doesn't remember. . . . Don't be too much surprised if some airplane will drop near there some day. . . .

We are considering leaving the farm. It should be a good time to sell now. So we had a chance to buy a small brick house at a bargain the other day and we will make arrangements to sell the farm. Mr. Musser contracted asthma lately and is unable to take care of this place. We have a large lawn which has to be mowed quite often during the summer and also we like to raise our own vegetables and it all takes labor. . . . We decided it would be best to move back to town. . . .

I suppose General Dwight is having a tough time. We are still hoping for victory. . . . We certainly appreciate all the nice things you have done for us thus far and also your acquaintance in honor of the old homestead. With best wishes,

Mrs. C. O. Musser.

Occasionally in letters to intimate friends, Aunt Amanda wrote about Dwight. Generally she directed her attention to affairs at home, where the members of the family were scattered, what they were doing.

· 4 ·

Birthplace of mother of General Eisenhower in Virginia

Leaving the eisenhowers in Pennsylvania, we make our next pilgrimage to old Virginia to visit the landmarks of General Eisenhower's mother's family. Eisenhower, like General MacArthur, comes on his maternal line from the grand Old Dominion which produced Washington, Jefferson, Madison, Monroe, Lee, and a long line of great Americans.

Our journey leads to Augusta County, Virginia, where General Eisenhower's mother, Ida Elizabeth Stover Eisenhower, was born on May 1, 1862, in the little hamlet of Mount Sidney, near Staunton (the birthplace of President Woodrow Wilson).

The Stovers, too, have been in America more than two hundred years. Pioneers in the New World, as were the Eisenhowers, they span the life of the nation, reaching back into the Old World to traditions fading away in the eleventh century.

Before going to Mount Sidney, stop at Staunton, set in the heart of the beautiful and historic Shenandoah Valley, in the foothills of the Blue Ridge Mountains. It is a city of some 12,000 people, with old homes of mellowed brick and impressive modern residences surrounded by foliage and gardens, with churches, educational institutions, industries and outlying farms and orchards.

20

Not far away are five famous caverns and near by is Natural Bridge and its neighboring town of Lexington, where General Robert E. Lee lived as president of Washington and Lee University, and where General Stonewall Jackson lived as superintendent of the Virginia Military Institute, from which General George C. Marshall, our Chief of Staff in World War II, was graduated.

General Eisenhower's forebears settled here in Augusta County sometime between the years 1727 to 1732. It was a stout and sturdy race that laid the foundations in Colonial days on the trail of Indian hunters. There was a great tide of emigration moving through here; forward-looking men and their families passed this way on horseback, or in carts and wagons, frequently filled with flaxen-haired children. When asked where they were headed they never failed to answer, "To the Ohio!"

Here the Stovers lived through the generations, through the American Revolution, the War of 1812, the Mexican War, the Spanish-American War, and the Civil War. From here Stovers went into World War I and are fighting in World War II. And here today are kinfolk of General Eisenhower's mother.

Go out now in apple-blossom time, while General Eisenhower is across the seas commanding the Second Front, and visit Mount Sidney. Here, on the hillside, is the old farmhouse where Mother Eisenhower (then Ida Elizabeth Stover) was born eighty-three years ago. Here she lived with her father, Simon P. Stover, her mother, Elizabeth J., and her brothers and sisters—there were nine in the family, her parents and the seven children.

The old house, photographed for this book, is typical of its time in the Shenandoah Valley. It is surrounded by fertile acres of farmland, with orchards and stately trees. In apple-blossom time, with cherry trees and peach trees in bloom, it is a vista of simple beauty. Not far away is the old Limestone schoolhouse where the girl who was to become the General's mother went to school.

We shall hear Mother Eisenhower relate some of her recollections about the old home and school when we meet her in Kansas, where she lives while her world-famous son is commanding his armies in the liberation of Europe.

Meet some of the folk who knew General Eisenhower's mother as a girl in Augusta County, and others who aided in giving us the historical facts. Here is the courtly John W. Wine, who was a childhood friend of Ida Elizabeth Stover. This is what he tells us:

"I am seventy-five years old and I knew Ida Stover and all her family intimately when they were living on a farm near me in Augusta County. We went to school together in the old Limestone schoolhouse. Ida was a very pretty girl with light hair, very vivacious and attractive, and indeed quite charming. Her brother, J. Worth Stover, was her schoolteacher. Ida was a bright student and very popular in our little community. She was the life of the parties we used to hold at each other's homes and attended the nearby Salem Lutheran Church, where she was quite active.

"As a boy, I used to spend much time at the old house where Ida was born. When her folks died, she went to live with her Uncle William Link. We all called him Uncle Billy. Ida lived with the Links from the time she was seven years old until she was eighteen. Years later I bought that old house from Uncle Billy and made it my own home. I remember when Ida's cousin, Mary Ann Link, married Emanuel Beam and went west and took Ida with them—she was just twenty. That's the last time I ever saw her. I've stayed right here in the farm country where the Stovers and the Links once lived. They were mighty fine people."

Mr. Wine acted as guide to the old Stover landmarks when John D. Crowle, Jr., president of the Staunton and Augusta County Chamber of Commerce, took the photographs of the

Birthplace of General Eisenhower's mother, near Staunton, Virginia.
Photo by courtesy of Harry Burnett, Clerk Circuit Court of Augusta County. Taken by John D. Crowle, Jr., President of Staunton and Augusta County Chamber of Commerce

Birthplace of General Eisenhower in Denison, Texas. Photo by courtesy of H. Bailey Carroll, Texas State Historical Association, and William D. Harwell, of the Denison Chamber of Commerce

Old Eisenhower homestead in Elizabethville, Pennsylvania. Private photo, courtesy of Ira P. Romberger, present owner

International News Photo

The upper photograph shows the invasion leader at the age of ten, with his
and mother and five brothers. "Ike" is at the extreme left. The lower photog
of the same family group was taken in 1926

Press Association

birthplace of the mother of General Eisenhower and the old Limestone schoolhouse which she attended. Mr. Crowle, a typical Virginian, in the insurance and banking business in Staunton, makes a hobby of "taking pictures" and graciously assisted in collecting historical records for this book.

Visit the Circuit Court of Augusta County, in Staunton, where you meet scholarly Harry Burnett, Clerk of the Court, who has been on duty in the courthouse for nearly fifty years. He knows everybody and is recognized as the authority on the history of this section of Virginia. With him you meet his wife, Bessie Burnett, who does the research in the office.

Delving into the old birth records we find this entry: *"May 1st 1862—White—Female—Parents, Simon P. Stover—Elizabeth J. Stover."*

No name is given for the child, she apparently had not been named when the birth was recorded, but this is the baby girl who was to become the mother of General Dwight D. Eisenhower.

Among these records we dig up the will of Simon P. Stover, General Eisenhower's grandfather, proved on January 26, 1874, leaving his estate in the hands of his son, Charlie, to care for the family from the proceeds of the farm.

Continuing our search, we come upon the "settlement of Daniel Stover," General Eisenhower's great-grandfather, dated January 18, 1862, which gives the heirs of his son, Simon, as follows: "John F.—Jacob W.—Charles W.—Joseph W.—Simon C.—Elizabeth."

And here is another will, dated August 13, 1811. It is the last testament of an earlier Daniel Stover, General Eisenhower's great-great-grandfather. He left his property to his sons, Jacob —David—Daniel—Simon—Samuel (all Biblical names) and a daughter Elizabeth. To Daniel he left "my German Bible."

The earliest of these Stover records is that of Jacob, who evidently arrived in the 1730's and later obtained a grant of "5,000 acres in East Rockingham." This was the great-great-great-grandfather of General Eisenhower.

Researches at the Virginia Historical Society, in the historic Lee House, in Richmond, reveal confirmative information. Mrs. J. A. (Rebecca) Johnston, assistant secretary, says, "This society was among the earliest to give the line of General MacArthur's mother. We are equally glad to give leads about General Eisenhower's mother's family. The Stovers were very numerous in Augusta County. You will find much of interest about the Reverend John Caspar Stoever, first minister of the German Lutherans in Augusta County. He had come (early in the 1730's) as a missionary; his son, a theological student, accompanied him."

We discover that a Peter Stover in 1799 (the year of George Washington's death) left land and $10,000 to the community of Strasburg, in the Shenandoah Valley, which was at one time known as Staufferstadt (Stovertown). And again we come across the record: "In 1729 Jacob Stover received a grant of 5,000 acres along the South Fork of the Shenandoah River at the base of Massanutten Mountain"; also the statement that "a group of German-Swiss settlers founded along the river a colony known as Massanutten Town."

This Jacob Stover, as we have seen in the Court House records at Staunton, was the direct progenitor of General Eisenhower six generations back. This brings the Stovers into Virginia three years before Reverend John Caspar Stoever arrived. It is probable, therefore, that he was a brother or relative of Jacob. This record would further indicate that these migrating Stovers came from the branch in Switzerland, kinfolk of the Stovers in Bavaria and Baden. That they were all of the same family is indicated by the fact that they came to the same region about the same time. There are further records that point toward Jacob Stover first going to Pennsylvania before coming down to Virginia.

General Eisenhower's maternal forebears, who had settled in the wilderness with the first white men to trod this ground, found themselves on the "road of history."

George Washington, after making a trip to Augusta County, said, "The western part of Virginia, more especially around the Blue Mountains, in my opinion will be considered, if not considered so already, the garden spot of America. Forasmuch as it lies between the two extremes of heat and cold, partaking in a degree of the advantages of both without feeling much the inconveniences of either—and with truth it may be said it is among the most fertile lands in America east of the Appalachian mountains."

Thomas Jefferson sought to inaugurate at Staunton the chief emporium of an infant industry—the manufacture of nails. The first cut nail ever made in the United States was made at Staunton. It was the center of an iron district for a hundred years. Out of this region came iron for the guns that thundered at Cherubusco and Monterey in the Mexican War and later for Civil War cannon.

Genealogist Hughey, one of the Stover kin, has made a valuable collection of data in her "Stoever Genealogy." It will be the duty of future genealogists to straighten out the lines of these first Stovers in America, many of whom moved westward with the surging tide of migration.

The records show that the Reverend Johann (John) Caspar Stoever arrived in Philadelphia, in September 11, 1728, on the ship *Good Will* (David Crockett, master) of Rotterdam, having sailed with ninety Palatines from Deal on June 15—a three months' voyage by sailing vessel across the Atlantic. He was forty-three years old when he landed in America. With him was his son, John Caspar Stoever, Jr., the young theological student.

Documents give this further information. He was born in 1685, at Frankenberg, in Hesse. His father, Dietrich Stoever, conducted a mercantile establishment. His mother, Magdalena, was the daughter of Andrew Eberwein, pastor at Frankenberg. One of his baptismal sponsors was John Crist. Eberwein, pastor and headmaster in the Pedagogium at Geissen, which position was held later by a relative of Stover's, John Philip Fresenius. In youthful years, Stoever was a teacher at Amweiler, at the eastern slope of the Hardt Mountains. . . . He also attended to the playing of the organ and there probably first engaged in theological studies.

Here are extracts from an interesting letter, dated May 11, 1736, written by Councillor Koehler of Pommerania to a Professor Francke in America, while Reverend Stoever was back in Germany.

"Delegates of the congregations in Virginia . . . together with their minister, Mr. Stoever, have arrived here and from here will go to Danzig and Koenigsberg. They have collected a rich harvest, more than two thousand thaler (a German dollar worth about seventy-three cents). . . . I represented to them . . . the main purpose of their transplantation to America . . . to make known the Gospel of Jesus Christ in all places and parts of the earth . . ."

The good Councillor continues: "On his return he (Stoever) intends to buy twelve Negroes as slaves . . . to clear enough land so that he together with another minister and assistant could live on it, without being a burden to the congregation. . . . He is now paid a salary of three thousand pounds of tobacco. . . . He thinks hundreds, nay thousands of slaves will be brought from heathen ignorance to Christ."

This letter further infers that John Caspar Stoever, after arriving in Philadelphia in 1728, preaching there for a time, had returned to Germany and came back to America on a second voyage in 1733, via the West Indies.

The most revealing of all the Stoever documents is dated

March 10, 1734, at Graven Precinct, North Carolina, probably on his second arrival in America by way of the West Indies. This is a remarkable agreement between "John Caspar Stoever and His Wife."

"Since the holy state of matrimony is not only a holy and Divine Ordinance . . . I, John Caspar Stoever (minister of the Evangelical Lutheran German Congregation in Virginia) and my spouse Maria Magdalena, between whom and me hitherto hath been some difference, I have agreed as follows, to wit:

"1st. The married persons promise each other to live in this holy state of matrimony (according to God's will till Death shall part them) peaceably and in union as behooves Christians, and totally forget and bury in oblivion all what has formerly past between them, and to travel together to Virginia where ye sd Stoever's congr. is & he lives.

"2ly. The husband promises heartily to love and honour his beloved wife, Maria Magdalena, and to provide for her maintenance and cloathes according as his station and condition will afford & as behooves Christian husband also.

"3ly. Maria Magdalena promises to love and honour her husband and in all things, & in love & faithfulness to obey his lawful commandments as a Christian wife ought to do.

"4ly. In case the husband agt. his wife's will should travel to any other place, and contrary to expectation leave her there, half of his Estate to fall to her share, without that she be the cause of his so leaving her.

"5ly. I, Stoever, have promised to give unto my son (John Caspar) & Daughter (Elizabeth Catharina) by the first marriage, a certain part of my estate for their entire exclusion, and to make this present wife & ye son got (together with what children God shall be pleased to give me) by this second marriage, sole heirs of what estate I shall leave, so that they shall have no one to divide it with them.

"6ly. Stoever promises during the life of his mother-in-law to maintain & cloath her & to shew her all love and faithfulness due from a child; in consideration of which she promises as well to be careful of not giving offence herself, as to admonish her Daughter to beware from offending & giving occasion of quarrel or strife, especially to leave off all evil speaking, backbiting & slandering which occasion offence, and truly to behave herself so in all things towards her child and son-in-law as becometh a loving & Christian mother. To the end the congregation may not be offended nor no new strife may be raised in the house."

General Eisenhower's kinsmen at times apparently had wars in their own household. And some of our readers may agree that these domestic wars (when they do break out) can be equally as fatal to the parties concerned as combats in World War II.

According to tradition the Stovers or Stauffers owe their origin to a generation of knights called Stauffacher at Hohenstauffen before the year A.D. 1000. They were of Alsatian ancestry and founders of the House of Hohenstauffen in Suabia, Germany.

We find in ancient Old World records that Frederick, founder of the Hohenstauffens, died in 1105 and his heirs ruled the family dynasty until 1268, when after a period of splendor and glory it was suddenly seized by a dreadful calamity and hurled into the darkest night of oblivion. The last of the house, Conrad by name, at the age of fifteen, attempted to enforce his right, gained several battles and was finally defeated at Teglicozzo, taken prisoner, and beheaded on November 29, 1268.

The leading authority on these Stauffer origins, Frederick Raumer, states, "Legend has it that at the time of the prosperity of the House of Hohenstauffen their ancestry was traced back to the Ancient Emperor of France as far back as the reign of Charlemagne."

While the Stovers in America have not traced their origin directly to this ancient house, there are traditions that make it an

interesting possibility. Records state that upon the beheading of
Conrad, the members of the Stauffer, or Stover, family took
flight, one group going to Baden, another to Bavaria (the Palatinate where the Eisenhowers lived), and a third to Switzerland,
where they were living at the time that William Tell won his
great victory.

We find these facts established: During the early 1700's, while
religious persecutions were raging in both Baden and Bavaria
(where a branch of the Stovers had taken refuge), Baron Graffenreid, agent of Governor Spotswood in Virginia, urged those
of the Lutheran faith to go to America and thus escape the
persecutions. The Baron had a motive: Governor Spotswood
owned coal mines in Virginia and needed workers, for which he
was willing to pay a "fair commission" to Baron Graffenreid.

Thirty-two families left for the New World and after many
setbacks and disappointments finally arrived in Virginia. Governor Spotswood offered them seven years of tax exemption to
work the land and establish a community, also offering them
employment in his coal mines. We find these Palatinates in 1714
settled above the falls of the Rappahannock on the southern
branch in a horseshoe peninsula. They named their community
Germanna, in the Parish of St. George. It was palisaded with
stakes stuck in the ground, strong and close to repel musket shot
and bows and arrows of Indians. Nine houses stood like sentinels
all in a line. Twenty feet in front of each house was a small shed
for hogs and hens. There was a blockhouse within a pentagon
with loopholes, a retreat from Indians, which was also used for
divine services and prayers every day, with two sermons on
Sunday. This was the existence of pioneers who trod the bleak
wilderness to blaze the trails for the generations of Americans to
follow.

Twenty more families of Evangelical Lutherans, consisting of
about eighty persons, fled the religious persecution in Alsace and

Palatinate Germany, coming to Germanna in Virginia in 1717. After passing through many trials, during which they became increasingly impatient with the exploitation of Governor Spotswood and his failure to provide them with the promised land grants, the colony settled in Spotsylvania at the most distant boundary of Virginia.

A third colony of Germans had come to the New World between 1717 and 1720, forty more families who settled in the forks of the Conway and the Robinson rivers in the present county of Madison. This land entry was made in 1718 and patented to the Germans in 1724. Their aged pastor, Reverend Henry Haeger, who had for sixteen years been unable to perform his duties, died at the age of eighty-eight years in 1733 and left them without any spiritual leader.

Here it is, in 1733, that we find Reverend John Caspar Stoever, arriving in Virginia to join his fellow countrymen as their pastor. The German colony had taken up a grant of 193 acres in the fork of the Rapidan River. The new pastor was said to be a relative of an earlier Stover who came to America in 1728 and became a minister in Lancaster County, Pennsylvania, and at Philadelphia.

Reverend John Caspar Stoever saw the possibilities in the new America. After a year with his little flock in Virginia (as we have witnessed in documents), he made a return voyage to Germany to collect funds for a church. He came back with his wife and over three thousand pounds (a great increase from the first two thousand thaler). With the surplus a new tract of several hundred acres of land was bought. But on this return voyage he had become seriously ill, and died in 1738.

While Pastor Stoever had been collecting funds in Germany, and during his illness, Reverend George Samuel Klug, born in Prussia and ordained in Danzig, acted as pastor. The German colony now numbered about three hundred. After the death of

Pastor Stoever they built, with the money he had turned over to them, what they called the Hebron Church in 1740. It stands today on a beautiful hill in the forks of Robinson River and White Oak Run, where it has been continuously used for Lutheran services for more than two hundred years.

Soon after the death of Pastor Stoever the records in the *Virginia Magazine of History and Biography* state, "They have a beautiful large church and a school, also a parsonage, and a glebe of several hundred acres with seven Negroes who must cultivate the minister's land."

The Old Virginia where the first Stovers lived, according to the charter given by King James to the London Company for Virginia, extended "to the Pacific Ocean and one hundred miles into it." Its dimensions were "400 miles wide on the Atlantic and of the same width from sea to sea with all the islands in both seas within 100 miles from the shores thereby."

On the same year that Pastor Stoever died (1738) the County of Augusta was laid out. The Augusta County Court, where we obtain many of the records for this narrative, was organized and held its first meeting in 1745. In examining Chalkley's extracts of original court records from 1745 to 1800 we find the Stovers frequently mentioned.

There were lawsuits in the Courthouse in 1804 over the land of Jacob Stover which was encompassed in the original five-thousand-acre tract that Jacob settled on. Jacob Stover was now an old man, still living on a small part of the land. Small parcels of the land had changed hands repeatedly, and of the original five thousand acres Jacob now held only four hundred acres on which he lived.

Mary Gilmer sued to get control of the Stover land. Augustine Price, eighty years old, maintained squatter rights. He claimed that he was driven from his home in New River in the year of Braddock's defeat by Indians, then encamped on

Mrs. Gilmer's land, which was owned at the time by John Madison. Robert Hook, an aged crony of Price, made a deposition for his friend which stated that he "has known the walnut tree for sixty years." Further depositions state that Jacob Stover deeded the land on Cub Run to Christopher Francisco in 1741. More deeds were signed over to Peter Bowman for other tracts. The Judgment Book of Augusta County fails to bring us further light on the deposition of the dispute property.

The Stovers were much interested in the development of communities beyond Augusta County. Joseph Stover conducted a lottery, along with some friends, to build a Lutheran Church in Strasburg.

Thus in the glorious valley of the Shenandoah, in historic Augusta County, where the mother of General Eisenhower was born, we have followed in the footsteps of his maternal ancestors.

As we walk again through the old Stover farm in Mount Sidney we indulge in another flight of imagination. Under the apple blossoms we fancy we can see little Ida Elizabeth romping through the green fields, her golden hair gleaming in the sunlight.

When she was born in this old home in 1862 armies were fighting not far away in the Shenandoah Valley. In this same year Lincon was writing the Emancipation Proclamation; Grant was fighting the Battle of Shiloh; Lee was leading the armies of the Confederacy in which her kin were fighting; the battle of Antietam was fought on the road to the gates of Washington.

Ida Elizabeth was a war baby. The Union armies came down to Augusta County on their raids through the Shenandoah. Staunton was twice occupied by Federal troops. This was the supply base for the Army of Northern Virginia and Stonewall Jackson's valley campaign.

The little Virginian who was to be the mother of General Eisenhower was only three years old when the Civil War ended and Lincoln was assassinated. In her first year in school the Germans were fighting France, in 1870; her future son was to fight to drive the Germans out of France in 1944.

When she was eighteen years old the Russo-Turkish War had just ended in faraway Europe. We leave her here in her twentieth year as she starts with her cousin, Mary Ann Link, the bride of Emanuel Beam, for the Great West. The year is 1882. As they stand in the doorway of the old Link home at Mount Sidney they bid good-by to their happy childhood. She little knew that a young man named Eisenhower, whom she was to meet and marry in Kansas, had gone ahead of her from his home in Elizabethville, Pennsylvania, but four years before.

We see her for the last time in Virginia as she kisses Uncle Billy Link and all the Links, waving to them in smiles and tears as she starts on the great adventure that was to end in romance and fame.

· 5 ·

Eisenhowers on the pioneer trail to Kansas

Westward ho! The long trail of covered wagons had been crossing the frontiers for a generation. Since the days of the Gold Rush of '49 adventurous men on horseback, mule, and afoot had followed the trails—fording rivers, winding their way over mountain passes, along the precipitous canyons, over plains and deserts to the Promised Land.

The Eisenhower family from Elizabethville, Pennsylvania, were on their way in the summer of 1878. And the Stovers, from Mount Sidney, Virginia, started four years later.

Stories about their making the journey on horseback, in covered wagons, and stage coaches are romantic but not history. The steam engine was now conquering the continent, railroads were stretching their glittering rails across the prairies, over bridged rivers and through tunneled mountains.

The Eisenhowers and Stovers were pioneers of this new age. We shall hear how Ida Elizabeth Stover and Aunt Amanda made their journeys, how they settled on the plains along the famous cattle trails and "grew up" with Kansas, which derived its name from the Sioux Indians, meaning "People of the South Wind." The Eisenhowers were the forerunners for the religious group, the United Brethren, coming out of the East into the building of the West.

34

Let Amanda, the little sixteen-year-old girl from Elizabethville, now an eighty-two-year-old woman, Mrs. Amanda Eisenhower Musser, first tell her story. In her home in Dickinson County, Kansas, her brilliant mind recalls the days before her distinguished nephew, General Dwight David Eisenhower, was born. She has written her reminiscences for this book.

"I feel highly honored that you think of me, as a little eighty-two-year-old lady with only a common country-school education, to give a few facts that will help you in your work. There are only two of the Jacob Eisenhower family living any more, myself and one brother who lives in California. I miss my brother David Jacob Eisenhower, Dwight's father. His mother is living not far from our place. We as a family all admired her; she was a good mother and a wise instructor of her boys. She had seven, one dying in infancy.

"I am very glad you had the privilege of visiting the Eisenhower homestead in Elizabethville, and I want you to know that home was always a house where prayer was offered night and morning ever since I could remember from my childhood days. I hope it might be so to this day.

"My father was always a farmer. We children were brought up on the farm. I had three older sisters than myself and three younger brothers. When my father heard of all this beautiful land he thought this was the place to go with his boys, and now I am the only one of the family living in Kansas. God has graciously prospered us. So we have no lack for anything.

"As I said, my father was a farmer and expected his boys to do the same; but my oldest brother, David Jacob Eisenhower, Dwight's father, decided he wanted an education. He went to college and met and fell in love with Ida Elizabeth Stover, who was a native of Virginia. She was left an orphan at an early age and went to live with her uncle, then later came to Topeka, Kansas, and attended the same school as David Eisenhower.

"You want to hear about our journey to Kansas in 1878. Some things I remember very distinctly. There were only seven of the party who left Elizabethville. We went first to the small town of Millersburg. I think the agent, a Mr. Bender who was at the head of the party, ordered it that way. With us was my grandfather, Frederick Eisenhower, my father and mother, Jacob F. Eisenhower, myself and my brothers David, Abraham Lincoln Eisenhower, and Isaac composed the party until we arrived at Harrisburg where others joined us.

"I was then in my sixteenth year and it was rather hard to leave all my friends and schoolmates, but I held back the tears and sobs until we were on the train, then my heart really did break. A stranger sitting close by inquired as to what the matter was. I remarked, '*We are going to Kansas!*'

"At Harrisburg five other families joined us. John Gish and family, Wash Jury and family, Samuel Pyke, Jacob Pyke, John Pyke, and their families. Now we were on our way to go somewhere we didn't know.

"This would almost make a book should I go into all the details. My father, as you know, was a minister. My grandfather, Frederick Eisenhower, was a weaver by trade; he wove bedspreads, tablecloths, linens which were used for men's shirts, pillowcases and towels; some few are still in our families.

"My deepest impressions on our arrival in Kansas were the continual blowing of the wind and that we could buy fresh country eggs at five cents a dozen. We youngsters had our fill, believe it or not.

"I remember how in 1879 a large colony came from Pennsylvania and settled close to where we had bought our first home, twelve miles south of Abilene, our trading point. My father soon got hold of a pair of good ponies, and how they could travel over these ungraded roads! It wasn't such a hard task to go twelve miles to do our weekly trading.

"And so it was we grew up with Kansas, and we love it today as our home. I know you don't want me to tell the history of this grand State, which is our history, so I'll have my husband tell you about his recollections."

Dear Aunt Amanda smiles benevolently and the young man she married in Kansas, Mr. C. O. Musser, now a gracious gentleman of eighty-one years, writes his reminiscences for us in firm, clear handwriting as vigorous as his beloved wife's:

"I came to Kansas on the twenty-first day of March, 1884, and started to work with a farmer. The farm was close to the Belle Springs Cemetery. I found out that Frederick Eisenhower, great-grandfather of General Eisenhower, was buried the sixteenth of March, 1884, a few days before I arrived. He was nearly ninety years old. I heard he had two brothers, and the three of them had outstanding military records in their youth.

"In the summer of 1884 I kept calling at the Eisenhower homestead, and I married Amanda Eisenhower on November 30, 1884. We spent the winter of 1884 and 1885 in Pennsylvania and returned to Kansas in the spring of 1885 and moved on a farm.

"I knew the Eisenhowers in Elizabethville and often went to the old homestead to hear Jacob Eisenhower preach. He spoke mostly in the German language. When he moved to Kansas with his family these meetings were continued in his new home until 1894, when meeting houses were built. He was a member of the 'Brethren in Christ,' afterwards named 'River Brethren.' He was past eighty years when he died.

"I remember the summer in 1885, when David J. Eisenhower was married to Ida Stover; they were both students at Lecompton College (Lane University) conducted by the United Brethren.

"About the winter of 1885 and 1886, David J. Eisenhower and a partner by the name of M. D. Good started a merchandise store at Hope, Kansas. My father furnished the money, but in a few years they closed up and sold out. Mr. Good took Eisenhower into failure, and I stepped in and assumed the mortgages my father held. I also became owner of 160 acres of land. It was after this that my brother-in-law David and his small family moved to Denison, Texas, where Dwight Eisenhower was born.

"In the fall of 1889 the Belle Springs Creamery Company built a plant at Abilene, Kansas. I was appointed foreman of the plant and in 1891 I asked my brother-in-law to come back to Kansas. We worked together in the same factory for over twenty years. Dwight's father was a good engineer and mechanic. He took sick. After he was restored in health he was employed with a telephone company for over twenty years. Four or five years ago he was laid off work and was given a pension. For several years he was in ill health and he died a little over two years ago.

"Dwight Eisenhower was about two years old when he came to Kansas with his parents from Texas. Years later he worked for me, with some of his other brothers, in the creamery, washing cans and doing odd jobs when they were quite young. The boys were all industrious.

"I was superintendent at the Sunday School when Dwight and the other brothers attended. He had a teacher by the name of Mrs. Ida Hoffman, and she told me some of her experiences with the boys. After Dwight left for West Point, he very seldom returned home. Of course he went to the Philippines and to Europe. There were seven boys in the family, one by the name of Paul died in infancy. It is a long-lived family—Frederick Eisenhower 89 years, 7 months—Jacob Frederick Eisenhower 80 years, 4 months—David Jacob Eisenhower past 78 years.

"The Eisenhowers, as you know, were of German descent, settling in Switzerland and some generations later moving to America. The Engles, Hoffmans, Mussers, Brubakers, Eisenhowers, and many others, became what is called the Pennsylvania Dutch. These Pennsylvania Dutch left Germany because of military requirements.

"I was born near Mt. Joy, Pennsylvania, in 1863. Amanda and myself will be married sixty years the thirtieth of November, 1944. My wife is two years older than I. We are, of course, very happy that our nephew, General Dwight David Eisenhower, is making such a notable record in the world's history."

Here is what Historian Andreas has to say in his authoritative *History of the State of Kansas* of the conditions in Kansas about the time that General Eisenhower's father arrived on the plains:

"The number of new settlers coming into the (Dickinson) county kept increasing each year until 1879, when one of the most complete and perfectly organized colonies that ever entered a new country arrived in Dickinson County. In point of numbers and equipment it far exceeded anything that had preceded it. All told, they numbered nearly three hundred persons. The leaders of the movement had been traveling through Kansas for some time seeking a location and finally decided upon Dickinson County.

"When they had selected the lands for the colony, they immediately set to work and had a large frame building erected in Abilene, 20 × 80 feet, for the accommodation of the colonists upon their arrival, until suitable buildings could be erected upon their lands. On Friday, March 28, 1879, the first company arrived in Abilene, which consisted of thirty persons from Frederick County, Maryland, and on Saturday morning upwards of two hundred arrived from Lancaster, Cumberland, Dauphin, Lebanon, and Franklin counties, Pennsylvania; these were followed later by others.

"In religion they are what is known as 'River Brethren,' and in order not to be deprived of their privilege of worship, they brought with them a minister, Reverend Benjamin Gish, and a bishop, Reverend Jesse Engle, so that from the time they started, there was a perfect church organization in the colony. The colony divided on its arrival in the county, some settling north of the Smoky, and some south, in the vicinity of Belle Springs. They brought with them fifteen carloads of freight, and in noting their departure from Pennsylvania, the *Marietta Times* said that they took with them not less than $500,000 in money."

This eminent historian, writing three years after the Eisenhowers arrived in Kansas, gives this picture of the country in which they settled: "A more beautiful prairie country would be difficult to find. . . . Streams of pure, clear water are found at intervals of a few miles along which grow ash, walnut, hackberry, elm, oak, and cottonwood. . . . Timberland embraces three and one-half percent of the county. Scattered over the face of the county are a great many artificial groves and fine orchards, which tend to break the monotony of the scene. . . . There is little wasteland, and the acres are but few which are not susceptible to cultivation. The soil is excellent and exceedingly deep, all of its alluvial, upland as well as bottomland, subsoiled with lime and clay. . . . Valleys of many of the Eastern rivers, such as the Connecticut and Mohawk, sink into insignificance compared with those of the Smoky Hill. In many places a man can stand on his own threshold in these valleys and view tracts of land three and four miles square, the soil of which is not only unexcelled but unexcellable."

In the early days, the area now covered by Dickinson County was included in the blank sections on maps called "The Great American Desert." This myth of the "desert" prevented early settlement such as occurred in eastern Kansas as far west as Manhattan and Fort Riley. Dickinson County, where the Eisenhowers settled, lies only a few miles from the precise geographic center of the United States. It is 130 miles west of the Missouri River and is strictly a prairie country, the surface of which is undulating. There is little or no diversity of scenery over most of the county, though there is some broken and bluffy country in the northwest and southwest portions. Almost bisecting the county, a mile or so south of Abilene, is the Smoky Hill River. Along this river, and the larger creeks, are valleys one to three miles wide.

Settlers came in slowly for several years, until the Kansas Pacific railroad reached the area. Abilene became the western terminus of the road, and one of the most luridly violent frontier communities in the whole history of the western frontier. This extremely "wild" period extended from 1867, when W. K. McCoy and Brothers of Springfield, Illinois, established a stockyard for Texas cattle in Abilene, until 1871, when the big cattle market moved farther west with the railroads. More than three million cattle were driven into Abilene in this period.

The Texas longhorns came up the thousand-mile Chisholm trail, laid out by Jesse Chisholm, extending from Texas across Oklahoma and southern Kansas to Abilene. The drive took months. Hundreds of thousands of cattle, driven by hundreds of cowboys, came into Abilene every season. The cowboys were wild characters, eager to "let go" after weeks and months of desperately hard work on the trail. They "let go" with a vengeance in Abilene. Killings became a common occurrence. Saloons and bawdy houses ran day and night.

The "tough district" was located a mile and a half north of town and consisted of twenty-five or thirty one-story frame houses, each with ten or twenty rooms. The district was known as "McCoy's Addition" and "Devil's Half-Acre." When conditions were at their worst in 1871, just before the removal farther west of the big terminal market, the *Abilene Chronicle* (now known as the *Reflector-Chronicle* and published by

Charles Moreau Harger, the Eisenhower's closest friend in Abilene) stated that there were more cutthroats and desperadoes in Abilene than in any other town its size in America.

When Abilene was incorporated in 1869, an effort was made to clean it up. All of the first town marshals, however, were either killed or driven out of town. Finally Tom Smith, of Kit Carson, Colorado, applied for the job and promptly became one of the legendary figures of the Old West. He was polite, even deferential, soft-spoken—but he was a dangerous man in a fight. By sheer force of character as well as by physical prowess, he managed to enforce the ordinance against deadly weapons and the ordinance requiring the licensing of saloons.

He was succeeded after a few months by Wild Bill (James Butler) Hickok, a Union sharpshooter in the Civil War and a notorious frontier figure. At the time of his appointment as Abilene town marshal, he was reported to have killed forty-three men (not counting those shot in the war). His skill with revolvers was fabulous. He could dent a coin tossed into the air, drawing and shooting with marvelous speed and with either hand. He could keep a can dancing in the dust with a steady stream of bullets from a revolver in either hand. He always carried a pair of six-shooters. While serving as town marshal in Abilene he once killed two men fleeing in opposite directions and did it with such rapidity that a boy witness swore on oath that only one shot was fired.

Some old-timers claim that Wild Bill killed over fifty men during his term in Abilene. He himself had no compunctions regarding the killing of men. He once said, "Killing a bad man shouldn't trouble one any more than killing a rat or a mad dog." He himself was killed, in 1876, in Deadwood, South Dakota, by a drunken gambler named Jack McCall, who shot him in the back of the head as he was playing poker.

By the time the Eisenhower family arrived in Dickinson

County, the wild cow-town days were ended, but the tradition of violence and sudden death remained and—glamorized now—will remain. It is a major part of the folklore of the community in which General Eisenhower was raised. Mementoes of the wild days are scattered all over town, and undoubtedly this "Wild West" romancing aroused that sharp interest in the child Dwight which still persists in the man; his favorite reading for relaxation consists of "Wild West" stories and novels which he devours with amazing speed and in amazing quantities.

This old "Wild West" is in strange contrast with the arrival of the Eisenhowers on the scene. They, as stated, were members of the religious sect known as "River Brethren." This denomination was formed in Pennsylvania (about 1770) among Swiss emigrants who lived along the Susquehanna River. They believed in trine immersion, the washing of feet, non-resistance, and non-conformity with or to the world. They had a distinctive old-fashioned dress—the men in plain dark suits, the women with long plain dresses and bonnets.

Hence, the Eisenhower family had, from religious conviction, a strong pacifist tendency which, judging from the family name, is at odds with the family's career in earlier times. According to a portion of the family records, written in the hand of the General's father, the name Eisenhower means "iron hitter" as distinguished from Eisenhauer, "iron hewer," and Eisenschmidt, "iron smith." According to other sources, the name Eisenhower stems directly from Eisenhauer. Family tradition has it that the name originated with mounted warriors in one of the medieval German armies.

The Frederick Eisenhower who is General Dwight Eisenhower's great-grandfather was born about 1787 in Pennsylvania, as we have recorded. The family tree listed in the back of the "baby book" of Milton S. Eisenhower, Jr. (son of the present president of Kansas State College), records that his great-grandmother's maiden name was Barbara Millerin. This family tree is based on Dwight's father's recollections. The "baby book" lists her birth date as 1786, rather than 1789. Another authority gives the name as Barbara Miller and claims she was a blood relative of General Winfield Scott.

A competent researcher, Mr. J. W. Howe, now in the real-estate business in Emporia, Kansas, but formerly editor of the *Abilene News*, a weekly paper, says the "Eisenhowers came to Abilene, with all their worldly goods in a freight car, and came from Texas to Kansas City and then on the Union Pacific to Abilene."

Whatever future researchers may reveal, we know that the Eisenhowers from the first were among the most respected people in their community. The River Brethren in general (like most such "cultural islands") were notably thrifty and prosperous, self-reliant and absolutely honest in their dealings with the world.

As we have mentioned earlier, Jacob F. (General Eisenhower's grandfather) had a good deal of property. He had half-interest in a small bank, a general merchandise store at Hope, and some farms. The property was all lost, apparently through a failure in the Hope bank. The story is that a partner absconded with funds. The Eisenhowers, attempting to cover the losses of depositors, lost their own property.

Uncle Musser and Aunt Amanda have told us that young David Eisenhower, the General's father, met Elizabeth Stover, from Virginia, in a college romance at Lecompton College, which was also known as Lane University, operated by the United Brethren and located at Lecompton in Douglas County, Kansas. It is uncertain what courses he studied, though he seems to have taken a general course. The institution has ceased to exist. It is believed, however, that he studied engineering there, and it is possible that he studied mechanics, for those early

Kansas schools set on the frontier were more in the nature of vocational training institutes than colleges like those of today. He did not take a degree.

David and Ida were married in the summer of 1885. In the family Bible we find their first son was born in Hope, Kansas, on November 11, 1886, and christened Arthur B. A second son, Edgar A. was born in Hope, on January 19, 1889.

The young father David worked in his father's store and bank until the collapse of the family property. He continued studying engineering through the *International Correspondence Schools*, specializing in "stationary engineering," or what is now called "mechanical engineering." He received his diploma and we find him obtaining a position in Denison, Texas.

· 6 ·

General Eisenhower's birthplace in Texas

THE GENERAL EVIDENTLY STARTED a war of his own right here at home the moment he stepped into world fame. His sudden rise to power caught the records unaware. There was no official record of his birthplace, as births were not recorded at the place and time when he came into the world. He was a victim of a mix-up in the cradle of facts.

Records in the War Department at Washington definitely stated: Tyler, Texas. Records at West Point stated: Denison, Texas.

The public press took its choice; most neswpapers and magazines accepting the War Department's record; only a few being advised of the West Point record, and neither group going to the one direct source of information—Mother Eisenhower, in Abilene, Kansas, and the family Bible.

We entered the controversy and instituted our own researches. Strangely enough, the same division existed in Abilene. A family friend first informed us that Tyler was the place. The decision was left to Mother Eisenhower. She emphatically said Denison, and she had the family Bible to corroborate her.

Merely as evidence as to what can happen to a man when he suddenly emerges from the comparative "unknown"—and how little was known about him when we began our researches—we

46

make this record of the conflict which soon reached a peaceful solution.

G. D. Fairtrace, City Manager of Tyler, with the rose as its emblem and the "Heart of East Texas" as its motto, was taken unaware, too. He turned the dispute over to V. F. Fitzhugh, General Manager of the Tyler Chamber of Commerce. Mr. Fitzhugh gave us this statement:

"Although the War Department records reveal Tyler, Texas, as being the birthplace of the distinguished Commander of Allied Armies, European theater, General Dwight D. Eisenhower, we have been unable thus far to establish any basis for such a claim. Shortly after his appointment as commander of the European forces, a number of newspapers and magazine articles credited this city as being the place of his birth. Denison, Texas was likewise supported by some writers as General Eisenhower's birthplace."

Mr. Fitzhugh thus proved that this was a newspaper war, not one between the two cities. His position, therefore, was arbitrator for the press. He communicated immediately with the General's mother in Abilene, Kansas. Here is his letter:

"Dear Mrs. Eisenhower: As you perhaps have noticed, Tyler has been credited by some writers as being the birthplace of your now very famous and capable General Dwight D. Eisenhower. This report has resulted in several inquiries from people interested in obtaining as much information as possible on his early life. Although the preponderance of writers now credit Denison as being his birthplace, most of them say he spent several years in Tyler during the early years of his life."

And here is Mother Eisenhower's reply: "(1) Name of city in which General Eisenhower was born and date—*October 14, 1890*, Denison, Texas. (2) During what year and on what date did his family move to Tyler? *His father was on train service to Tyler but never lived there.*

"The family Bible records the birth of Dwight Eisenhower as above. The records left by Mr. Eisenhower do not mention anything about his employment in Tyler, but he had spoken of his train service to Tyler."

We shall find later a similar controversy over his name, whether it was David, or Dwight. These apparently unimportant details become of importance only to show how little is known of a man until he becomes celebrated. Throughout our nation-wide researches we found these frequent discrepancies, with many conflicting versions of the same stories.

Through the valued aid of H. Bailey Carroll, of the Texas State Historical Association, at Austin, the oldest learned society in Texas, we directed our investigations to Denison. Here, Mr. William O. Harwell, Manager of the Denison Chamber of Commerce, gave us this information:

"A photostatic copy of General Eisenhower's birth certificate is not available since, at the time he was born, Texas did not have such a system of recording vital statistics. Our mayor is communicating directly with General Eisenhower's mother in order that she may prepare the necessary affidavit to secure a birth certificate for General Eisenhower as is provided under the present Texas law. It is our understanding that General Eisenhower's father was employed by the M-K-T Lines as a machinist while here."

He further referred to *Who's Who in America* which in the latest edition had correctly given Denison the decision over Tyler in the rivalry for the birthplace of General Eisenhower.

Millard M. Cope, editor of the *Denison Daily Herald*, a historian interested in everything pertaining to Texas and the nation, made this comment in his authoritative journal: "At the time the General was placed in command of American troops in England, the tip came through a news service source that he was born in Denison. Later newspaper and magazine articles listed his birthplace variously as Denison and Tyler. Denison began to get uneasy over the prospects of losing such an outstanding distinction. . . . As the final verdict, Denison today is saluting a native son with its Eisenhower Day observance.

"Denison can't claim much more than that the General first saw the light of day here: but that's enough. His family, while he was a small baby, moved to Kansas. The 1890–91 edition of the Denison City Directory lists David J. and Ida Elizabeth Eisenhower, parents of the General, as living at the northeast corner of Day street and Lamar avenue. Owned today by Mrs. Frances Wertz, the house occupies that site, and from all available information was the birthplace fifty-two years ago of the man today leading the Americans in the most sensational development of the war to date. The yellowed city directory, in a collection belonging to Harry Tone, lists the father as an engine wiper at the Katy roundhouse."

The nearest that we come to finding anyone in Denison who remembers the Eisenhowers a half century ago is James Redmon, a retired engineer, who is the "man who went for the doctor at the birth of General Eisenhower." Here is his story as he told it to the *Denison Press:*

"Yes, I remember it quite well, the night I went for the doctor to be the man to be honored with bringing a baby into the world to a mother who was at the time nursing not a child, but a leader who was some day to be at the head of the invading forces set on destroying the camps of Nazism, with the avowed purpose of freeing a world from despotism, and of saving democracy and the right of life and liberty.

"I was living in the home of the Eisenhower family in the old home as it now stands. I was an engineer on the Katy and had apartments upstairs, and was in from the run on the night that baby Dwight D. Eisenhower was to be born. Several women had gathered in to do what they could as they did in those days.

Midwives were plentiful also and, in case a doctor could not reach the house in time, they generally did what they could for a prospective mother.

"I do not quite recall all the details, you see, as I had no idea a celebrity was being born, and that the man who was to lead the forces of the world in arms against the worst Mephistopheles of all ages was to be announced at that time.

"I recall the room, it was downstairs—the northwest one— where the mother was confined and the child was born. I was the only available man on the place with the exception of the husband, and so I hustled out of my apartment and went for the physician. I do not even recall the psysician who was the lucky one, but at the time Doctor Acheson was the prominent physician here and he might have been the one. He did a lot of practicing for the railroad boys and it could have been him.

"It was a cold night in October, the fourteenth, when the birth took place. He was the only baby in the locality for a while and many of the neighbors came in and nursed the little fellow and kept 'company' for Mrs. Eisenhower.

"I am glad the move is on to make a shrine of the house in which the baby was born, and hope it will be visited by many thousands in the days to come. I lost track of the family until they came into prominence through that son, now famous for his ability as a general in the United States armed forces. Some day I would like again to renew the acquaintance of the Eisenhower family and maybe, after the old home has been made a shrine, they will come back to visit here and I will have that privilege. I will then, if the General himself ever returns while I am alive, get to shake the hand of a man who as a baby I have held in my arms."

Mr. Redmon retired several years ago and lives quietly at his home here, and although physically unable to get about as in younger days, his mind is alert and he is proud of the fact that he had a little part in days associated with the babyhood of this now great General Dwight D. Eisenhower.

Mother Eisenhower, in Abilene, recalls these "events" with deep interest. She says, "Dwight was born in Denison, Texas, on October 14, 1890. We lived there but a short time, less than two years. We had two other little sons in our family then and I was kept busy as a young mother at home. There was no time to make the acquaintance of many people, and those who might know us would probably be in their eighties now. Dwight's father, David, was an engineer, employed by one of the railroads. We went to Denison in 1889."

Here arises the controversy over General Eisenhower's name. As stated, there is no birth record in Denison. And the family Bible names him as *David* with Dwight as a middle name. He was named David in honor of his father.

The explanation is both plausible and practical. His mother soon found that when she called David, both the father and the son answered. Therefore, she began to use the middle name Dwight and ended the confusion. She didn't like "Junior," and so he became Dwight. The names were reversed from that time and have remained so throughout his life.

Mother Eisenhower also had another reason. She dislikes the shortening of boys' names: she knew David would soon become Dave. It annoyed her when her son Arthur was called Art—and her son Edgar had become Ed.

"I knew there was no short cut for Dwight," she explained.

But she was ironically to be foiled again. Not only did Dwight become Ike, but all her sons becames Ikes, a nickname from the first syllable of Eisenhower, distorted as these nicknames frequently are. Many boys receive even more incongruous appellations.

When there were six of these little Ikes they went to school in pairs. The oldest, as we shall see, became "Big Ike," the youngest "Little Ike," and the boys between were various gradations of Ikes, "Red Ike," etc., according to their characteristics. When other babies arrived they assumed the throne of "Little Ike," and for a time the General was just "Ugly Ike," during his awkward, gangling years.

Thus we find Dwight first opening his eyes on this bewildering world in Texas—a young Texan from the Lone Star State, the largest in area in the Union, named from the Indian word Tejas, and strangely enough meaning "Friends or Allies," with "Friendship" for its state motto.

If there is anything in a name, Dwight's life has certainly exemplified it. And if the stars have anything to do with directing our lives, Dwight, born under Libra, has had his lucky stars with him. These, fortified by inheritance from pioneers, home environment, fortunate associates, natural inclinations and native ability, with the developing events, have made him the man he is today.

It is interesting to note also that Texas is in itself an empire larger than many of the countries which General Eisenhower is leading as an Ally or those which he is liberating or invading. With its 267,339 square miles, it is larger than Germany, larger than France, twice as large as Italy. Norway, Denmark, Holland, Belgium, Switzerland, and all the small countries of Europe combined could be lost in Texas.

Texas is an empire larger than Austria, Hungary, Rumania, Bulgaria, and Greece combined. It is larger than Czechoslovakia, Poland, and nearby Slovak neighbors combined. It is more than twice as large as England, Wales, Scotland, and Ireland combined. Four Englands could be embraced in the arms of Texas.

When General Eisenhower's forefathers came to America as pioneers, Texas was called "New Spain," nearly one and one half times as large as Spain itself. It was a land in which buffaloes and wild horses ranged over its dominions. The early pioneers lived behind heavily buttressed walls with presidios or forts to protect them from the Indians.

Texas was a part of Mexico when General Eisenhower's grandfather was born and later became an independent nation with Sam Houston as President of the Republic of Texas. These were the times of the Texas Rangers and the cattlemen—the days of Stephen Austin, "Old Sam" Houston, and David Crockett and the Alamo.

It was at this time that "Old Sam" gave a slogan in sixteen words which won one of the decisive battles of the world: *"Victory is certain! Trust in God and fear not! And remember the Alamo! Remember the Alamo!"* This old battle cry is carried by General Eisenhower's Texas boys into World War II.

Here at the Alamo, in San Antonio, Dwight Eisenhower was to be stationed at Fort Sam Houston when he received his first military commission in 1915, here he was to be made a first lieutenant, here he was to meet the girl he married, and here she was to live while her famous husband was leading the Allied Forces in World War II.

Denison, the birthplace of General Eisenhower, is in the Red River Valley in Grayson County, Texas, near the border of Oklahoma. It is a city of flower-bordered esplanades, giant trees and wide thoroughfares, with a population around fourteen thousand—a progressive American city.

The famous old Butterfield Stage Line used to pass through here with its heavy stage coaches on their route from St. Louis to San Francisco. This was a trading post for buffalo hunters, cattlemen, and traders. As a landmark of these pioneer days there is a granite shaft in Denison in memory of Justin Raynal, famous gambler, who left his estate to "build schools in Denison." Nearby rise the spires of many modern churches.

This section was the rendezvous of white trappers and Indian fighters. Kit Carson, "Old Misery" Beck, Jim Bridger, John

Colter, and their breed of adventurers visited the town. Old Colonel Coffey had his trading post but a few miles from here. His friendship with the Indians frequently enabled him to free many of the white captives who were taken in raids.

When the railroads began to come through Denison, it became one of the principal shipping centers for the produce from the Red River Valley. And it was on these railroads that the father of General Eisenhower was working when Dwight was born.

Here in the house in Denison young Dwight first stood on his own feet and learned to walk. Here he spoke his first words and learned to talk. The first two years of his life were spent in Denison. When he was taken to Kansas to "grow up" he was still the young Texan with a love for the Lone Star State.

Much of his military career, until he went to Washington and the Philippines, was spent at army posts in Texas. It is not surprising that those who know him best speak of him as the Texas-Kansan with the blood of the Pennsylvania Dutch and the Virginia pioneers in his veins.

As Governor Coke Stevenson said, when in the magnificent State Capitol at Austin he wrote an introductory statement for this biography: "The State of Texas takes keen pride in the fact that it has given to the Nation and the world one of its great sons as Commander of the Allied Forces on the European Front in World War II. . . . I take this opportunity to extend around the world our greetings from Texas to our great General and all Our Boys under his valiant leadership."

Dwight D. Eisenhower as President of the School Athletic Association at High School in Abilene. At his left is Harry Michaels Makins, Vice president; at right is Herbert Calvin Sommers, Secretary

On the Abilene High School Baseball Team (1909). Dwight Eisenhower is the tall fellow in center of front row with the bat in front of him. Both photos on this page from the Eisenhower family collection

Dwight Eisenhower at twenty-two, and a cadet at West Point

Lieut. Col. Dwight Eisenhower in World War I. Both this photo and the one above are from the Eisenhower family collection

Boyhood of "Little Ike" in Abilene—typical American home town

THE LITTLE TEXAN, with the Pennsylvania father and the Virginia mother, was now to become a Kansan. Could any combination make a better American than this? Four great States in the making of a man who was to lead forty-eight States in the defense of human freedom.

We follow David and Ida Eisenhower with their babies as they leave Texas to return to Kansas in 1892 and establish their lifelong home. Uncle Musser, as he has told us, had offered David "a good job in the creamery in Abilene," where the boys could begin to "help out" as soon as they were old enough.

Little Dwight, two years old, was taking his first trip on the train. His wondering eyes looked out on the "big world" which some day was to hail him as its liberator. The little toddler, who had just learned to stand on his own feet and chatter a few childish phrases, was going to Abilene, and Abilene was to make him the man who was to be acclaimed in capitals of the world.

What makes a nation great? We find the answer again in the little home towns like Abilene! Just as Dwight's father grew up in pioneer days back East in Elizabethville, so the son grew up at the gateway to the Great West. In him was bred the strong character of these pioneers.

Here in the Sunflower State, whose motto is, "To the stars through difficulties," Ike's boyhood and youth were lived until he was twenty years old. This still is his home. He says: "When my work is finished I hope to go back to Abilene and spend my days."

Walk through the streets of this home town and you will realize the truth of the old adage "as the twig is bent, so grows the tree"—and you will better understand what makes America great.

Abilene, in the heart of Kansas, the home of the Eisenhower family, is a typical prairie town of nearly six thousand people. It derived its name, Abilene, from the scriptural term of "Grassy Plain" from ancient Syria. It is located on the flatlands of the Smoky Hill river bottoms, with the northern section running back into the hills. Its streets are lined with elm trees, some forming a bower over the highway. Its homes are set back from the street as in old New England, with velvety lawns and flower gardens.

Waving fields of wheat, corn, alfalfa, and generous farm homesteads surround the town. One enters it directly from the clean sweep of the farmlands. Settled soon after the Civil War, it awoke from its primeval slumbers, when in 1867, the Kansas Pacific Railroad (now the Union Pacific) built west from Kansas City.

In Texas were tens of thousands of fat cattle on the range, gathered during wartime when there were no means of driving them to market. Abilene became a shipping point, and soon thundering herds came in an unending stream across the Indian territory, now Oklahoma, to the hastily built yards at the trail's end. This terminus is marked by a huge boulder on Main Street, the gift of the Daughters of the American Revolution.

Through 1867, and until 1871, when other shipping points were opened farther west, the influx continued. Along with the herds came the cowboys, jaded by their long trek and with their pay checks uncashed. For their amusement a whole city of dance halls and saloons sprung up on the southern edge of the city. The nights were filled with roistering and the days with the lowing of cattle.

This was the borderland of the "Great West" in its birth throes, the first birth pains of a continent aroused from the æons, a giant struggling to its feet to march on to vast conquests. We have noted that Abilene, now a city of churches and schools and cultured homes, was once known the country over as a "bad" town. It was but human nature in the raw: rugged pioneers bringing vigorous life to the plains. To curb the disturbances two policemen fully attired in uniforms were imported from St. Louis. They were so stoutly treated that they stayed only one night, and left for more quiet pastures.

We have told you how Tom Smith, a brave enforcer of the law, tried it. He disarmed the cowboys and kept a semblance of law and order, until one night he was found dead in a dugout where he went to arrest a murderer. A large boulder in the Abilene cemetery erected by a grateful citizenry marks his grave.

Then we have seen "Wild Bill" Hickok, touted as quick on the trigger and with a record of courage and nerve. "Calamity Jane," a woman of note in the annals of western desperadoes, accompanied him to Abilene. He lasted a few months, sending to the happy hunting grounds the more obstreperous of the frontiersmen. He and Calamity Jane lie side by side in the Deadwood cemetery in South Dakota.

Some three million head of cattle had been shipped from Abilene when the heyday of the trade vanished. Then Abilene commenced to rebuild. When Dwight Eisenhower came here, an infant, twenty years later, it was a steadily growing community. As he grew up into the new century, Abilene took on new habiliments and became a community of peaceful homes. During his childhood its social activities were homemade: the people depended upon themselves for amusement. Home talent plays, school plays—in one of these Dwight was a swaggering hero—horse races, county fairs, cultural organizations which discussed poetry and art, community dances, an occasional stock company playing *The Count of Monte Cristo* at the "opera" house.

Those were the halcyon years for the ambitious village. It lived a community life. All shared its activities. In this environment Dwight and his brothers took a large part. They were popular, energetic, likeable. The fact that they worked their way through school did not count: wealth did not count in those days. When, as we shall see, Dwight expressed a desire to go to West Point, the whole town helped and rejoiced at his winning the appointment.

Returning occasionally, he finds a new Abilene of six thousand population: paved streets, an eight-story hotel, handsome school buildings, public library, federal building, artistic railway stations, an attractive city park, $150,000 swimming pool instead of the "Old Swimmin' hole" in the river. The business district is almost wholly rebuilt and modern homes set on spacious lawns. Abilene is a thoroughly modern American city.

General Eisenhower's home town in his youth was a city of some forty-five hundred people. It had dirt streets, mostly board sidewalks, perhaps a dozen motor cars, a half dozen churches and was building new schoolhouses. The center of a rich farming country, its youths found jobs in summer on the rural acres. This the Eisenhower boys did. They were a clan of their own. They worked together, played together, and Dwight, the third in age, was liked by everyone.

When he came home on his infrequent visits as a captain, a brigadier general, he found companions he had left behind and loved to fraternize with them as of old. On a sunny morning one would find him sitting with a group of old-time cronies in a favorite confectionery store, passing jokes and reminiscences.

He did not wear a uniform on these stolen meetings, but put on civvies so that he would not be conspicuous or make his friends self-conscious. He visited the stores and offices of those he had known—such as were still left in the city—and received warm greetings everywhere, for the town is very proud of Dwight.

Dwight was one of the most popular among the youths of town. He was jolly, generous, with initiative. In school and in the social doings he was always a leader. He seemed to have the social instinct tempered with respect for his associates.

As one walks down the prosperous looking streets today with their comfortable homes, you come to the post-office lawn at the edge of the business district and stand before a boulder marking the terminus of the old Chisholm Trail—the end of an era. Youths who gather about it today come from the many colleges—the percentage of boys and girls attending college is higher in Abilene than in most of the nation's communities.

Abilene, like all progressive American communities, has its home-town newspaper, one of the best-edited in the United States. Step in and meet Editor Harger, lifelong friend of the Eisenhowers, as he sits in the office of the *Abilene Reflector-Chronicle*. With the latest news from World War II coming over the tickers of the Associated Press and the United Press, he keeps Abilene informed on every move that Ike makes on faraway battlefields.

While the villagers call him Charlie, he is in reality Dr. Charles Moreau Harger, L.H.D., Litt.D., a distinguished poet and author as well as journalist, the "William Allen White of Abilene." This scholarly gentleman is an authority not only on the Eisenhowers but on the history of the state and nation. More than four score years have not lessened his energies.

Editor Harger gives us this insight into the background which molded the strong character of General Dwight Eisenhower. "The General's outstanding characteristic is his love for the simple things of home life," he remarks. "His youth was among the modest people of our town. They were workers, money was scarce, it was no disgrace to work at anything honest. They lost nothing of caste among their fellows, for most of them were in the same category.

"One summer Ike worked in a creamery, emptying milk cans, delivering ice and proving his energy and resourcefulness. Between times he and his brothers tended garden on the four-acre home place to which service men today take walks to look at the Eisenhower cottage.

"One of his attainments was cooking. He fancied himself a chef and proved it. While his parents were at church he and his brothers, himself as leader, would prepare the Sunday meal. It is related by his mother that sometimes she would come home and find the boys tossing dough to one another or vying with each other in the perfection of their viands.

"His ambition was to make a pie. After many trials he accomplished it. The pie was declared satisfactory by his parents, and Dwight was greatly pleased by his triumph. He added pancakes and vegetables to his menu and enjoyed the task.

"The dish washing was done by the same tossing method by which the dough was handled. From hands to hands the crockery went the rounds, with only occasionally a crash. When he came home the first room he visited was the pantry, and he longed to try his hands at cookery again. His wife tells of his prowess yet. In their Washington home he frequently took the preparation of meals into his own hands. He prided himself on the perfection with which he could cook a steak.

"At the camps where he has been stationed he always, if possible, set out a garden, raising vegetables for the mess. It was amusing to his comrades, but he went at it seriously. On the home lot he and his brothers raised potatoes, tomatoes, beans and similar products and sold them around town, thus obtaining money for their clothing and school demands."

Mother Eisenhower soon found herself with six Eisenhower boys, of whom the General is the third. They were called by their playmates "Big Ike" and "Little Ike," with such varied exceptions as "Ugly Ike," for the General, and "Red Ike" for the readheaded Earl. Mother Eisenhower disclaims all knowledge of these nicknames. When asked as to the whereabouts and doings of "Ike" she asks blandly, *"Ike? Who's Ike?"*

Dwight was "just about the most normal boy" you could imagine, according to his brother Milton. If there was any clean fun, he was in it. Several of his companions in those days claim he had a temper which he managed to keep pretty well under control. He was strong and healthy—quite notably strong—though his brother Edgar, almost two years older than he, always "licked" him when they scuffled. After Dwight got to West Point, he took up scientific boxing and wrote to Edgar, challenging him to a scrap. Edgar, however, had by that time become an undergraduate at the University of Washington (where he took his law degree) and was better prepared to do his scrapping with words than with fists; he declined Dwight's offer.

Dwight used to swim in a hole in Mud Creek, which meanders through Abilene. In the winter, if and when the stream froze over, he played hockey—or "shinny" as they called it—on the ice, using a tin can as a puck. When he grew older, he "graduated" to the Smoky Hill River, where the older boys took their sport, fishing and swimming. He attended Lincoln Grade School in Abilene and was considered one of the best athletes in school.

A friend of the family, Kenneth S. Davis, a young writer who has collected much data for this book with the family's approval, informs us: "The boys were raised in a home which took Christianity very seriously. Their Aunt Amanda was their Sunday School teacher and the boys attended Sunday School regularly. They did not, however, attend church services as a general rule, for Sunday was the parents' 'day off' and the boys had all the cooking and housework to do that day.

"Dwight and Edgar were the official cooks. All of the boys were encouraged to make games of their work, though if the work was not done well, it had to be done over at once, and the cooking of Dwight and Edgar was no exception. However, it is doubtful that the family as a whole would have enjoyed the pastries the two prepared if they had known just how those pastries were made.

"On one occasion, Dwight and Edgar were making an apple pie. Edgar made some 'crack' about Dwight. Dwight let fly a handful of pie dough at Edgar. The two played baseball around the kitchen with the dough, dropping it on the floor once or twice. In the process, the dough turned several shades darker than it should have been. The kitchen was a mess when the boys heard their father and mother drive up. Dwight, in a hurry, collected the somewhat grimy remains of his pie dough, dumped it back into the bowl, and made his pie, while Edgar rapidly policed the kitchen. The over-browning concealed the grayness. The family pronounced the pie 'pretty good for a kid cook.' Not until a long time afterward did Dwight and Edgar tell the true story of that pie."

Mr. Davis tells us that the Eisenhower orchard raised all the different kinds of fruit that grow in Dickinson County—apples, cherries, pears. The Eisenhower garden raised potatoes, sweet corn, cabbage, peas, beans, tomatoes, berries, practically all the vegetables, including celery, which was blanched by placing boards on both sides and packing the boards with soil. The garden was about 100 by 150 feet and was irrigated and intensively cultivated. Dwight and Edgar were the family gardeners. Neither of them particularly cared about gardening, though Dwight likes to garden now. But they seemed to have "planters hands"; they had the "feel," and things grew well for them.

Each of the boys had assigned chores, but these were changed every week to avoid boredom. For instance, the boys took turns by weeks in getting up at 5:30 in the morning to build the kitchen fire and put on the mush, then driving their father to work. They took turns selling and delivering eggs, chickens, vegetables, and fruit. The money, of course, was turned over to the family "banker," who was the father. Stories have been told that Mother Eisenhower was the banker: this was one thing she never did.

The older boys took jobs on neighboring farms or in the Belle Springs creamery, helping finance the growing family. Arthur, the oldest boy, is reported to be the only one of the six who didn't milk the cow. Always dignified and careful of his dress, he preferred to do extra work to make up for not doing his share of the milking.

Life for the Eisenhower boys was not all work and no play. After their assigned tasks were done (and even these were frequently made into a game) the boys were free to follow their bent, subject only to the limitations of respectable conduct.

To understand Dwight today—his absolute lack of pretension, his genuine friendliness, his talent, amounting to genius, for handling men of all types and making them almost worship him, his tough "fighting heart"—you have to understand his upbringing as one of six boys. No one raised with five sharp-eyed, sharp-tongued brothers is likely to have much pretense left in him by the time he leaves school.

The one thing normal boys hate above all else in their fellows is "conceit": the assertion, conscious or unconscious, of any individual's "superiority." Dwight's hatred of conceit and vanity was particularly strong. This stems from his father, whom all the boys loved dearly; he was a modest and retiring but deeply self-respectful man.

The Eisenhowers are distinctly a "family." The family is the basic unit, within which the individual Eisenhowers have their being, and it is highly cohesive. The boys still think of themselves more as a family than as individuals. When any of them does anything outstanding (and all of them are continuously doing outstanding things), he thinks first of how pleased the family will be, and derives his greatest pleasure from that. The boys keep in close touch by correspondence, and each of them has made an effort—usually successful—to visit his mother in Abilene at least once a year.

The six Eisenhower boys learned, and learned early, that success in life must be earned; that nothing worthwhile can be gained save through effort. All the boys had regular assignments of work. Thus their family income was supplemented by home-grown vegetables and fruit, with dairy products and poultry produced by mother and sons. This work required of the boys was also a deliberate technique of their mother's. She was concerned with building character. She was all too aware that idle, healthy, fun-loving lads are likely to get themselves into serious trouble. She provided them with disciplined, useful outlets for their healthy energies.

Abilene, the home town, took the General's rising popularity with a cumulative appreciation. For years he had been just one of the Army officers. When he was made a member of the war staff at Washington, the town first commenced to take notice. His appointment to London, the North African invasion, his promotion to a four-star general, and his becoming Supreme Commander of the European Forces, thrilled the town.

The Chamber of Commerce ordered five thousand copies of a portrait, and his features greeted residents in hundreds of windows. It announced an "Eisenhower Day" in the Summer of 1942. The town was bedecked with flags, the band led a parade to the city park, and crowds gathered for the ceremonies. His long-time friend, Editor Harger, paid a tribute to the General. Girls sang songs in his honor. His mother, who had been induced to come to the celebration, was introduced and received cheers from the townspeople.

The General was made an honorary member of the Rotary and Lions Clubs, of the American Legion, and accepted the distinctions with brief cablegrams of appreciation. But the town wanted to do something more. So the Chamber of Commerce came to the front and adopted this resolution:

> Whereas: General Dwight D. Eisenhower, being reared and educated in Abilene, Kansas, has gained national and world-wide fame as a four-star general in the United States Army; and whereas: General Eisenhower continues to honor Abilene as his "real home town," resolved that the Board of Directors of the Abilene Chamber of Commerce requests the Governing Body of the City of Abilene, Kansas to pass an ordinance renaming Buckeye Street as "Eisenhower Avenue," thus honoring General Eisenhower as a military leader of world recognition.

This street extends for two miles through the business and residential districts. The Citizens Committee asked the City Commission to name the city park "Eisenhower Park" and erect proper signs so designating it. This city park covers some fifty acres, beautified with flowers and trees.

An oil painting of General Eisenhower decorates the USO rooms. It was dedicated with speeches. His picture dominates the billboard on Main Street with the names of some two thousand men of the county who are in the armed services. Abilene honors its most distinguished citizen.

Here is an anecdote about the Eisenhower family: It was mid-

January, 1943, when the General suddenly appeared in Kansas. He had left North Africa and come to Washington. No hint was given of his coming. After a few days in the capital, consulting with the General Staff, he took an inconspicuous car with a driver and went to West Point to see his son and only child, John, cadet in the Academy.

Driving into the grounds he parked the car under an overpass and slipped into the commandant's office. A call was sent to John to come immediately to the office. Young Eisenhower was in overalls in the machine shop, his hands and face discolored with grease. The order was to come as he was: and he did.

His surprise can be imagined when he saw his father, who, he thought, was in North Africa, standing there. After a visit the General drove back to Washington undiscovered. A few days later he appeared in Kansas, greeting his younger brother, President Milton S. Eisenhower, of Kansas State College, at Manhattan, forty miles east of Abilene.

He arrived at Fort Riley on a plane at dusk and sent word ahead. With only a driver he went to Manhattan where his mother and an elder brother, A. S. Eisenhower, vice president of the Commerce Trust Company, Kansas City, and his brother Milton awaited him. The dinner was embellished by favorite foods, including the well-known Pennsylvania "puddin" brought from home by his mother. An evening of visiting followed. In the conversation the matter of a soldier's responsibility under shock or weariness came up and the General told of an experience in North Africa never before related.

He had gone farther to the front than was wise and was in danger of being surrounded by the Axis troops. In a jeep loaded with extra gasoline he and an orderly started hurriedly on a far course over the desert. Driving for hours and hours, making a wide detour to get back to camp, they took turns at the wheel. The orderly was at the wheel when the General went to sleep:

and propably the driver did also. Suddenly they found the jeep off the road and partly overturned in a ditch. Neither was hurt. After a long struggle the machine was righted and they could proceed.

"What did you do to the orderly for going to sleep?" he was asked.

"Do? Poor chap, when we returned I sent him to the hospital to sleep to his heart's content."

That was the human side of Ike Eisenhower.

After a few happy hours with his mother and brothers in Kansas, the General slipped away. Because of threatening bad weather, he left in the early morning and took his plane back to Washington. No one in central Kansas except the family knew of his visit.

The news came in a day or two that he was in London—he had jumped the Atlantic in an airplane to take up his duties as Supreme Commander of the Allied Army. Then it could be announced that he had been on his home soil and had visited his mother. His mother and her woman companion, the brothers and their families, breathed no word of the visit until it was all over. They were good censors.

Thus we can see that we have in Ike Eisenhower and his brothers a mixture of Tom Sawyer and Huckleberry Finn with a dash of Tom Brown. We can readily understand the General's love for his home town.

He grew up in exciting times: when Buffalo Bill was a boyhood idol, when Carrie Nation was smashing saloons in Kansas with her hatchet, precursor of prohibition years to come. His greatest hero was Teddy Roosevelt and his Rough Riders. He followed the Spanish-American war with childhood interest.

When Ike heard of Admiral Dewey's great Battle of Manila Bay in the faraway Philippines, he little knew that some day he would be in these same islands with MacArthur, a lad born in the neighboring state of Arkansas—that in World War II they would both be making history on opposite sides of the earth.

And we can see in Ike some of the qualities of Abraham Lincoln, who, when he thought of home, penned verses which are little known, in which he expressed this same deep sentiment:

> My childhood's home I see again,
> And sadden with the view;
> And still, as memory crowds my brain,
> There's pleasure in it, too. . . .
>
> The friends I left that parting day,
> How changed, as time has sped!
> Young childhood grown, strong manhood gray;
> And half of all are dead. . . .

· 8 ·

School days in Abilene—with recollections of his neighbors

THE PEOPLE OF ABILENE are walking encyclopedias; what they don't know about our nation's history isn't worth knowing; and what they know about Ike Eisenhower would fill an encyclopedia.

Editor Harger's newspaper office is the center of all information, past, present, and future. We will visit him again and listen to some of his reminiscences.

"A favorite gathering spot for the young men and some oldsters in Abilene for many years was Joner's place, a modest candy, news, tobacco, and fountain and confectionery store on the main street. 'Joner'—his real name B. L. Callahan—was a boyhood friend of the General, later was mayor of the city, and is one of the most loyal worshippers of Dwight in the community. One corner of the store has walls covered with pictures, letters, and newspaper clippings of the hero—in his youth and after.

"Here every morning a dozen or more patrons meet informally to sip their 'cokes' and discuss the events of the day. Once they collected money and sent a cablegram of congratulations to the head of the army on his birthday; they have also sent hundreds of cartons of cigarettes. When the North African campaign opened, the 'gang,' as they like to call themselves, sent this cablegram: 'The gang and all Abilene endorse the United Nations' choice of leadership. Fight 'em, Cowboy! Joner.'

" 'Fight 'em, Cowboy,' is the playing slogan of the Abilene High School teams of which Dwight was a member. When Eisenhower came home on visits during the twenties and thirties he always spent an hour or two at Joner's. There the old playmates and schoolmates would crowd the little cafe and talk over old times and the events of early days. Nothing was said about army life. He wanted to get away from all that. To inquiries he merely said he was stationed so and so. This was when he was aide to General MacArthur in the Philippines or commandant of important military posts in the Northwest. Writing home from London once, he said, 'I wish I could go down to Joner's this morning and have a coke with the gang.' "

Joner's is gone now: Callahan has moved to more commodious and sophisticated quarters. But he still has an "Eisenhower corner" fixed up with pictures and letters and clippings where the "gang" hangs out of mornings and listens to the radio accounts of their hero. His return will be the occasion of much rejoicing.

Editor Harger tells how the autograph fever struck Abilene when the General became famous. The friends who received letters were besieged for the signatures. It did not matter that mostly they were signed "Ike," they still had a value. A friend wrote to Dwight telling him of the demand for his autograph. When he sent them back (as related elsewhere) on a sheet of paper on which he had written "Ike" some twenty times, they were cut apart and given to the schools to help in a bond-selling campaign.

The children fought over this new currency and piled up stamps and bonds until all were gone. One girl bought $230 in bonds to secure her longed-for autograph. All this was in addition to a number of letters written to children and classes, all of which are treasured by the recipients and will be handed down to their grandchildren some day.

Ike's promptness in acknowledging communications is a wonder to those who know the strain under which he labors. The cablegram of the Rotary Club telling him he had been made an honorary member of that organization, the cablegrams from the "gang" extending congratulations on his birthday and on his promotion, received replies the next day.

To the Rotary Club, he said, "Gentlemen: Your cablegram stating 'Honorary membership voted you today' arrived yesterday. I deeply appreciate the spirit which prompts the tender of this honor. I hope you will not have cause to revoke the membership, as when the war is over I would like to attend sessions of the Rotary Club of my real home town."

He writes to his correspondents, "Keep the mail coming. I will try to do my part."

"General Eisenhower is about the least impressed with having his picture in the paper or on posters of any prominent person alive," Editor Harger tells us. "When his home town ordered five thousand copies of a gaudy portrait, and hundreds of them were placed in windows, a friend wrote to him, 'They are the worst pictures of you I have ever seen. They show you with a mouth like Joe E. Brown and features like nobody at all.' However, he added more favorably, 'It is a splendid picture of a uniform.'

"Back from North Africa came this reply: 'If it is in order, I will apologize for the appearance of the picture poster you tell me about as floating around Abilene. The artist may have done a bum job, but, after all, he didn't have a hell of a lot to start working on. Anyway, what was the occasion for the picture? Am I supposed to be selling a particular brand of cigarettes, or is the war-bond drive still on?' "

Editor Harger relates: "One day when Ike was not so prominent he arrived in town and sputtered the indignation he felt. He had just got off the train and it must have been full of isolationists. He was boiling mad over the apathy of our people. He said people ought to learn what the hell was going on; that Japan had been preparing for war for ten years, and were going to jump on us one of these days and we'd have nothing to fight 'em with. He said he had intended retiring that year and moving back to Abilene, but that he had decided not to because this country soon would need every soldier it could scrape up.

"Have you heard about the incident on the General's visit to the Cairo conference?" asks Editor Harger. "Ike told it in a letter to his home folks. At the conclusion of the conference the General flew to the Holy Land and was met by the Very Reverend Paschal Kinsel, O. F. M., President of the Terra Sancta College, conducted by American Franciscans. Father Paschal escorted his guest on a tour of the holy places, including the Holy Sepulcher and Mount Calvary. At the tomb of the Saviour, the General met Brother Francis Kreutzer, O. F. M., a native of Kansas. Later the military leader sent Brother Francis a large photograph autographed 'from a fellow Kansan.'

"General Eisenhower and Father Paschal visited the Garden of Gethsemane and the Mount of Olives before going to Bethlehem, where the Allied Commander prayed in the Grotto of the Nativity. At the Grotto, he was greeted by a fellow Texan, Brother Camillus Liska, and the two had a short visit. The General and his religious guide had lunch together, after which Ike expressed his gratitude for the privilege of an ideal pilgrimage to the holy shrines following an arduous time in Cairo."

We leave Editor Harger to see some of the old "gang" around Abilene—to hear what some of his schoolmates have to say and some of the "old timers" who knew him in his schooldays.

One of Ike's boyhood friends is Orin Snider, now a farmer in

Abilene; he was coach of the football team on which Dwight played in his high-school days and recalls the characteristics of the young devotee of athletics.

"He was just another average chap," Orin tells us. "He was a capable player and in his post-graduate year in 1901 was the best tackle on the team. Although only weighing 155 pounds, he won the honor of being the best tackle in the Kansas Conference. Dwight worked hard and did not have much time to practice. He fired furnace in the creamery and ice plant, earning enough to keep him in school.

"In the regular school years Dwight played end; his brother Edgar was really a better player. But in the final showdown Dwight won out. Young Eisenhower was always ready to admit mistakes. He quickly diagnosed the trick plays of the opponents and was invaluable in planning an offensive, a characteristic that has been shown in his army life. The team had homemade uniforms, some with sweatpads swiped from livery stables for shoulder pads and old stocking caps for headgear."

This boyhood friend says of Ike as a baseball player, "He played center field on the baseball team, but was just another player. One thing he always demanded, that the team show good sportsmanship, whether winning or losing; and every man on the team respected him. He was president of the school's athletic association in his senior year and drew up the constitution by which the association has lived for forty years. When he went to West Point he slipped naturally to his old place on the football team, this time as halfback."

Remembered vividly by the old "gang" is a feat of prowess that endeared Ike to the sporting crowd in the home town. It seems that one Dirk Taylor, a Negro heavyweight, had achieved something more than local fame as a fighter during Ike's absence. Dirk was a handyman around town, mowing lawns, doing odd jobs, and acting as porter in a barbershop when he wasn't fighting or training. Dirk was good, all right, but he was cocky about it. Husky, belligerent, and boastful, he declared he could "lick any man in Kansas."

Dwight arrived home on a brief leave. He had taken up boxing at West Point and the boys appealed to him to take some of the wind out of this heavyweight.

"We've been badgered by this 'champion' too long," they told Ike. "He thinks no one in this part of the country can stand up against him for one round. Why don't you take him on?"

Dwight was much lighter, but wiry, and had become known as one of the best boxers at the Academy. He took off his cadet uniform, changed into old clothes, and went over to the barbershop to get a shave. Dirk glared at him out of the corner of his eyes and mumbled, "I can knock out any man in Kansas." Ike listened quietly as he sat lathered in the barber chair.

When the shave was finished he surprised everybody by stepping from the chair and remarking, "Dirk, I know you're good, but how'd you like to go across the street to the basement of Stirl's clothing store while we see just *how* good you are?"

"Sure," replied Dirk. "There aint nuthin' better I'd like ta do."

With Cadet Eisenhower and Dirk the entire crowd in the barbershop, with the exception of one poor barber who had to stay behind, trooped across the street. In a few minutes they all trooped back again, carrying Dirk. The "champ" had been knocked out in the second round. Ike had boxed with precision against Dirk's power. Dodging a terrific uppercut, Ike came back with a solar plexus that laid the town's boaster flat on the floor. The claims of the invincible heavyweight were exploded. But there were no hard feelings. The two were good friends. Dirk became one of the town's most ardent admirers of Ike and called him a "swell fellow." And Ike gave Dirk many recommendations that got him extra jobs.

Incidentally, it should be said that in Abilene, as in most of

Kansas, there is seldom any racial prejudice. Ike has never had anything but friendship for the "colored brothers" and they are his staunch friends. Negroes played on the high school team with Dwight. His bout with Dirk was but a "sporting event": there is no color line in the boxing world. We shall see later Ike's kindly consideration for his colored soldiers in World War II.

So many years have gone by since the General's early school days that the teachers who had charge of his classes are mostly gone. Miss Annie P. Hopkins, now retired and living in Arkansas, gives us this picture of him:

"I remember Second Lieutenant Dwight, just graduated from West Point, when he came home to Abilene in the summer of 1915. He was en route to Fort Sam Houston, Texas, to report for his first duty in the army. I talked with him at his home early in September. He was a fine-looking, strapping fellow then, very boyish in his talk and in his actions.

"I recall very distinctly that he mentioned one woman mathematics teacher whose classes he had attended in high school. She tutored him for a while before he took the entrance examination for West Point. He spoke very highly of her and said, 'I'd like to see her again to thank her for what she did for me. How she did dress me down for the mistakes I made. She didn't handle me with gloves on.'"

He was a rollicking student, good-natured and popular with his classmates, a good student but no prodigy. One of his classmates, Mrs. R. I. Parker, now living in Hinsdale, Illinois, says, "Dwight was something of a whiz in history." She got out the year book of the high school to prove it. Under the picture of the serious-faced boy the line reads, "Little Ike is now a couple inches taller than Big Ike [his brother—all the Eisenhower boys were called Ike]—he is our best historian and mathematician."

"He always knew more than any of us," she commented. "He

always did lots of reading on his own account and could talk about the kings and generals of the past for hours. In the prophecy we printed at the end of the course it was set down that he would be a professor of history at Yale.

"I remember that he played in our parody of *The Merchant of Venice*—our senior play. He was clever and amusing and kept the remainder of the cast in stitches, much to the dismay of our coach."

There is extant a program of the high-school senior-class play in Dwight's senior year at high school. The play was *The Merchant of Venice Up-to-Date*, and Dwight Eisenhower played the role of Launcelot Gobbo, servant to Shylock, who is described in the synopsis as the "hero of the occasion." The modernized version was reported to "center around the rivalry between Captain Antonio of the Abilene High School football team and Shylock, a former player on the Chapman team."

The girls in Abilene looked upon Dwight as an "up and coming young man." Some of them thought he was "handsome"; others called him "manly." Here is what one of his old girl friends says about him: "I was with him in high school. He was always a natty dresser. He kept himself neat and up-to-date with the latest fashions in youth's clothing, always in good taste. We girls considered him the most presentable boy in the school.

"And," she adds, "we admired his light hair, blue eyes, and wonderfully white teeth. He taught me to swim and took me dancing. He was just a jolly good friend, a perfect gentleman."

When Abilene people recall young Dwight now, their anecdotes seem to center on his high-school days. He managed to carve out an athletic career second only to that of his older brother, Edgar ("Big Ike"), who was in his school class. He gave some indication, in his senior year, of the organizing genius which was to mark his military career. We find this story in the section on "Athletics" of the Abilene High School Annual, called *The Helianthus*, for 1909, written by and signed by Dwight Eisenhower.

"Early in the fall of 1908," wrote the youthful Eisenhower, "the high school boys organized an Athletic Association for the year. After electing Dwight Eisenhower president, Harry Makins vice president, and Herbert Sommers secretary and treasurer, we proceeded to do business. Deciding not to play any baseball, we started on football at once," Dwight continued, and then went on to tell of the football record that year.

Prior to Dwight's senior year, sports were not officially connected with the school. The teams had worked out at the county fairgrounds, bought their own uniforms, and employed their own coaches. Dwight, by laying the foundations of the school's Athletic Association and obtaining the approval of the high-school administration, helped inaugurate a new era in Abilene's athletic history. The high school ever since has been notably strong in football. It was a proud day for a school from another town if it could beat Abilene. Ike was President of the Athletic Association, 1909; football, 1907, 1908; baseball, 1908, 1909.

Classmates of Dwight describe him as "strong as an ox" and the "scrappinist" kid in school. In one football game—the last game of the 1908 series—he is reported to have "roughed" about half of the Salina High School line because his friend and teammate, J. F. (Six) McDonnell (who now lives in Abilene) had been accidentally knocked out by Forest Ritter, a Salina player.

Salina High had come down to Abilene that year with an unbeaten team. It was prophesied that Abilene would lose by a big score. McDonnell, who played quarterback for Abilene, called a fake play, faking a pass to one Bud Huffman, who was playing right half, and then started around left end himself. Ritter came charging through and hit McDonnell hard at the knees, laying him out. It was then that "Little Ike" went to work tearing up the Salina line—and the final score was 18 to 0 in favor of Abilene.

"Little Ike" incidentally had tried out for football in his freshman and sophomore years, but hadn't made it because he was too small. He was an end in his junior year—though he was not as big a star as his brother Edgar, and again in his senior year. Both boys were high-school heroes.

"In his school work, Dwight was not outstanding," his old schoolmates tell us. "He made about average marks in grade school, and slightly better than average in high school with the exception of history and mathematics. Some reports have it that he knew more mathematics than the high-school teachers. He was so intensely interested in history that his teachers had to give him extra long assignments in order to give the other students a chance."

This interest in history is one of the first things that people who know Dwight will tell you about him. It is said that he knows in detail the history of every important military campaign, ancient or modern, that has been recorded. It is through and because of his study of history that he developed those studious habits, the passion to *know*, which has characterized the military career of the man.

Among those who knew Dwight well when in high school is Mr. J. W. Howe, a prominent member of the school board and civic leader. He gives us these recollections: "My first contacts with Dwight came about 1907, but it was a year later when he and his high-school gang, as they called themselves, began to be frequent visitors at my office, the *Abilene News*, my weekly newspaper. This contact came about rather oddly. I had taken a boy, who had little opportunity in life, to work in the office. He was a baseball pitcher, a left-hander, and for one of his age was above his class. He and Dwight became close friends and were together a great deal. Ike came to my office as did many others. I was single, a member of the school board, and had time to sit around and discuss many subjects with them.

"In those days," Mr. Howe explains, "all a newspaper editor had to do to get exchanges was to write a letter to the paper he desired and ask for an exchange. It was generally done. So I had dailies from New York, Cleveland, Kansas City, St. Louis, as well as many of the Kansas dailies and weeklies. Ike began by looking through them—then to read them. Most of the time he read newspapers from a distance. He said, 'I like to read about what is going on outside of Kansas.'

"I also had a large library," Mr. Howe continues. "Many books I bought, but I also received many complimentary copies from publishers for reviews. They wanted to 'get the small-town view of the publication.' Many of these books dealt with educational matters. The boys would come to get a certain book to get information to write some essay, theme, or thesis. It was a bright and intelligent 'gang' of boys that came to my office. Ike was among the top line with them. He had his school difficulties like the others and many times asked me to help him out with his work. And, as school boys do, was sometimes of the opinion that the teachers had it in for him.

"I do not recall his ever being in any serious trouble. In fact the 'gang' never went that far. However, I never knew him to miss a Hallowe'en round-up or any other event wherein he could expend some of his surplus energy and have a good time. I never knew of his going out to hunt up the town bully just to lick him. I never knew of his being a rodeo rider or a cowhand. He was a good boxer and I used to watch him and the other boys box in a little room I had provided for them. He was not revengeful. He never went out looking for trouble, but at the same time, if he became unexpectedly involved, he never ran away from it. I think his grin saved Ike a lot of trouble.

"I always wondered why the 'gang' called him either 'Ugly

Ike' or 'Little Ike' instead of a more attractive name like 'Smiling Ike.' Dwight had a good personality. He was generally well liked and made friends easily. He never rubbed it in on some boys who were unfortunate, or who from no fault of their own became involved in some difficulty. He was not vindictive. However, he did resent certain slurs or underhand 'shots,' as the boys called them, and would come back with an appropriate retort.

"He had self-assurance but never in all my contact with him did he ever show any conceit. He resented this in other boys more than anything else. In fact, he would dislike a boy for being conceited much more than for something he had done. He had a good physique, wore his clothes well, never overly dressed but usually had good material in his clothes, for he had to make them last. Ike had to work at all times when not in school. He would take any job he could do and seldom complained about the work being too hard.

"To me the outstanding point of his character," Mr. Howe points out, "was that he never showed any bitterness about having to work. He took this for granted. However, in sessions of his 'gang' he took the attitude that a better equalization of economic affairs should be made. As I stated, he made friends with many people, but still and all he had, of course, his select group. The Eisenhower family had no special pull anywhere, and never asked for any.

"Dwight had two outstanding qualifications which, when properly applied, will mean success to most people in almost any vocation they may choose. He was especially observant. He could walk through a plant, or a building or manufacturing establishment, or watch someone who was adept at his work and be able to tell you everything he had seen.

"The other outstanding quality was his ability to listen to a conversation and then at the proper time ask questions that would bring him the information he wanted. He liked to debate subjects and had the faculty of asking controversial questions so as to confuse his opponent and make him come forth with some outstanding facts. If, in the discussion, he was being cornered he would come forth with some witticism and put on his best smile. In that way he generally ended the debate by disposing of his opponent's argument.

"One occasion I vividly recall was a football game," Mr. Howe relates. "It seemed that Ike and a couple of other boys who were players on the high-school team had it intimated to them by the high-school principal that they might not get to play the Friday afternoon game. This was a blow because they were playing a neighboring town—the one town they always wanted to beat. Accordingly they called on me. I was supposed to be the boys' friend and also a member of the school board, and they insisted it was my duty to compel the school authorities to let them play. They, of course, had been behind in their schoolwork.

"I endeavored to explain to them that I was not responsible for their not complying with school requirements. I told them I could not see where I came in, and that it was not my fault. However the argument was of no avail. They told me that I was a fine school-board member and that I certainly lacked the school spirit. I gave them no satisfaction, so they left the office, slamming the door and telling me they would not come back nor would they ever ask me to do anything for them again. However, they all came back. They played in the football game.

"Another occasion of this kind was when some of the boys, including Ike, went skating or hunting during the time school was in session. They were instructed what they must do in order to return to school. The boys thought it too hard a task. So I was again called upon to intercede. About the same arguments were made pro and con. I was again charged with not being their friend. However, they came back in a day or so. I mention these things to show that Dwight was firm in his demands, yet even as a high-school boy he could see, after thinking it over, he was wrong and the authorities right.

"Two incidents stand out in my mind that apply directly to Ike. I had a book, *The Life of Hannibal*. It started out with Hamilcar telling Hannibal what was expected of him. It told of some of his war strategy. Ike got to looking at it and then later began reading it. I do not know whether he ever finished it, but my reason for remembering it was that several other students looked at it and remarked it was too deep for them.

"The other incident was after Ike's appointment to West Point and was preparing for his examination. He came into the office one evening after school and wanted to know if he could borrow my *Century Book of Facts*. He said he guessed he would have to do some real studying now. He afterwards remarked that it certainly helped him.

"At the 'gag' sessions in the evenings, when national, state, county, city, school, and civic affairs were discussed, as well as sports, and many times the conduct of various citizens of the town, someone would start to sing. Now that was one place Ike got into trouble. He at that time had to struggle to carry a tune and the boys used to insist he was the discordant note. There were others, as far as that goes, but Ike evidently is a much better general than he was a singer.

"Dwight was a good athlete. He was a good ballplayer—playing left field mostly, I think. He was a good football player. He played the game with all the vim and enthusiasm he possessed. He was not what the boys called a 'dirty' player. He took advantage of the opponents' weaknesses, but that's about all. One of the rules that we laid down to the boys whom I sponsored—and there were about thirty of them—was that there was to be no rough stuff in any game."

In summing up the life of Dwight Eisenhower as a high-school student, Mr. Howe says, "We found him going along the average road. He never impressed his knowledge on others, nor did he approve of their doing that to him. He respected his elders. He was always for the underdog, if he thought the boy or girl was right. Money was not his aim. The rich and poor alike respected the Eisenhower family and on several occasions I have seen Ike go to the rescue of some boy who he thought needed help. He, as everyone else, became angry, but soon cooled off. In other words, he was a real boy, associated with real boys, did the usual boyish pranks, and was in no way susceptible to flattery. In fact he hated flattery and conceit more than anything. Reading of some of his acts as a General I find he has not changed."

Dwight Eisenhower's graduation from the Abilene High School was a "great event." There were thirty-one members in his class. The commencement address was delivered by the Hon. Henry J. Allen, then editor of the *Wichita Beacon*, and later elected governor of Kansas and United States senator. He was a friend of the late William Allen White whose many books include *The Martial Adventures of Henry and Me*, describing a trip they made to France during World War I. Superintendent of Abilene schools, W. A. Stacey, presided at the exercises.

Eighteen-year-old Ike was there, as he said, "in all his glory." His family sat in the audience and looked upon him with pride as he received his diploma. He was starting out on a career, no one knew where. Ike himself didn't know. He worked around Abilene for more than a year, helping his father and doing various jobs as a fireman and refrigerative engineer—and all the time he was "planning."

Finally he decided. He was intrigued by the biographies of great military leaders. His decision took his family by complete surprise.

"I'm going to enter the service of my country," he announced.
The Eisenhower family were religiously opposed to war.
The United Brethren, like the Quakers, were pledged to peace.
Here after centuries of "living together in brotherhood" they
were to have war brought right into their own household.

Dwight, however, insisted he knew what he was about, and
no amount of persuasion could change his mind. His ancestors
had felt "called to the ministry": Ike felt "called to the service
of his country."

Two pals had reached their decision together. Ike and his
friend, Everett Hazlett, were going to Annapolis and enter the
Navy. Hazlett passed his entrance examinations, but it was discovered that Ike, twenty years old, was a few months over age.
He bid his friend, Hazlett, good-by and went into a secret
session with himself.

Again Ike came out with a decision: he would go to West
Point and serve in the army. Immediately he lost himself in all
the documents and official information he could obtain about
the United States Military Academy. Ascertaining the qualifications required, he began to study day and night. Finally he
felt assured he was equipped for his first battle with the examinations.

Appointment to West Point required political confirmation.
Ike enlisted two family friends, Editor Harger, of the *Abilene
Reflector-Chronicle*, who knew everybody and was held in
high esteem throughout the community and the state. If Ike
could "win him over" he would have the strongest possible
support. Editor Harger, admiring the determination of the
youth, consented to help him. Ed Heath, postmaster of Abilene,
a position of political importance in the community, joined
Ike's forces. Other influential citizens were lined up. Ike now
had his first fighting squad ready for action.

United States Senator Joseph H. Bristow was a power in

state and national affairs, a leader on the floor of the Senate. And on October 11, 1910, Dwight David Eisenhower received from the War Department an appointment to West Point. This official document created quite a sensation at the village post office when Postmaster Heath handed it to Ike.

Young Dwight passed his examinations with flying colors against eight competitors. Abilene extended its congratulations to "our boy who is going to West Point." His schoolboy friends shook his hand with exclamations, "We knew you'd do it, Ike!" And the girls were thrilled with the prospects of their former classmate coming home in "a cadet's uniform." The Eisenhower family was now resigned to the inevitable.

On that June day in 1911 Dwight Eisenhower, surrounded by friends at the railroad station in Abilene, stepped on the train "to go East." He waved to the group on the platform as the train chugged out of sight. And something told them, "We'll hear from that boy; he's heading out for a great future."

Two boys from the home town were now to "make good" in the service of their country: Midshipman Hazlett at Annapolis was to become a commander in the United States Navy—Cadet Eisenhower was on his way to West Point, finally to become a general in the United States Army. Thus the Army and the Navy were to be united in two boys from Abilene.

· 9 ·

Visit to Mother Eisenhower in the Old Family Home

WHEN SOLDIERS come to Abilene they ask one question: "Where is the house where General Eisenhower lived?" The dwelling has become a shrine. Though it is a considerable walk from the center of town, day after day groups of uniformed men stroll to gaze at the modest boyhood home of their hero—hoping also to gain a sight of the mother.

When it was built the Eisenhower house was well out in the suburbs. The idea of the father was to have plenty of space in which to bring up his energetic flock. It is still in the far southeast part of the city on a four-acre tract which the Eisenhower boys tilled intensively.

The visitors see a white, two-story dwelling of simple architecture, with bowers of roses in the well-kept yard. It is like thousands of other houses in the villages of the Middle West, a lean-to at one side, a porch in front. It has no gables, no fancy doorways—it was constructed for use and not for show.

In summer the eighty-three-year-old mother may be sitting on the front porch calmly knitting and thinking of her sons so widely scattered—and especially of one guiding a large part of the nation's fighting forces.

International News Photo

Mrs. Eisenhower and Cadet John S. Doud Eisenhower, United States Military Academy, returning from their Christmas shopping in Washington, D. C.

Acme Photo

Mrs. Eisenhower pinning a medal on her husband when he was a colonel. President Manuel Quezon, of the Philippines, looks on

Inside you find a thoroughly homey atmosphere. There are chairs and tables fifty years old, the walls nearly covered with photographs of the family—most of them of "Ike" in various poses and some of the entire group of six sons. The parlor has a davenport and some easy chairs with books here and there. Portraits of father and mother—and more poses of the sons. Somehow the spirit of parent-son relationship seems to be present more here than in ordinary homes.

To know General Eisenhower, one must meet his mother. A gentle old lady, with firm faith in God and man, her silver hair glistening in the sunlight, her hands folded in resignation, Mother Eisenhower awaits in her eighty-third year for the end of the war and the return of her famous son.

When one looks upon this kindly countenance, with its benevolent smile, there is no doubt whatsoever that this is the mother of the world's great general. The resemblance is striking. His features are but a masculine replica; he has the same firm but kindly mouth, the same penetrating blue eyes, the same keen intelligence of expression. Even in her venerable years, she retains the magnetic personality and dominant qualities that characterize the General.

To give you an intimate acquaintance with the mother of General Eisenhower we combine here a visit by her lifelong friend, Dr. Harger, (for this book) with other visits to the old homestead by townspeople and pilgrims who have journeyed to this new American shrine. Owing to her venerated years, her family desire to protect her as much as possible from the fatigue of sight-seers. There is a family agreement that she shall not be burdened with questions. Therefore, these anecdotes are largely a composite of many interviews.

Here, in the sunset of life, we meet the Ida Elizabeth Stover who left her home in Virginia more than sixty years ago and "came West." There is still the same pioneer spirit in the nobility of her soul. She is, as one commentator has said, "a truly great woman in her own right."

"Perhaps," says one of her visitors, who recently painted a vivid word-picture of her for the American press, "Ida Elizabeth Eisenhower is today's strongest influence for world brotherhood. Not directly. But her influence operates through her famous son who is following her teachings."

Mother Eisenhower points with pride at seven pictures in her long, low-ceilinged living-room—one of her recently deceased husband, "My David," and the others of her six sons. She lives here alone, with her companion and family friend, Naomi Engle, and these photographs of her beloved family. Two are dead— Earl and Paul—"gone with their father."

Through the recollections of Mother Eisenhower, as related during the years, we are able to come into intimate friendship with this family—the mother, father, and six sons. We look into the heart of a mother as one of her boys rises to world fame. To her, Dwight is still "my boy." She sees him only as "a good son."

When Mother Eisenhower heard that her Dwight had been made Commander in Chief of the mighty Allied Forces in World War II, she sat silently and is said to have remarked, "I feel sad when I realize that the responsibility was delegated to Dwight on the Eve of the coming of Christ."

It was Christmas Eve, and her mind was with the Saviour of humanity who nearly two thousand years ago had come to the world as the Prince of Peace. It seemed impossible to her that she could be living in the world's greatest war, with her own son leading the fighting forces. But she knew it was for a "just cause" and that "truth and justice" would eventually triumph.

Dwight to her was "just another soldier"—another mother's son. She did not think of him as a general. When she saw the boys in uniform, passing her home in Abilene, her neighbors say she remarked gently, "*I have a boy in the Army, too.*"

Mother Eisenhower has been quoted as saying, "I hate war. War is wrong!" But she realizes that this war was not instigated by us, but was forced upon us; therefore it is right that we should defend ourselves and go out armored in what she believes is the cause of righteousness and justice.

She satisfies herself with the conviction that we are fighting to create a new age of human brotherhood in which there shall be no wars. And she is proud that her son is leading in the "great crusade." To her it is like the ancient crusades to recover the sepulcher of Christ from the hands of the modern pagans.

"My mother, back in Virginia, grieved herself to death when I was a little girl eleven years old because of the Civil War," she has told friends. "I have hated war ever since."

Her memory goes back to old Virginia as she has recalled her childhood. "Yes," she says, "I was born at Mount Sidney, in Augusta County—Ida Elizabeth Stover. My father, Simon Stover, and my mother, Elizabeth Link, died when I was quite young.

"I was five years old when my father died. My seven brothers and I first went to live with my grandparents, until my mother died. Our farm was ten miles from any town. But we were a happy family."

We can see them now around the family table. She learned early to work around the household. When she was seven years old, she was a good cook and would stand before the brick bake oven and roast ducks or chickens or ham and bake pies for the family of ten.

"It would never do to burn any of the food or take it out underdone," she laughs. "That was sure punishment."

She remembers the old apple orchard and the meadows where she used to play. The youngest child, she adored her brothers. Everything they did, she tried to do. She loved to go horseback riding with her brothers. They would ride through the woods and then sit down under a big tree and tell what they were going to be when they grew up. They decided they would all go away together—somewhere—a long way off. It was agreed that Ida was to go to college.

Even then they realized the value of an education, but she had to keep her ambition a secret because their elders told them that a girl should be seen but not heard—listen, but not talk. She would steal away and read every book she could lay her hands on. Ida went to the country schoolhouse where her oldest brother was a teacher. It was known as the Limestone School-house—built of logs and rough timber on the edge of the woods. Here she learned the three R's—reading, 'riting, and 'rithmetic. It was nothing more than what we would call a shack today, a barren room with rough board benches.

When Ida was not at school, or cooking meals at home, she was generally found in the bare room upstairs making quilts. They were always making quilts. That was the winter pastime. There was no heat in the room and her fingers would get so cold that she would often botch the work and then have to pull it all out and do it over again. It seemed that they were keeping everlastingly at it. If you could cook and quilt that was about all a girl had a right to know.

When she was in her teens, Ida decided to go out into the world. She went to Staunton, near Mount Sidney, where there was a large school and earned her way by baking chickens and pies for the townspeople. There was a high school in Staunton where she studied until she was twenty. This is why some of the old neighbors in Mount Sidney say she left for Kansas when she was eighteen. She really left for Staunton and did not come to Kansas until she was nearly twenty-one. Her brothers joined the Dunkard Colony and settled near Topeka. Ida followed with her cousin. They had kept their childhood agreement to go far away and build their own lives.

Ida found that there was a college called Lane University, at

Lecompton, Kansas, and she went over there and matriculated in September, 1882. She was going to get an education and do big things—filled with burning ambition. Here she met a young student named David Eisenhower, who was studying to become somebody. Well, they fell in love and got married. Then, somehow, books didn't seem so important.

Ida had two ambitions now—the first to be a good wife and mother, the second to advance world brotherhood. She had become imbued with the ideas of Lincoln when he emancipated the slaves. She was eager to wipe out racial prejudices, to raise the Negro to the status of equal citizenship. David agreed with her that all races and nationalities were our brothers.

It is interesting to note here that her son, Dwight, still believes in these principles and demands that "all races be represented equally and undiscriminatingly on the battlefronts."

Mother Eisenhower has many times related their early struggles in raising a family. David had studied engineering at the University and later took a correspondence-school course. When his father lost his fortune they went down to Texas where Dwight was born.

Then after two years they came back to Kansas where David worked as an engineer at the creamery. It was operated by the River Brethren. They had to raise much of their own food in the big vegetable garden. And kept two cows and pigs and chickens, a horse, and a dog—one dog at a time and always a small one. They also had a little orchard. The boys did the chores and also helped earn money by working for farmers near-by.

The boys not only did all the outdoor work, but much of the housework as well, since there were no girls in the family. The driving force of the family was Mother Eisenhower. The father was at work most of the time, and he was also a much less dynamic personality than his vivacious wife. Quiet, modest, retiring, he was almost shy.

He was absolutely trustworthy and capable in his work and was immensely liked and respected both by his superiors and the men who worked under him. In his quiet way, he had immense determination. Once he had decided upon a course, he followed it through. While not a fighter by temperament, he could fight when necessary without yielding, without even considering the possibility of yielding.

The mother, however, was the driving force of the family, and chiefly responsible for the boys' upbringing. She it was who saw to it that the boys had regular schedules of work at home, that they kept up with their work at school, and she was the family disciplinarian. She rarely used the rod, but when she did it was with such effect that Dwight, for one, still remembers. Dwight and Edgar once got a severe "licking" from their mother for neglecting to deliver lunch to their father at his workplace one noon. They "got to playing and forgot." They never forgot again!

Their father, during this period, left the creamery and became an engineer in the gas plant. Later, he was manager of the local plant, which became part of the United Public Utility Companies; thus he had worked himself up into the white-collar class. Before his retirement in 1931, he served as chairman for the employees' benefit and savings plan for all the United companies—a big and responsible job.

When Mother Eisenhower was told, "It's a big job to bring up six fine sons—you've accomplished something great yourself in the world," she replied, "Well, I tried to raise my boys dependable."

She insists that a mother must be not only a good manager and diciplinarian, but the most intimate friend and companion of her boys. She must keep herself in their confidence. Her firm religious principles made her a perfect mother.

Vegetables from the garden were the family diet. Milk, simple, home-cooked foods. They had healthy appetites and consumed enormous quantities of mush with syrup—and puddin—yes *puddin*, not pudding. This was Dwight's favorite dish—he was brought up on puddin.

It is an old Pennsylvania Dutch dish, consisting of all the last scraps from the hog at a country butchering, preserved in lard and melted out in the cold winter days to eat (preferably) with fried mush.

"It was cooked in this big iron kettle," Mother Eisenhower explains. "We used yellow corn meal salted to taste, stirring the meal into boiling water, and cooking it three hours. We let it cool, sliced it, then fried it slowly. Next we poured puddin over it."

Puddin was part of the Pennsylvania Dutch tradition of both her and her husband's family. Mother Eisenhower gives us the recipe which has come down through the generations:

"Use bits of pork, ham hocks and such. Boil, together with bones, if any, for three hours. Let cool, then grind very fine, two grindings. Salt and pepper to taste. Brown in a pan that is covered to prevent spattering. Drain grease. Add water to make meat sauce consisting of thick gravy. Heat again and work into smooth consistency. Spread on slices of fried mush, or bread. After each use, cover or seal what remains with grease to keep fresh indefinitely."

Every kind of fruit known to Dickinson County was produced in the orchard, and in the garden corn, potatoes, peas, cabbage, tomatoes, beans and berries grew aplenty. The garden was intensively irrigated and cultivated. There was also an alfalfa meadow which helped to feed the two cows, the team of horses, the pigs, the chickens and the rabbits which the family owned.

The boys did the chores on an alternating schedule. One of the chores was getting up at 4:30 and starting the kitchen fire, putting on breakfast, and driving Father Eisenhower to work.

They also took turns in selling the farm produce, and later took part-time and summer jobs as farm hands or in the creamery.

Although the boys were mighty busy their recreational opportunities were not neglected. With six brothers, supplemented by a few boys from across the street, there were always enough to start a good baseball or football game.

"When all the boys were home, each was given a chore that would take him from early morning until one or two o'clock," the neighbors say. "They worked hard because then they could play football or baseball or go to the river, about two miles south. Dwight was very industrious about hoeing and tending the vegetables. He disliked the job of shaking the bugs off the potato vines."

Mother Eisenhower tells of Dwight's visits home after he went away. One of the last times he brought his son, John. Together they worked for a long while making a new concrete walk behind the house and fixing a chicken coop.

The General's gardening experience came out again in 1941 when he was stationed at Fort Lewis at Tacoma, Washington. There was ground available there where some of the officers had planted flowers. The General took the opportunity to plant corn, tomatoes, radishes, cucumbers, peas, and beans as well as other vegetables.

Running true to the form of all cooks, Dwight has some secret recipes which he reveals to no one, not even to his mother. These include formulas for potato salad and a vegetable soup, in the creation of which he combines the mysteries of a magician and the fastidious housewife. He also likes sandwiches, leaning in preference to the fried egg sandwich and the old beef and onion. The creation consists of several thin slices of extremely rare beef and a three-quarter-inch slice of Bermuda onion, and heaven help the hindmost. The bread is whole wheat.

One of the Eisenhower brothers once asked his mother, "How, Mother, did you ever manage to bring us up?"

"Didn't you ever catch on?" she asked confidentially. "Don't you remember there was always lots of work to do around the place—and that you were always busy doing it?"

This is Mother Eisenhower's secret formula for making men —strong and independent and self-sufficient men. Whenever they found their own work done, she encouraged them to "help out the neighbors." Dwight worked as a farm hand and even as an ice-puller in the local icehouse.

"Boys are the best investment in the world," Mother Eisenhower has been quoted as saying. "They pay the biggest dividends. We had a careful banking system, worked out by their father. The boys were our bank. We invested in them every spare penny we could save."

"It is always wrong—war or no war—to waste anything," is one of the important provisions in the Eisenhower constitution. "Wastefulness is but another way of becoming a spendthrift." Their family adages are as wise as old Benjamin Franklin's.

Friends of Father Eisenhower say that he figured that we keep a dollar in the bank a whole year to earn less than a nickel; therefore, when we spend the nickel we are spending the savings of an entire year. He did not believe in penuriousness, but he did believe in thrift, in wise expenditure, not in throwing money away.

The General's letters to his mother are precious trophies of World War II. She and the family have bundles of them. Here is a typical line taken at random:

"Feeling fit as a fiddle. With a home in every city, like the commercial traveler, Affectionately, Dwight."

Mother Eisenhower chuckles with delight as she shows the copy of the cablegram the General sent to his townspeople when they were celebrating "Eisenhower Day." "If you folks try to high-hat me and call me by titles instead of Dwight when I come home, I shall feel like a stranger. The worst part of military rank is its loneliness that prevents comradeship. I wish I could be home with the old gang at the cafe."

When he writes to his mother he sends messages of good cheer, but in letters to other members of the family he is concerned over her advancing years and exceedingly solicitous of her health and happiness. His letters to neighbors are filled with tributes to her.

The sons were devoted to their father, a man of sterling character and love for his family. He was held in esteem in his community, where his integrity, honesty, and loyalty to home, state, and nation set a high standard for Americans to follow. Since he passed away in 1942, in the midst of the war, the sons have felt a deep loss whenever they come home.

Dr. Harger's keen and gentle observations, as an old family friend, give us the following picture of the old home and its beloved mother:

In that little room, chatting around the dining table, it was easy to see how mother love has absorbed the mind of the aging parent. Constantly her mind goes back to the goings on of the boys—their games, their household duties, their friendships. It is all her life now. When the General made a flying trip out to Kansas in the winter of 1944 and spent a night at the home of his brother, Milton, president of Kansas State College in Manhattan, forty-five miles east, Mrs. Eisenhower and her companion drove down to meet him. They arrived before the General. The other members of the household, in order that the meeting might be perfect, withdrew and left the mother alone at the door to welcome her noted son. Through the long evening she sat close to Dwight as if he belonged to her solely.

Frequently comes to her mind the fun the boys used to have —simple pleasures such as American boys had in those days.

They swam in Mud Creek, a stream that flows in crooked course through the town and occasionally floods the surrounding countryside.

Dwight graduated from the creek to the Smoky Hill River, a wide stream that flows toward the sea and which has been the delight of the youth of the town.

He spent his evenings "off" at the homes of various members of the school "crowd," some dozen couples who formed a sort of club which they named "Bums of Lawsy Lou." The name did not mean anything but the memory of its meetings still lingers in the minds of staid matrons.

"The initiation of a girl was that she should be kissed by every boy," explained one of the members. "On the night I was accepted I got the first kisses of my life from ten boys. And was I embarrassed?"

The Eisenhower home was not large enough for the parties and they were held at the homes of others, but the young folks often came to call to see the boys. Today they all take great pride in having been friends of Dwight.

In the tiny parlor is an upright piano, standing silent since the sons have gone. Milton, the youngest, used to play and was a solace to his mother who loves religious hymns. The piano is dusted and polished every day—perhaps in memory of the boys, and on the music rack is a hymnal.

Mother Eisenhower, despite her age, looks after the housework and with her companion keeps the rooms spotless and the belongings in their proper places. It is, we repeat, a typical American home of a typical American family with a sound background, a firm faith in the nation, and traditions that date back into the last century—like the lives that have been lived there.

The Eisenhowers are highly regarded by the people of the city; folks always have had a warm feeling for the family. It had little part in the social life of the city—rather it was imbued with religious sentiments and gave of its substance to the up-lifting activities of the community.

The State Federation of Women's Clubs has nominated Mother Eisenhower for the honor of being the "American Mother" and the selection would be a just one, for she typifies the true mother, devoted to her six sons and bringing them up as worthy citizens.

When an oil portrait of the General was unveiled with cere-mony in the USO room she refused to go. "Let *them* honor Dwight," she declared. But she did go when a great gathering in the park paid tribute to the General on his first advancement in North Africa. She sat in a car near the stand with tears in her eyes as the words of praise were spoken. When introduced she refused to go to the speaker's platform—but received gratefully the scores that pressed forward to grasp her hand. On the way home she said, "It was the pleasantest evening of my life—and it was *all* for Dwight."

Guests—and they are many—are received in the little dining-room which is the gathering place of the family. Mother Eisen-hower is frail, slight, but wears her years with dignity. Her blue eyes shine, she has a ready laugh, and impresses you as one who has borne the struggle of life bravely. Constantly in her conver-sation she recalls stories of her children's youth—those years more than half a century away seem to be like yesterday to her.

Some one raised the question, says Dr. Harger, as to whether or not the Allies would win the war. Up spoke the defender, "Of course, everything will come out all right—because Dwight is there!"

She has a supreme faith in his ability and is sure he will solve all problems. It is a sublime evidence of a mother's faith. Con-stantly, she expresses her assurance of the safety of Dwight and

MICHIGAN STATE
LIBRARY

relies on the big family Bible—a prominent feature of the room —for her faith.

Uninvited guests come these days—all receive the same gracious welcome, and she gives freely of her remembrances with a genial smile.

She has posed for scores of pictures—though she always deprecates the action. Only when some one comes who wants to exploit a commodity does she draw the line and politely show the intruder the door. Plans to have her appear on radio programs, to go to New York or elsewhere for appearances are frowned upon. She desires that she shall be—and the sons insist —left as much out of the public eye as possible. But it is not easy to accomplish completeness in this—she is too important in today's history.

An example of the thoughtfulness of the entire family was the visit of the General's wife to Abilene in the autumn of 1943. The town knew that the General's wife was a visitor and was duly excited. She might have stayed at the hotel and called on her mother-in-law but instead she left her baggage in her room and spent two days in the old Eisenhower home, sleeping in the room that used to be Dwight's and visiting with the mother and neighbors who called.

What does Mother Eisenhower think of the great honor that has come to Dwight as commander of the Allied forces in the European theater? Looking up at the General's picture she said to her friend, Dr. Harger, "There is sorrow when I realize the terrific responsibility delegated to Dwight. My highest hope is that Dwight may be an instrument in bringing peace to this troubled world.

"I know he will do his work well. Dwight learned to shoulder responsibility early. He did his assigned tasks well as a boy and has never lost sight of his personal responsibilities as he has advanced to greater tasks.

"I hope and pray that his work may fit into the plan, ordained by God, for the restoration of peace and goodwill throughout the world."

In the family Bible we find the record of this happy home; the explanatory notes in parentheses are ours.

David J.—Born Sept. 23, 1863, (Elizabethville) Pennsylvania.
    Died March 16, 1942.
Ida Stover—Born May 1, 1862, (Mount Sidney) Virginia.
(Married September 23, 1885, at Hope, Kansas, by Rev. E. B.
    Slade, pastor of the United Brethren Church)
Children:
Arthur B.—Born Nov. 11, 1886, Hope, Kansas.
(Vice-president Commerce Trust Company, Kansas City,
    Missouri)
Edgar N.—Born Jan. 19, 1889, Hope, Kansas.
(Attorney at law, Tacoma, Washington)
David Dwight (later changed to Dwight David)—Born Oct. 14,
    1890, Denison, Texas.
Roy J.—Born Aug. 9, 1892, Abilene, Kansas. Died June 15, 1942.
(Pharmacist at Junction City, Kansas)
Paul A.—Born May 12, 1894, Abilene, Kansas. Died March 15,
    1895.
(Baby who lived but ten months)
Earl D.—Born Feb. 1, 1898, Abilene, Kansas.
(Electrical Engineer, Charleroi, Pennsylvania)
Milton S.—Born Sept. 15, 1899, Abilene, Kansas.
(President Kansas State College, Manhattan, Kansas)

Graciously Mother Eisenhower speeds the parting guest. "Come again, please," she says.

Looking back at the white dwelling one wonders at the miracles of human development. Out of that home have come not only a great military leader but five other sons who, without wealth, without influence, have taken prominent places in the world. It is a real example of American opportunity, and American accomplishment.

And so, we leave Mother Eisenhower here in the sunset of

a long and beautiful life, waiting for the trumpet call to join her husband and loved ones in the Great Beyond. We bow in reverence to the mother of General Eisenhower—a woman with faith in God.

We can see her with her Bible in her hands as she sits looking out of the window in her peaceful home. There is sublimity in her aged face—a smile of farewell. And we feel that in her heart she is reciting her favorite Psalm:

"He that dwelleth in the secret place of the most High shall abide under the shadow of the Almighty . . . *He is my refuge and strength: My God, in Him will I trust. . . .*"

· 10 ·

Intimate insights into General Eisenhower

GENERAL EISENHOWER's devotion to his home folks and his neighbors back in Kansas, while engaged in the world's greatest war, is a true insight into the measure of his own greatness. With battles raging around him he never forgets the old home town of Abilene.

While at his headquarters in London, when laboring under the stupendous burden of the Second Front, a twenty-three-year-old private walked into headquarters and asked an M.P., "I'd like to see the General, if he's not too busy."

"What do *you* want to see him about?" growled the M.P.

"I'm Private Walter J. Thorpe," the soldier replied. "Tell the General I'm from his home town."

Ten minutes later, after much telephoning, messengers going back and forth, and inspection of Thorpe's credentials, General Eisenhower stepped out smiling.

"So you're from Abilene? Come right in."

The General and the private from his home town were closeted for twenty minutes at Allied Headquarters. Thorpe came out, shoulders erect, and a happy grin on his face.

"He remembered me," he exclaimed later. "We talked about things back home. I'd met him while I was working on his brother's farm in Kansas. The General asked me how I liked the army and how long I'd been stationed in Northern Ireland. He noticed I wasn't wearing any stripes and asked me how many months I'd been in the army. I told him two years and explained I had missed out on a technician's rating back in the States. We talked quite a bit about Kansas wheat and about farm folks we knew back in Abilene.

"Twenty minutes later I figured I'd taken up about enough of his time," Private Thorpe explained, "so I got up and got ready to leave. Then I thought about those guys in my hut, and I asked the General whether he'd write me out something to prove I actually had seen the Supreme Commander of all the Allied Forces. He wrote a note and handed it to me. Then he said, 'I'm glad you came to see me and if you're here again, drop in. You're always welcome.' Then he shook my hand."

Private Thorpe proudly displayed the note. It read, "Dear Thorpe: I'm delighted that, as a fellow citizen of Abilene, Kansas, you called at my office to see me today. (Signed) Sincerely, Dwight D. Eisenhower."

In moments before and after a great battle, Ike frequently scribbles a few words in his bold handwriting, or occasionally dictates on his official letterhead plain, homey messages to his friends and neighbors. With the eagerness of a doughboy he looks forward to letters from home. In this the General and the common soldier are of the same rank—all boys from home.

Ike's letters are treasure-troves to the folk in Abilene. They horde them like gold. When one arrives at the post office everybody in town hears about it. They call each other on the phone to ask, "What's the latest news from Ike?"

A modest man, who dislikes these penetrations into his private life, the General will undoubtedly regret that historians must probe into personal sources to reveal the heart and soul of a man. But General Eisenhower now "belongs to the ages," as was said of Lincoln, and every letter or anecdote will be treasured by future generations with the same avidity as those of Washington and Lincoln. He cannot escape history.

It will be noted that in these letters to his intimate friends he seldom speaks about himself or the war but confines himself to the simple things of the simple life—the great General in command of armies becomes the common citizen of Abilene.

Here is a letter to our friend, Editor Charles M. Harger:

"Dear Mr. Harger: My thanks are due you again—this time for your nice letter of July 10 and for the article you wrote and had published in the *Kansas City Star*. The article itself is, of course, far too flattering to me. But I am particularly pleased that you brought into your article the one idea that I consider worthy of mention: namely, that my father and mother, as sturdy, God-fearing, straightforward and self-reliant parents, brought up a large family of boys, each of whom has made a respectable place for himself. This, as I see it, is the real achievement of the particular Eisenhower branch to which I belong, and the mere fact that Milton and I have received a bit more publicity than have the others of the family is a matter of relative insignificance."

Editor Harger treasures a letter written to him a few days before the great victory in Tunisia. This is one of the few instances where the General talks about the war. The letter reads:

"Things are going along quite well here at the moment but sometimes I get a bit dismayed when I hear that many of our 'leading thinkers' at home are saying, 'We have won the war but are losing the peace.' I have no quarrel with those who see the necessity of planning a lasting peace, but I deplore the acceptance of the winning of the war as a foregone conclusion, as it indicates a very dangerous misconception of facts. We have a lot of war yet to fight, a lot of lives to be lost, and it is considerably less than magnanimous of those at home thus to sell our boys short."

There are many of these letters in Editor Harger's possession. Ike looks upon him as the most intimate friend of his family, and since his father's death "Uncle Charlie" seems to have taken the place of a father in Ike's heart. When the editor wrote to him that "the letters must be a too heavy drain on your time," the General replied, "It is an odd thing—your asking me how I find time to write letters. It is almost my only relaxation. Moreover, there is nothing from which I get more real enjoyment than hearing from old friends. I like to keep in touch with them. The feeling that they are rooting for me and my soldiers is too precious to lose."

Among the Eisenhower "war letters" in Abilene are many being preserved as historical documents by Mrs. Maude Hurd, widow of Ike's closest friend, Arthur Hurd, the leading hometown lawyer, who died just before the General conquered Sicily. Here is one received by her husband a few days before his death:

"Dear Art: I am more than astonished that an autograph of mine should have been used as a prize in a bond-selling campaign. However, if it worked, I am all for it. One of these days I will have typed up another set and sign them as I did before. Undoubtedly George's [the Hurds' son] homecoming was a big event in your life. I can imagine that you two had a lot of fun talking over the war, even if he is fed up with his Washington assignment. After all, someone has to do that kind of job. Give my best to Charlie, Mr. Harger, and the rest of my friends. As you can tell by the papers, all our news right now is very good, and active fighting in this region should be completed shortly."

Mrs. Hurd in explaining this letter to a friend relates, "My husband and Dwight frequently wrote to each other. After Dwight first came into prominence, one of our acquaintances here called up to ask if he might have the General's autograph for his little boy. Arthur gave it to him and then wrote Dwight to kid him about his growing fame among Abilene's school children. Dwight replied that he couldn't imagine why anyone—even a child—should want his autograph, but if anyone did, there certainly wasn't any reason why he shouldn't have it. He enclosed a separate sheet on which he had written his signature twenty-four times. Arthur cut them apart and gave them to the schools where they were auctioned off to help in the war-bond drive. That's what Dwight refers to in this letter.

"It never made any difference to Dwight what your standing was or what his was. Once friends is always friends with him. My husband wrote to him and said, 'You must be tremendously busy now. Don't bother to answer my letters.'"

Then she shows Ike's prompt reply: "Butt out, old horse. I'll decide how often and to whom I want to write."

Another precious letter in Mrs. Hurd's possession is in reply to her husband's worry that the General's "pay" might not be able to stand the strain of keeping up with the British nobility when King George VI bestowed upon him the Grand Cross of the Order of the Bath.

Ike wrote back, "Dear Art: Please don't worry about the expenditures I will make to support any decoration that may be conferred upon me. Since I am not an Englishman, the normal titles and necessary expenditures that go along with the Grand Cross do not devolve upon me."

One more of these Hurd letters was written immediately after the capture of Pantelleria.

"Your letter was written on May 29, which was before we took Pantelleria and Lampedusa. We planned a very careful campaign against those two places, which were supposed to be the Italian Maltas in the middle of the Mediterranean, and everything went off exactly as scheduled. We picked up quite a number of additional prisoners (which in itself is not important) but what is important, is that we have removed two obstacles to our free use of the sea route. I must confess it was a great relief to me that the Pantelleria operation went through without a hitch."

One of the rarest collections of Eisenhower letters in Abilene is owned by Miss Frances Curry. Her childhood home was less than a block from Ike's. She is the youngest of the six Curry sisters who have known Ike, as she says, "since he was knee high." As Frances runs in to see his mother nearly every day she writes to the General about these visits. Here is one of his replies:

"Dear Frances: Your V-mail letter of April 18 reached me here May 10. You have a genius for crowding into one short letter all the things that I like to hear about my mother and the folks at home. I cannot possibly tell you how much I appreciate the trouble you take in writing to me. The story of sitting in the dining-room with the sunlight streaming through fairly made me homesick for mother, the old home, and the whole town. The next time you call on or phone my mother, tell her I am well and miss her all the time. I only wish that planes flew fast enough that I could spend one day with her and be back here the following day for work. I would go A. W. O. L. that long!"

The General frequently thanks Miss Curry for her visits to his mother and says, "All our friends in Abilene have been so kind and considerate that I shall always be in their debt. It is difficult to realize how much we depend on friends until we are miles away from all the ties that bind so closely."

Miss Curry holds in her hand fondly a letter in which General Eisenhower confesses he gets "homesick." Here are extracts from it:

"It has not taken me fifty-two years to discover that at heart I am nothing else but another Abilenite and damned proud of it. The other day I was wondering how many of you Curry girls still live in Abilene. I know that Mae went away when she was married, but I think Cecelia, Agnes, you, and Helen still live there. Am I wrong? Recently I had a letter from Lois Harger and just yesterday one arrived from Nelle Graves. I wonder if you would remember her [Miss Curry is quite a bit younger than Eisenhower]—she was a little auburn-haired girl who was a classmate of mine in school. Her name is now Lutton (at least that is the way I make it out from her letter), and she is living in Illinois. I have had letters from Mr. Stacey, who used to be our Superintendent of Schools, and from several of my old teachers in high school.

"The people in town that I usually correspond with are Arthur Hurd, Charlie Case, Mr. Harger, with an occasional letter to others. Every time I inspect any troops, I am constantly looking for boys from Kansas. So far I have had very little luck, but occasionally run into one. We have also a number of WAC's and Red Cross girls; but of the few that work around my immediate office, none is from my State. My love to all your sisters, to Gladys Brooks, Maud Hurd, and any of the other girls you remember as friends of mine. When I write to Art Hurd, I usually ask him to remember me to the masculine crowd, so I will ask you to do the same for the ladies—I hope you don't mind."

The neighbors in Abilene all turn out to see the news-reels in the motion-picture theater—"just to see Ike." As he walks across the screen they applaud vociferously. One night they were watching as the French General Giraud pinned on him the Grand Cross of the Legion of Honor. General Giraud stepped up and gave General Eisenhower an accolade, a kiss on both cheeks. Miss Curry wrote him that the townspeople were somewhat shocked.

The General replied, "At the time that General Giraud gave me the French Grand Cross, one of my old friends asked me what Abilenites would say if they ever saw a picture showing me getting kissed on each cheek. While I admit that I was just a bit terror-stricken at the prospect, I figured out at the same time that those who knew the Eisenhower tribe of boys would be sure that it was something I wasn't seeking, but to which I could scarcely object. At that I'll bet there was a chuckle around the audience the night that you saw it."

Ike's devotion to his mother is shown in many letters. He frequently says that he owes everything to her for whatever he may accomplish in the world.

In another letter to Miss Curry he writes, "Dear Frances: You have a knack of giving me a picture of my mother in her home that is almost as vivid as if I could see her myself. It is quite true that Mother would like to take a long plane ride—sort of a junketing trip. Nothing would give me more fun than to start on such a journey with her. Maybe I could get you to go along and keep the diary."

And at the bottom he scrawls in longhand humorously, "Love to all the girls and remember me to Joe. Tell my mother she must stop this night-club life—I can't have her out in the hot spots at nine in the evening."

Among General Eisenhower's old friends in Abilene who tell stories about him and write letters to him is friend Callahan, the former "cowboy" mayor of Abilene, who conducts the corner smoke shop where the males of the town gather to talk about Ike. They chip in and buy cigarettes to send to Ike's soldiers.

He shows this letter with pride: "Dear Joner: Every time I receive renewed evidence of the way the Home Front is standing behind my fighting men, it gives me a warm feeling inside. So far as you possibly can, please thank every one, in my name, who sends a carton of cigarettes through your system."

The General further sent a personal note to each of twenty donors in which he said, "I have just received the two special packages of cigarettes you sent to me and my men as a Christmas present. I assure you that no present could be more grate-fully received, and in the name of all of the men who will enjoy them, as well as in my own, I thank you sincerely for the gener-osity and thoughtfulness of your action."

The children in the public schools in Abilene write letters to "the great man who went to our school." All the children in the second grade in the Garfield School made birthday cards and sent them to the General. They jump with joy as they show the answer they received from him.

"Dear Youngsters: Your very nice teacher, Miss [Janice] Polley, sent me a letter not long ago to tell me of the birthday cards all of you had made for me. The cards arrived today and I appreciate them more than I can tell you. Best wishes to each of you and many thanks for the cards."

The Citizenship Club of the sixth grade at the Garfield School have a letter "which money could not buy." They got together and sent a Christmas box to "some soldier overseas who might not otherwise receive one." It was addressed to General Eisen-hower with the request that he "give it to one of your friendless boys." His reply to Evelyn Lady, secretary of the club, is the priceless memento.

"Dear Evelyn: Thank you very much for your letter and for the nice Christmas box which, as you requested, I am sending to a soldier who will propably not be expecting any Christmas present this year. To you and to all other members of the Eliza-beth Mallot Barnes Citizenship Club I send my very best wishes for 1944."

This record of Eisenhower's letters could be continued for many pages, for we find them in many homes.

At Eisenhower's headquarters across the seas his military aide reports that letters from home give the General great inspiration for his day's work. When the mail comes in he inquires eagerly, "Anything for me from home?" He is as delighted as any G.I.

as he tears them open and eagerly reads them, frequently re-marking, as he once wrote Miss Curry, "I cannot possibly tell you how much I appreciate the trouble you take in writing to me."

Thus in these letters we see the *real* Eisenhower—a plain man of the people, loyal to his friends, with gratitude in his heart for even the smallest consideration. Weighed down with the re-sponsibilities of the greatest war in history, he always finds time to keep in touch with the folks back home.

We now administer to the world-famous General the severest of all the "penalties of greatness"—penetrating into the inner-most circles of family. But, as an ideal example of the relation-ships between father and son, we feel our duties would be amiss if we did not give some insight into this phase of the Eisen-hower character.

As we have related, his only son, John Doud Eisenhower, is following in his father's career. Graduating from West Point, in June 1944, he enters the army at twenty-one years of age. We met this upstanding, soldierly young man at West Point while pursuing researches for this book. He is a "chip from the old block"—a typical Eisenhower to carry on the family name. He, too, has the Eisenhower dislike of the spotlight. With deep ad-miration for his father, he pleads to be allowed to remain "far in the background."

When appealed to "for the sake of history," however, he agreed that to the extent of establishing the "relationships of father and son" he would give us some insight into the General's fatherly advice as expressed in their correspondence. These records from letters, therefore, are for the purpose of giving other American fathers an historic example of the perfect com-radeship between father and son. Here is a typical letter from General Eisenhower to his young son about to become a second lieutenant.

"Dear Johnny: This is written from my advanced C. P., during the early days of the Sicilian attack. The papers keep you fairly well informed of our operations, so you know that this whole force is hard at it again. Strangely enough, for me personally, the beginning of one of these major pushes is a period of comparative inactivity, because there is so much waiting for reports, while I'm removed from my main headquarters where there is always something to keep one hustling.

"The main purpose of this note is to wish you well on your birthday. You will be twenty-one—a voter if you were a civilian! I wish I could be there to shake you by the hand and say 'Good luck.' As it is, this note will have to do; although possibly I'll get to send you a teletype also.

"You will note that the ink seems to soak into this paper. That is because of the dampness in this tunnel where my office is located. The weather outside is hot and dry. You may be sure I spend as little time as possible in this hole—but occasionally I have to have conferences, etc., here. . . .

"It's time to go see the admiral. He's one of my best friends —and a great fighting man. Good luck, and again, congratulations. Devotedly, your Dad."

Here we see fatherly advice in its noblest attributes, a great General and his son in perfect accord as he makes suggestions for the boy's future, the good fellowship of two brothers, two soldiers in the ranks. To further establish this relationship we give a facsimile of one more letter which we present as a classic example of this comradeship.

We trust that the good General, who has command over the great Allied Forces in World War II, will pardon us for our invasion on his privacy. But the greatest generals through the ages have met this same fate in the hands of biographers. The only power that exceeds their authority is history, in which "the pen is mightier than the sword."

ALLIED FORCE HEADQUARTERS
Office of the Commander-in-Chief

8 September, 1943.

Dear Johnnie:

Had a nice note from you today written August 8. You
were just about to go to Pine Camp. But I have had later
news from you because Mamie wrote me about your visit to
Washington after you had completed your Pine Camp tour.

I see that your mind is made up to go into the Infantry.
Naturally, having been a doughboy all my life (although I
must say with very little chance to stay in it), I cannot
quarrel with your choice. I still believe, however, that
what I told you about the Field Artillery is sound.

By the time you get this letter you will know that today
was a very full one for me and crowded with anxiety. However, being made as I am, it is also crowded with hopeful-
ness. I am probably the most optimistic person in this
whole world. Everybody else sees all the risks and dangers
and I guess I am just a wishful thinker, because I just
shut my eyes to such things and say "We will go ahead and
try to win". One of these days I will probably get a very
bloody nose -- but I hope it isn't this time.

This isn't much of a letter but I will do better at an
early date. In the meantime, best of luck and I really
hope that you don't give up your tennis entirely. It is
a fine sport.

As ever,

Devotedly
Dad.

· II ·

General Eisenhower's Wife and Son

WITH THE EYES of the world on General Eisenhower, every phase of his life and character must be revealed under the penetrating glare of fame. As we have said, he belongs no longer to himself but to posterity. Hesitantly, we enter into the privacy of his home life, but this, too, is now a part of history.

General Eisenhower's charming and brilliant wife, in her desire to escape the spotlight, closed her home in Washington while the General is in Europe, and now lives in retirement in San Antonio, Texas, where as Marie Geneva Doud, she first met Dwight David Eisenhower.

Mrs. Eisenhower, a lady who "walks in grace and beauty," is a true symbol of the American wife and mother. Her intelligence and culture, and the eminent position which she now holds, are intermingled with her simplicity and love of people. She never loses touch with the common heart of humanity and feels that every boy fighting for our country is "her boy" and every mother is "her mother." Her days in comparative seclusion since leaving the nation's capital are devoted to war work, letters to soldiers, and whatever she can do to "help out on the home front."

In her letters to us, she expressed cordial cooperation with the wish that all the attention be focused on the General and

114

that she be left in the shadows. This, however, is impossible in fulfilling our duties to history. Therefore, we are giving our readers whatever side lights we have been able to obtain from authentic sources.

Mrs. Eisenhower is a brunette, with gentle eyes and a velvet complexion. She is lithe, graceful, and animated. For all her small size—her weight never exceeds 108 pounds—she has a dignity livened with a gracious manner. Her hair is a crown of waves and is worn in bangs. She wears a platinum and diamond wedding ring and a charm bracelet which holds mementoes of her husband's career.

The vivacious Miss Doud had left Iowa, her birthplace, and gone to Denver, Colorado, during World War I. Her parents were in San Antonio, Texas, and she went to visit them. The story in the Eisenhower family is that when young Dwight met her—he was stationed at Fort Sam Houston at that time— he decided then and there, "This is the girl I'm going to marry."

It is further said that on the night Mamie, as he calls her, first met Dwight she had a date with another man and was anxious to get away. Together with her parents and a neighboring judge and his wife, she was having dinner at the officers' mess. Mamie didn't want to stay. Her mother told her they would be polite guests—Mamie's young man could pick her up at the post after dinner, or not at all. There was to be no argument about the matter. Mamie stayed. She was a beautiful eighteen-year-old girl and extremely popular with young men.

This was on a Sunday night, and Dwight was at the officers' mess. He and Mamie got along well from the beginning. Before her date, Mamie walked around with Dwight to inspect the first sentry. The next night Dwight called the Doud residence again and again. Mamie herself had gone to a picnic. When she returned the maid told her a Mr. "I Something" had been calling every fifteen minutes. The telephone rang again and Mamie answered it.

"He asked me to go to the show at the 'big night' at the Majestic," she admits. "Well, all of us girls were always dated up for that night, so I told him it would be four weeks before I had an evening open."

After much futile argument, Dwight took the engagement four weeks ahead, but he says he managed to arrange some dates in advance of the big event. The courtship started in October, in December they were engaged. The marriage took place in Denver, Colorado, on July 1, 1916, the day he was made a first lieutenant.

Mrs. Eisenhower says that Lieutenant Dwight scared all her other beaux away during his courtship. After she married him he never brought his military problems home, but let her run the house while he attended to his business. Her chief domestic problem was fitting a collection of Persian rugs into her home. The General, a man of simple tastes, has always had a fondness for Oriental rugs.

Mrs. Eisenhower has many interesting anecdotes about these youthful days. She says that the wedding was the only occasion at which she ever saw her husband nervous. He was so afraid that he might crease his white pants that he refused to sit down until the ceremony was over. She insists, however, that while the General is a neat dresser he resents all appearances of being a Beau Brummel. While they were stationed in the Philippines, he shaved his head as well as his face because, he said, "It feels cooler."

The life of the war bride from that time on was at army posts in all sections of the country—East, West, North, South— at the Panama Canal, in the Philippines, in Washington, until the General went to England.

Their first son was born, as related elsewhere, at Fort Sam

Houston, in Texas, September 24, 1917, the year following their marriage. Mamie was then twenty years old. The boy, whom she named Doud Dwight Eisenhower, died at three years of age while they were living at Camp Meade, Maryland, on January 2, 1921.

Two and a half years later a second son came to the Eisenhowers, at Denver, Colorado, on August 3, 1923—the John Sheldon Doud Eisenhower, whom we shall soon meet. He was reared at army posts, going to the Philippines with them when he was twelve years old and attending school there until he was seventeen years of age.

Mrs. Eisenhower reveals that the General's nickname "Ike" has always been a thorn in the side of his mother. She has never been able to save her boys from their childhood appellations. Once when the General's wife sent his mother a letter saying that she and Ike were traveling and hoped to stop off in Abilene, Mother Eisenhower replied that she was looking forward to welcoming them, but would like to know "who this 'Ike' is with whom you are traveling."

She sympathizes with his mother now that her own son, John, is currently known as "Eisey" at West Point.

The General's wife regrets the military order that when men go off to war they must leave their wives behind them. This applies equally from generals to privates.

"I would like to be in the war with him," she says regretfully. And then adds, "But this war is bigger than I or any other person. I feel no different from any other woman whose husband has gone to war."

While living in Washington as Chief of Operations, Eisenhower usually arose at 6:30 and walked a mile and one-half to his headquarters at Fort Myers. Usually he did not get home until eleven o'clock at night. His social life was diminished to nil. He only went out five times during his entire stay in Washington. His recreational activities were limited to bridge, at which he is an expert, and to reading Westerns, his favorite relaxation. His wife still sends an occasional parcel of Western thrillers to his European headquarters.

She writes the General copious letters. "Men like quantity, not quality," she remarks. What she terms fervent *notes* of five or six lines come to her in return from her husband at the war front.

Mrs. Eisenhower has a keen sense of humor and laughs gleefully at this story. One morning she called the grocer early in order to place an order for early delivery. By noon the order had not arrived. She called again.

"This is Mrs. Eisenhower, and I've got to keep an appointment in a hurry. Won't you rush my order over, please?"

"Listen, lady," the clerk replied, "don't you know there s a war on?"

"Mister," she exclaimed, "*you're telling me!*"

When the General was appointed to lead the invasion forces, Mrs. Eisenhower was with her son John. The news surprised them. A few minutes later she remarked, "He has been in there to finish the job from the beginning. This is the greatest reward they could have given him."

Mrs. Eisenhower learned years ago that Army life is not easy. The year prior to the General's going overseas she had to move five times. She always had difficulty keeping maids because the General's work makes his life and working hours rather erratic affairs. He usually had breakfast at daybreak, and was gone often until nearly midnight, when dinner would be waiting for him.

His wife, with whimsical smile, relates in "strict confidence," "He eats anything on these occasions except parsnips. He used to be allergic to fish and onions, but he got over the onion allergy and now consumes them between slices of bread."

His whims run in many directions. His dislikes include the city when he can have the country, a crumpled morning newspaper, and unquestioning agreement from subordinates. He enjoys social amenities traditional with Army jobs, and his friends love him as much as they respect him. His orderlies worship him. The General does not drink. He says, "It is hard enough keeping valuable information in my head sober. It is a responsibility which can brook no oiling of the tongue."

That he is a man of action is clearly demonstrated in this observation by his wife. "We can always tell when Ike is about to be off somewhere, because he comes whistling down the street. Wherever he is, he is a very busy man."

Mrs. Eisenhower plays the piano by ear, and was often joined by her husband, who could pick out chords. "His favorite song," she says, "is *Abdul the Bulbul Amir*, to which he can sing about fifty verses."

"And," she exclaims, "he never forgets an anniversary. For the first anniversary I received a silver jewel box shaped like a heart. It still lies on my dressing table."

The General's wife lived for a time after he left for Europe in a roomy apartment in a Washington hotel, and she spent her time in war work and in studying Spanish. She is collecting material for a scrapbook which, she says, "I will paste up during my old age." She does not go to the movies, because seeing her husband walking across the screen saddens her. She sends him all sorts of presents. His most recent wish was for a pair of "grass slippers."

Mrs. Eisenhower is genuinely lonely while both her husband and her son are away. She follows the war religiously and longs for the day when Ike will come back and they can relax and sit opposite each other at dinner and just take it easy—general or no general.

"Nobody knows how I miss him," she confides. "But every

other wife misses her husband and every mother misses her son just as much. In this we all have everything in common.

"It is a joy to hear him talk," she says. "He is informed on almost everything. He's a brilliant conversationalist." She confides, "I've lived with him and listened to him for twenty-seven years—and *he still fascinates me.*"

The General has greenish-blue eyes which sometimes turn completely blue. When he is intensely interested they flame with fire. His face when animated radiates intelligence, warmth, and good fellowship. When he is lost in deep thought it is strong and severe. He is alternately handsome in kindly repose, but grim and awesome when "things don't go right." His voice is gentle in conversation, but can be aroused to a cannon roar when the necessity arises. These later revelations were not made by the General's wife, but come from intimate friends.

Now meet Cadet John Sheldon Doud Eisenhower, Company B, First Regiment, at West Point, when his distinguished father was commanding the Second Front in Europe. He is a tall, upright, handsome young soldier following in his father's footsteps. He looks you straight in the eyes with penetration, but there is a genial smile on his manly face. His modesty and self-effacement are outstanding characteristics. He has no desire to stand in the light of his famous father, but prefers to stay far in the background and earn his way up from the ranks.

This erect young Second Lieutenant, graduating from West Point, in June, 1944, his Aunt Amanda informs us, is "a brilliant young man with deep devotion to his father and mother, who have unbounded love for their only son."

"Johnny," as his father calls him, is a youth with Chesterfieldian courtesy. While he graciously says, "I hope that I can be of some tangible assistance to you and assure you that I will do my best," his remarks are restrained by his desire to leave others to reach their own conclusions about his father on the merits of his accomplishments.

"What are my impressions of my father?" he repeats from our direct inquiry and then answers with simplicity.

"Dad is about 5 feet 11 inches tall, weighs about 175 pounds. The last time I saw him he looked, I thought, considerably heavier. He has extremely big bones and powerful hands and arms. His ring is several sizes larger than mine. He moves easily but sometimes has a slight limp due to a football injury.

"His hair, in a fringe around the side of his head, is light brown. The sparse growth on top led him once to shave it, in disgust, and he kept it that way about two years in the Philippines. He tried once to do it himself with a safety razor, and his nicked head was a pretty sight.

"His eyes seem gray to me, and his nose is rather small. He is extremely direct in speech. His voice is clear and powerful and even in ordinary conversation he talks with all his attention. No hemming and hawing, no 'ers' or uhs.' "

Here in a few deft strokes we have a son's picture of his father—no biographer could do better.

"Dad's general interest in everything is remarkable to me, who am inclined to be easygoing," John continues. "He relaxed on the trip home from the Philippines—at times. That is, he did what he called relaxing all the time. In the mornings he would sit and watch the sea, but in the afternoons he was up on the bridge learning from the captain how to navigate the ship. He was slightly impatient because I was willing to look at the sea all day long.

"His physical endurance is his biggest asset. One thing that astounds me is how Dad can think of home even under pressure. His letters illustrate this.

"Dad is a four-star general; I'm two months short of a second lieutenant. Although he has been my idol all my life, his position is his; I have nothing to do with it. I'm just an average cadet, and any literary association between Dad and me would really have to be an example in contrasts.

"Dad was never very tough with me," he says, laughingly. "He had me well frightened from the start, and always boasted that he never had to lay a hand on me to make me mind. So far as I can remember he never did. However, when he told me to do something *I did it!*

"He likes to tell one story, unverified by the rest of the family, about when I was small. It seems that I loved to play records on the electric phonograph. The women of the family would come around and pick all the records off the floor when I was through. One day he was sitting in the room while I was playing them, and when I was through he made me pick them up.

"This was a new idea to me, and I didn't like it. I sat and howled and the rest of the family looked at him as if he were beating me with a ball bat. But he made me pick up every record and put them away.

"When I was through, the whole family were good and peeved at him. But he left the room to go to the basement for some reason, and I ran after him asking if I could come along and watch him. The family practically silenced us for the rest of the day.

"Dad has a perfect ability to relax," explains the son. "I have mentioned how he enjoys boat trips because of the lack of responsibility and worry, and how going across the Pacific he would sit on deck for hours and just look at the water or read a book. Dime Westerns and sport magazines are great relaxation for him. He goes through a pile of them in one night.

"You have Dad's athletic record, and can probably see why he has always encouraged me as much as possible along those lines. Though I am no athlete myself, he always said he would buy me any athletic equipment I wanted, and has carried it out to the letter.

"It seems that he has tried his hand at about every game there is. When he does, he doesn't fool around. He improves as much as he can, and claims that improving oneself is all the fun in playing.

"Dad is a great lover of music. By this I do not mean Chopin and Beethoven, but songs such as *Abdul the Bulbul Amir*, *The Old Spinning Wheel*, *The Last Round-up*, *Casey Jones*, *Steamboat Bill*, and, above all, *The Beer-Barrel Polka*. Though he plays no instrument, he has the virtues of a powerful voice, ability to carry a tune, good memory for words, and lots of enthusiasm.

"He loves to cook. His vegetable soup, which he likes to spend Sunday afternoons making, is the best I ever tasted. He also makes fine potato salad. It was always a great treat when he would allow me to help him when I was very young, and would entrust me with the important mission of peeling the potatoes.

"One of my earliest recollections of Dad is of his lying on a bed trying to pull his boots on—in a fury. In view of his injured knee, I believe his language could be excused.

"He was always far from a dude, however, and believed that cleanliness and neatness were all that is necessary in dress. For that reason, he hated to go to parties. I can still see him sitting out in the front room, dressed up and looking very uncomfortable, chewing nails while Mother sat in the back room fixing her hair.

"When she got him to the party, however, and he got to singing and talking with some friends, she had a very difficult time getting him to go home. He likes people and likes to exchange ideas with them, but he sure hates to doll up to do it.

"Dad enjoyed West Point very much. In contrast to earning

a living shocking wheat, he thought this was an easy life, and I agree with him. He liked the athletics, and, being a great lover of history, he was very much impressed by the traditions of the place. He always swore he wouldn't force me to go to West Point, and always pretended to try to talk me out of it. However, he gave himself away when he made me do foot exercises because my feet were too weak to pass the entrance examinations."

The General in his letters to Johnny urges him to play tennis, in which the father excels. He advises baseball, football, boxing, fencing, and all outdoor athletic sports. As in the letters we have read to other members of the family and to his friends in Abilene, he seldom mentions the war, merely the flash of a thought here and there.

When, in the turmoil of the Second Front invasion of Europe, General Eisenhower catches a few precious minutes to write home, he seems to have the remarkable ability to transport himself instantly from tumult, clamor, and bloodshed to the peace and quiet of family life.

This inherent quality, probably a quality inherited from his peace-loving forefathers, is an interesting study in psychology. It shows the General's ability to retain all the higher spiritual values in a world of physical and material chaos. Here is the repose that makes a great man.

John, named after his grandfather Doud, is a composite of Douds and Carlsons, Eisenhowers and Stovers—all pioneer families. His mother's folks migrated to Iowa shortly after it entered the Union as the Hawkeye State with the motto "Our liberties we prize" and the wild rose as its emblem.

The Douds came from New York State. Researches in the New York State Library at Albany, through the cooperation of Edna L. Jacobsen, head of Manuscripts and History Section, have not been sufficiently completed to trace their arrival in

America. At the Jervis Library in Rome, New York, Helen Salzmann, librarian, says the record of John Sheldon Doud is not found, as birth notices were apparently not recorded at that time.

We find, however, in Iowa State Department of History and Archives, through the courtesy of Lucretia E. Garretson, librarian and genealogist, interesting records relating to the wife of General Eisenhower.

Marie (Mamie) Geneva Doud, wife of General Dwight D. Eisenhower, is a native daughter of Iowa. She was born November 14, 1896, in Boone, Iowa. Her father, John Sheldon Doud, was born in Rome, New York, on November 18, 1871, and migrated to Boone and Cedar Rapids. Her mother, Elvira Matilda (Carlson) Doud, born also in Boone, Iowa, May 15, 1878, was the daughter of Carl and Marie (Anderson) Carlson. Her maternal grandfather, Carl Carlson, was born in Hallan, Sweden, July 11, 1841, a son of Peter and Johanna Carlson, born in the early 1800's.

Her grandfather, Carl Carlson, came to Boone, Iowa, in 1868. That same year he had married, in Sweden, Marie Anderson, the daughter of Ander and Breta (Larson) Anderson, of Hallan County, Sweden, who came with him to Iowa, where they reared and educated their children, among whom is Elvira Matilda Doud, the mother of General Eisenhower's wife.

The biographical record of Boone, Iowa, has this to say of Mrs. Eisenhower's grandfather: "Among the worthy citizens that Sweden has furnished to Boone County is numbered Carl Carlson, one of the old settlers of this portion of the state and a man of strong purpose and upright life, who by his well directed efforts has won success in his business undertakings and gained the respect and confidence of all with whom he has been associated."

Carl Carlson owned farms and flour mills. It is said in Iowa that the Douds were also interested in mills. Thus we find Elvira Matilda Carlson and John Sheldon Doud marrying in Iowa, and through their daughter, Mamie Geneva Doud, becoming the mother-in-law and father-in-law of General Dwight Eisenhower.

The General's only son, John Sheldon Doud Eisenhower, is therefore the true product of American democracy, the mingling of many strong races and nations, German, Swiss, possibly Dutch, intermarried with Scotch, Irish, English in America, on his father's side—and the powerful Scandinavians who settled the Middle West on his mother's side. All nations blended into one and inseparable.

This, again, is Walt Whitman's America, which caused him to chant: "Race of races . . . built of the common stock, having room for far and near. . . . This America is only you and me . . . the Many in One. . . . Shapes of Democracy. . . . Shapes bracing the whole earth, and braced with the whole earth. . . . America always! Always me joined with you, whoever you are!"

· 12 ·

With Cadet Eisenhower on the hill at
West Point

WE NOW LEAVE THE EISENHOWER FAMILY and follow young Ike
to West Point, re-living his life there with him and starting out
on his life career from twenty years to fifty-two years of age—
thirty-two years of amazing experiences and adventures.

When Dwight Eisenhower, a rugged, bronzed youth out of
the West, stood before the portals of West Point on the fourteenth day of June in 1911, he gazed in admiration at the stately
structures standing like citadels on the rock-bound hills over-
looking the grandeur of the Hudson River. The boy from the
plains had come to the highlands.

Five feet eleven, weighing 170 pounds, twenty years and eight
months of age, he was entering the greatest institution of its
kind in the world, the United States Military Academy.

The scene was awe-inspiring, a vision of beauty. In this peaceful setting it was difficult to believe that World War I would
soon be sweeping the nations, and that this young Kansan would
some day be the Commander in Chief of great armies in World
War II. He was starting on a career far beyond his imagination.

At this same time youths from many nations, whom he would
later meet on battlefields, were entering the military academies

of their countries: English lads at the Royal Military College at Sandhurst and at Woolrich; French lads at *L'École Speciale Militaire* at St. Cyr in the forests of Fontainebleau; German lads in the *Kreigschule* at Potsdam, Dresden, Hanover, Munich, and Vienna; Italian lads at Rome, Naples, Milan, Modena, Turin.

On this glorious June day "Ike" was trodding on sacred ground of the past, following in the footsteps of men who had become great in war and peace from the days of the American Revolution. It was on this same ground that General George Washington, recognizing the strategic importance of its commanding position and "to save the colonies that had declared their independence from being cut in two," established his headquarters. Under the direction of the young Polish patriot, Kosciusko, the "lover of freedom," Washington had fortifications built. Here, too, the traitor, Benedict Arnold, had bargained to surrender West Point for $30,000. It was President Thomas Jefferson, who, in 1802, signed the act creating the United States Military Academy in the historic highlands.

In the distance young Eisenhower could see the ramparts of Fort Putnam, commanding a magnificent view of river and valley, unsurpassed by any vision of peace and quietude in the world. He looked at the cannon standing around him, grim reminders of all the wars in which his nation had fought.

West Point, like Ike himself, was in a state of transition. It was preparing for the future. The magnificent cadet chapel was being erected, an outstanding example of modern Gothic architecture, with heavy buttressed walls of native granite, a carillon of twelve bells in its tower, and under its graceful arches the largest church organ in the Western Hemisphere. A huge new gymnasium, where Ike was to make a notable record, was under construction. The largest riding hall in the world was being built from granite quarried on the reservation; here Ike, horseman from the West, was to give daredevil exhibitions of a lad at home in the saddle. Surveying before him the Gothic structures of imposing beauty, he walked into the administration building.

"Eisenhower from Kansas," he reported cryptically. The routine of registration proceeded. Facsimiles of official documents which he signed in his plain, bold handwriting are in the possession of the author of this book, but as these are marked "strictly confidential," only portions of them may be quoted.

After giving the details of his home and birthplace, the official record bearing the handwriting of Dwight Eisenhower continues: Studies pursued in primary school: *Geography, Arithmetic, U. S. History, Spelling, Music, Grammar.* Time: *6 years, 2 mos.* Highest grade attained and studies pursued in that grade: *Senior Year: Economics, Physics, U. S. History, English, Civil Government.* State if you ever wholly or partially earned your own living: *Yes. Partially for six years and wholly for two years as a Refrigerating Engineer. Also fireman.*

Among the many other entries appear these notations: Private or Preparatory School: *None.* Normal School or Academy: *None.* University or College: *None.* Teaching school: *No.* Special preparation for examination for admission to U. S. Military Academy: *3 months.* Where: *Home.* Did you have a competitive examination: *Yes.* How many competitors including yourself: *Eight.* Do you use tobacco in any form: *No.* Ever in Army, Navy, Marine Corps, Volunteers in U. S. Service or National Guard: *No.*

Ike then records his education up to this time and the textbooks he has studied: *Wentworth's Algebra, Wentworth's Geometry, White's Arithmetic. Solid Geometry is the highest point reached. Hoenshell's Grammar, Quackenbos's Rhetoric, Lockwood and Emerson's Composition, Johnson's History of English and American Literature. Senior year in High School highest point; German, one year; Davidson's U. S. History; Channing's U. S. History, West's Ancient, Green's English*

Candidate's signature Dwight David Eisenhower
(Write in full, including middle name or names.)

State appointed from Kansas No. of Congressional District 5th
(If by President write "At Large".) (If appointed by Congressman.)

If appointed by Senator, his name Senator Jos. L. Bristow

Candidate's legal residence: Town Abilene County Dickinson State Kansas

Candidate's date of birth Oct. 14, 1890.

Candidate's place of birth: Town Denison County State Texas.

Is your father living? Yes Is your mother living? Yes

Name of parent or guardian David J. Eisenhower

Occupation or profession of parent: Is or was Refrigerating Engineer
(If mechanic, state what kind; if merchant, dealer in what.)

Address of parent or guardian: Street and No. 201 E. South 4th Town Abilene

130

Nationality of father ..... American ..... Nationality of mother ..... American .....

Date of appointment (letter from War Department) ..... October 31, 1910 .....

Time of Attendance at Schools and Studies there Pursued.

Studies pursued in primary school ..... geography, arithmetic, U. S. History, ...

..... spelling, music, grammar, ... Time: ..... 6 ..... Yrs ..... 2 ..... Mos.

Public High School: Name of School ..... Abilene High School ..... Time: ..... 4 ..... Yrs ..... 0 ..... Mos.

State if you ever wholly or partially earned your own living, and if so, for how long and at what work? ..... Yes .....

..... Partially for 6 years and working for 2 years. .....

..... As a Refrigerating Engineer. Also fireman. .....

Hist., Myer's Medieval Hist. Physical Geography: *Two years in primary schools and one year physical geography in high school.* Drawing: *None.*

Young Eisenhower had acquired a sound basic education; he had beaten his competitors in entrance examinations for West Point; he had passed all the rigid tests and physical examinations with high marks. Here was solid American manhood in-the-making.

The records show that he lived in the old 26th Division Barracks. His roommate was Paul Alfred Hodgson, now of San Antonio, Texas.

The Texas-born, Kansas-bred youth was now the raw material from which soldiers are made. Upon his character was to be branded three words, *Duty—Honor—Country,* the motto of West Point. There is no institution that places greater emphasis on character. It builds men physically, mentally, spiritually.

The appraisal of a cadet begins with the moment of his rude plunge into the West Point system. Nature had saved a blast of record-breaking heat to welcome Ike when he arrived at West Point in 1911. Through the three broiling weeks that preceded the transfer of the new cadets from "Beast Barracks" to the summer encampment at Fort Clinton, they underwent a process of indoctrination which left its mark. The job was thoroughly done. The end of each strenuous day found the plebes only too glad to tumble into their bunks for a night's sleep before reveille summoned them to a new day's grind.

Taps inspection was hardly over when more or less rugged spirits asserted themselves. Bull sessions were under way. Ike's room became a favorite hangout for these after-taps sessions. Voices were kept low and a sentry was always posted to give warning of the approach of a first-classman of the "Beast Detail." In the darkness the day's woes became less important, the boners of some overzealous first-classman developed into a tidbit, and plebe life in general became more endurable. There were plenty of arguments, often ended by one of Ike's pungent comments. Before anyone realized it, Ike had been accepted as a leader.

He remained a leader when, a year later, the ebullience of the yearlings made summer camp a sore trial for the first-classmen responsible for the administration of the Corps. "F" Company Street, boasting more than its share of shade trees, and a comfortable distance from such control centers as the guard tents and the Commandant's headquarters, was an inviting retreat. But the "F" Company yearlings, led by Ike, and spontaneously organized into self-styled "Rangers," kept the company street clear of visitors. A wet drag (a thorough dousing under the spigot) was apt to be the fate of anyone who strayed into those precincts.

Ike never left any doubts about his official leadership; he never lacked confidence in himself. His shout down the "F" Company streets, summoning his cohorts to a raid on a "runt" company's "boodle" supply (forbidden eatables), brought his classmates tumbling out of their tents. On occasion, the runts were allowed to share in the consumption of their own canned goods and lemonade, but not too often. Too much generosity that way was apt to breed a spirit of independence among the victims, a spirit not to be tolerated by the "flankers" of "F" Company.

Like his classmates in "F" Company, Ike fitted easily into the tradition which, throughout the history of the Corps, has fallen to the company marching at the close of the parade column. The tradition is one which scorns "file-boning," "teeth-boning," and any such serious efforts for advancement in corps rank or academic standing. It seeks to discover such maximum of ease as is possible under the strenuous West Point system. On the other hand, it puts a high premium on athletic prowess. The physical brawn of a group of fit men, averaging six feet or more in height, lent itself to outstanding performance on the athletic field. That feature of the environment likewise suited Ike.

Ike was never a "bucking broncho"; he was always willing to take the saddle. But his spirit of the plains found that he had four years of hard riding ahead of him. There were many hurdles to be jumped: higher mathematics, military topography, surveying, languages, physics, history and government, organic chemistry, mechanics, tactics, engineering, economics, law, military science and strategy, with all the interrelated hazards that had to be mastered.

Hard work and rigid discipline in body, mind, and soul challenge every young man who enters the gates of West Point. If he has the right stuff in him he comes out not only a soldier, but a gentleman and a scholar; a man of courage and character in whom has been instilled a high sense of honor and whose powers of analysis have been developed so that he may meet the problems of war and peace with clear thinking.

Plebe Ike, like all novitiates, went through the elementary training in the "Beast Barracks." He quickly became imbued with the spirit of West Point and the traditions behind it. These are embodied today in the reverential Cadet Prayer and "Alma Mater," written by a lieutenant who was graduated in the year 1911, when Plebe Eisenhower was entering, and the stirring words of "The Corps," in which tribute is paid to those who have gone before.

When Ike arrived at West Point he was just another "Mr. Ducrot," "Mr. Doowhistle," or "Mr. Doowillie," names applied to unknown plebes. He found himself in a world of "sirs" where every upperclassman must be so addressed. He was put through the customary plebe catechism.

These, or a similar ritual in many changing versions, according to the times, are but specimens of what "plebe knowledge" is supposed to be. But they must always be able to tell how many names there are on the Battle Monument, how many lights in Cullum Hall, and how many gallons in Lusk Reservoir.

What do plebes rank? "Sir, the Superintendent's dog, the Commandant's cat, the waiters in the Mess Hall, the Hell cats, and all the Admirals in the whole blamed Navy."

What time is it? "Sir, I am deeply embarrassed and greatly humiliated that due to unforeseen circumstances over which I have no control, the inner workings and hidden mechanisms of my chronometer are in such accord with the great sidereal movement by which time is commonly reckoned, that I cannot with any degree of accuracy state the exact time, sir; but without fear of being very far off, I will state that it is so many minutes, so many seconds, and so many ticks after the Xth hour."

I do not understand! "Sir, my cranium consisting of Vermont marble, volcanic lava and African ivory, covered with a thick layer of case-hardened steel, forms an impenetrable barrier to all that seeks to impress itself upon the ashen tissues of my brain. Hence the effulgent and ostentatiously effervescent phrases just now directed and reiterated for my comprehension have failed to penetrate and permeate the somniferous forces of my atrocious intelligence. In other words, I am very, very dumb and I do not understand, sir."

One of the current questions in the catechism is, *How many days, Oh Cataline?* And the correct answer is, "X days and a butt, Oh noble Cataline, and may the great God in heaven speed them more quickly by the great Corporal Jupiter, and may the coming days be more joyous, but not for me, sir. May your classes be no soirees, and your sorrows negligible, and on your leave may there be some beautiful femmes, some canoes, lots of skags, full moons, and plenty of Coca Cola; hot darn—but not for me, sir!"

We find ourselves looking into the mouth of the *Howitzer,* the official year book in which the Corps bombards itself. With literary explosives it throws "deadly" shells into its own ranks. Here are its detonations against "Ike" Eisenhower in 1915:

"This is Senior Dwight David Eisenhower, gentlemen. . . . claims to have the best authority for the statement that he is the handsomest man in the Corps and is ready to back up his claim at any time. At any rate you'll have to give it to him that he's well developed abdominally—and more graceful in pushing it around than Charles Calvert Benedict. In common with most fat men, he is an enthusiastic and sonorous devotee of the King of Indoor Sports and roars homage at the shrine of Morpheus on every possible occasion.

"However, the memory of man runneth back to the time when the little Dwight was but a slender lad of some 'steen years, full of joy and energy and craving for life and movement and change. 'Twas then that the romantic appeal of West Point's glamor grabbed him by the scruff of the neck and dragged him to his doom. Three weeks of 'Beast' gave him his fill of life and movement and as all the change was locked up at the Cadet Store out of reach, poor Dwight merely consents to exist until graduation shall set him free. At one time he threatened to get interested in life and won his 'A' by being the most promising back in Eastern Football—but the Tuft's game broke his knee and the promise. Now Ike must content himself with tea, tiddlywinks, and talk, at all of which he excels. Now lead us in a long, loud yell for—Dare Devil Dwight, the Dauntless Don."

This record was written by his roommate, Paul Alfred Hodgson, a colonel at Fort Sam Houston, Texas, twenty-nine years later, during World War II. Today Colonel Hodgson looks with pride and admiration at his "wife" (West Point for roommate) as one of the world's great generals.

In this same edition of the *Howitzer* we find this self-portrait drawn in bold strokes by Cadet Eisenhower himself: "Dwight David Eisenhower, Abilene, Kansas. Senatorial appointee, Kan-

sas 'Ike.' Corporal, Sergeant, A.B. (an Area Bird being obliged
to walk punishment), B.A. (meaning B-Ache in complaint about
something, also Busted Aristocrat reduced to ranks). Sharpshooter: Football Squad, 3,2. 'A' in football: Baseball Squad 4:
Cheer leader: Indoor meet 4,3."

And then to this autobiography he adds: "Now, fellers, it's
just like this. I've been asked to say a few words this evening
about business. Now, me and Walter Camp, we think————"

Walter Camp was the greatest football coach of his times,
leading the Yale bulldogs to unprecedented victories. He was
young Ike's idol; his genius and strategy in commanding gridiron combats appealed to the same instincts in the West Point
cadet who later was to direct the strategy on the world's great
battlegrounds.

The records at West Point prove that this embryo military
genius was not according to the glossary of cadet slang a "bone
file," striving to beat his comrades in the classroom. He was
neither a "max" (top rank in studies) nor a "goat" (in lower sections of his class). He was "hivey" (quick to learn) but seemed
to be satisfied to remain with the "engineers" (a cadet in upper
sections in academic work). "Book larnin'" did not appeal as
much to him as comradeship and activity.

An examination of the scholarship ledgers gives Cadet Eisenhower these ratings. As a "plebe" in 1912 he ranked 57th in a
class of 212. In 1913 he was 81st in the ranks of 177 members.
In 1914 he climbed up to 65th. He was graduated in 1915 as
61st with 164 graduates. Thus he remained huddled in the center
of the upper section. He was neither a "bookworm" nor a classroom combatant, but rather a soldier in the ranks.

It was in military tactics, strategy, mathematics, historic campaigns, battles, that he showed deepest interest. He reveled in
problems of maneuver, organization and movement of armies,
the scientific rather than the academic. We find him in drill reg-

ulations getting 13.64 out of a maximum of 15—in practical military engineering getting 8.04 out of a maximum of 10. His total proportional rate was 697.04 out of a maximum 840. But all the while he was absorbing the human knowledge of soldiery and warfare, contacts and relationships with his fellowmen in which he excelled.

Strong disciplinarian that he later became, tempered by kindness and a high sense of justice and loyalty, young Ike chafed under the rigid discipline of routine. Whatever restricted his intuitive love of action was a challenge to his nature. Moreover, he was an individualist absorbed in human beings and human life, a natural-born leader with initiative.

These reactions make an interesting study in the "Skin Sheets," or "Quill Book," in the records at West Point. As a "beast," or a plebe, in 1911, we find him: "Late to target formation 7:05; absent at 8 A.M. drill formation; Sunday overshoes not arranged as prescribed at retreat; late at chapel; room in disorder afternoon inspection; late at guard mounting; tarnished brasses at inspection; shelves of clothes-press dusty; chair not against table at 8 A.M. inspection."

Simple as these "delinquencies" may seem, they are rigidly enforced in military academies. Here, for four years, youth is severely trained in rules and regulations. The slightest infraction is subject to punishment. Soldiers in the making are forged on the anvil of discipline. It is not surprising that vigorous youth has its problems of readjustment from the freedom of home life to the strict routine of soldier life.

The "Skin Sheets" at West Point reveal these further demerits in 1912: "In room in improper uniform 1:50 P.M.; alcove not in order; late at 9:30 gym formation; not numbering problems as required at written recitations in mathematics; shoes under bed dirty; police corporal tents aligned at inspection; failed to execute 'right-into-line' properly; late to breakfast; late to dinner;

dirty wash basin at retreat inspection; shelves of clothes closet dusty; waist belt too loose at Saturday inspection; absent at retreat formation."

The records for 1913 show but five infractions for the entire twelve months: "Broom in roommate's alcove; late at reveille; late to supper formation; wearing improper uniform to drill; dress coat in alcove at A.M. inspection."

This was Cadet Eisenhower's banner year and his classmates wondered if "he was sprouting wings and assuming perfection," but he redeemed himself in 1914 by: "Shoes under bed not shined; talking in mess hall while battalion was at attention; misspelling name in communion permit; dirty soap dish at A.M. inspection; full dress and dress coats not hung as prescribed; word misspelled in an indorsement; collar of dress coat unhooked in mess hall at supper; not wearing black tie at P.M. inspection; dress coat and gray shirt not hanging in prescribed places; not in prescribed uniform at 7:45 P.M. inspection; shoes under bed not properly shined at A.M. inspection."

We frankly ask the reader if his or her record for 365 days could equal that of Eisenhower. But as he neared his goal in his last five months at West Point before his graduation in 1915, he made a last grand drive down the field of valor:

"While acting First Sergeant at guard mounting, not saluting properly when reporting detail; visiting during call to quarters about 9:45 P.M.; hours of instruction not accounting for absence at inspection by second relief; late at breakfast; late at chapel formation; apparently making no reasonable effort to have his room properly cleaned at A.M. inspection; absent from retreat; hours of inspection not accounting for absence at P.M. inspection; hours of instruction not accounting for absence from room about 9:10 A.M.; not staying in area between tattoo and taps as directed." This is the last entry, twenty-seven days before his graduation.

There were two "slugs," according to Ike's classmen, that are not recorded in the "skin sheet," but can probably be found under "special orders." He was barred from the dance hall for thirty days for dancing ragtime. And there are intimations that he served five hours on a "walking slug"—standing erect, eyes straight ahead, marching back and forth like a wooden soldier— two hours on Wednesday, 3:30 to 5:30 and three hours on Saturday, 2:30 to 5:30.

The dignity and pomp of waltzes and two-steps did not appeal to this young man from the plains of Kansas. He could do them in a most gallant manner if the occasion required, but he much preferred to whoop it up in syncopated rhythm to the beating time of stamping feet and clapping hands, advance guards of the jive and hepcats which were to follow in the next generation. His courtesy with an "Army Brat" (daughter or son of an Army officer) was Chesterfieldian, and with a "Drag" (young lady) on his arm he could compete with an English lord, but his inherent fascination was that of the breezy Westerner, the spirit of the "wide open spaces."

His open frankness, candid manner, genial smile and hearty handshake, gained him immediate and lifelong friendships. His fidelity and loyalty were as solid as a rock. His honesty and integrity were inbred through generations of upright and straightforward Eisenhowers and Stovers. Here was a young American who could be depended upon.

· 13 ·

"Kansas Cyclone" wins his "A" in football battles

Kansas Ike left his name emblazoned on a bronze tablet at West Point. He attained the Hall of Fame, in the great tradition of the institution, on the field of combat as an athlete. Here valor and unconquerable spirit are intrinsic qualities in the measurement of a man. Ike came from a rugged stock of pioneers. Fortitude, hardiness, and courage were bred in him.

As we walk through the huge gymnasium, built in the year that Ike entered West Point, we come to the bronze tablet. In bold letters are inscribed the names of men who achieved greatness as athletes. There, among them, is the name Eisenhower.

It was in this gymnasium and out on the athletic fields that young Eisenhower made his first conquests. In boxing, wrestling, fencing, he met his adversaries with skill and prowess. And here, in the swimming pool, he developed the endurance which was to stand him in good stead. It was said of Ike that if he was challenged he would, if necessary, "swim the English Channel" to meet his foes face-to-face.

The coveted "A" won at West Point was the first decoration Dwight Eisenhower ever wore. Little did he realize that this in future years would be followed by the highest decorations of his own country and the leading nations of the world.

Eisenhower on the football gridiron was "fast and furious." As a halfback they dubbed him the "Kansas Cyclone." Sweeping down the field, he carried everything before him.

Army opened the season of 1912 by winning its first game: Army 27, Stevens Institute 0. It won its second game: Army 19, Rutgers 0. The Army was on its way.

The battle against Yale, however, stopped them on the "beach-head." Here was a stiff barrier. It looked as though the game would end in a stalemate until a bulldog named Flynn, forgetting he was a son of Eli and charging like a Marine, got into action.

"He was so fast," said one of the gray-haired generals in the officers' stand, "that he looked like a jackrabbit scooting for cover on a Western plain. I haven't seen anything like it since I was a young lieutenant out on the frontier. That Flynn can not only run—he can fly."

Whatever it was, the Army was checked by Flynn. The score was Yale 6, Army 0.

West Pointers who remember a certain Army-Yale game will never forget Ike's greatest athletic performance, one which led sport commentators to mark him as the most promising young back in the East. With the game nearing its close, Ike was sent in as a substitute halfback. In the next five minutes he tore a tired Yale line to shreds again and again; never, however, getting far beyond the secondary defense.

His drives carried the ball forward for some seventy-five yards. One more play, perhaps two, and the ball would have been over. The Yale defenses were crumbling. At that moment the timekeeper's gun came to Yale's rescue.

Army came back with a victory over Colgate: Army 18, Colgate 7. Eisenhower did not start in this game but replaced the powerful Hobbs in one of the periods. The sports writers said, "Eisenhower is rapidly developing into a strong back." Another scribe records, "Eisenhower in the fourth period could not be stopped."

Another great battle developed when the Army met the Carlisle Indians. West Point made the first score, but failed to convert for the extra point. The Indians put up a strong defense. Eisenhower and Pricard, for the Army, could get only five yards in two attempts. When Hobbs punted, big Jim Thorpe fell with the ball on his own 30-yard line.

Roughness marked the combat. Two of the star players were ordered to the sidelines. Powell, the Indian fullback, was sent off the field for a mix-up with Herrick, of the Army. Captain Devore, of the Cadets, drew a similar penalty for an encounter with Vedernack, of the Indians.

This description is given by an eyewitness: "Standing out resplendent in a galaxy of Indian stars was Jim Thorpe, recently crowned the athletic marvel of the age. Thorpe went through the West Point line as if it were an open door. His defensive play was on a par with his attack."

Despite the formidable Thorpe the Army on their first rush got their second first down of the game when Eisenhower carried the ball 12 yards to his own 47-yard line. Throughout the conflict Ike was in the thick of it, fighting as though this were the pass of Thermopylae. Bruised, scratched, covered with sweat and grime, he fought off the onsurging Indians who were really on the warpath. But when the battle ended, the Army had been buried under the onslaught: Indians 27, Army 6.

Throughout the struggle the Army continued to send in reinforcements. Fourteen substitutes took the places of injured or exhausted men. Eisenhower was one of the casualties. His friend, Altman, took his place as Ike limped from the field.

In this battle were cadets who later were to make eminent

reputations: Left End Hoge built the great Alaska Highway; Right Guard Herrick became one of the ablest colonels on the Army staff in Washington; Fullback Keyes gained distinction with the Army in the invasion of Sicily; Right Halfback Eisenhower became the first American General ever to lead Allied Forces in the invasion of Europe.

A week after the debacle with Carlisle, the Army redeemed itself in the game with Tufts. It regained its striking power, for here there was no rocky mountain barrier. Although scalped by the Indians, they vanquished their next foe to the score of Army 15, Tufts 6. It was in this conflict (not at Carlisle, as some reports state) that Eisenhower was "severely wounded." While making a brilliant attack he went down in a crash and was taken from the field.

Army surgeons discovered that a kneecap had been fractured. The gridiron hero was laid up in a cast, unable to get back into shape for the rest of the season. Later he became coach for the football squad at Cullum Hall.

The Army went on to one more victory: Army 23, Syracuse 7. Then in its final game with the Navy, in a terrific land-sea battle, the midshipmen triumphed: Navy 6, Army 0.

With heads bared, old grads sang the traditional ballad they always sing to "drown their sorrows" whenever the Navy defeats the Army—their tribute to Benny Havens, a beloved character who lived and died in the Highlands, and conducted a little shop, just off the post, known as the "House by the River," to which many of West Point's famous sons have made pilgrimages.

Come fill your glasses, fellows, and stand up in a row,
To singing sentimentally we're going for to go;
In the Army there's sobriety, promotion's very slow,
So we'll sing our reminiscences of Benny Havens, Oh!

Oh! Benny Havens, O! Oh! Benny Havens, Oh—
We'll sing our reminiscences of Benny Havens, Oh!

To our kind old Alma Mater, our rock-bound highland home,
We'll cast back many a fond regret as o'er life's seas we roam;
Until on our last battlefield the light of heaven shall glow,
We'll never fail to drink to her and Benny Havens, Oh!

May the Army be augmented; may promotions be less slow,
May our Country in the hour of need be ready for the foe;
May we find a soldier's resting place beneath a soldier's blow,
With room enough beside our graves for Benny Havens, Oh!

It was a grievous disappointment to Ike when his gridiron injury put him on the sidelines. Football experts said that the Army and the football world had lost "one of its greatest promises." The Kansas Cyclone had been destined for the football hall of fame.

His love for the game, however, quickly found a new outlet for his enthusiasm. He became a cheer leader. Long will he be remembered as he stood before the bleachers and aroused huge throngs to vociferous outbursts that echoed over hills and valleys. He wore his "A" with pride as he swung his arms like a master conductor of a vast philharmonic—the Toscanini of the grandstands.

Ike's voice boomed out like the roar of a cannon: "Rah! Rah! Ray!—Rah! Rah! RAH!—West Point!—West Point! AR-MAY! —Ray! Ray! Ray!—RAH! RAH! RAH! RAH! RAH! RAH! —West Point!—TEAM! TEAM! TEAM!"

The spirit of the Army was in Ike's soul. He led the throngs on the football fields as he was later to lead armies into battle. In mighty chorus we can hear them singing: "We are the kings of the gridiron, the conquerors of ev'ry foe we meet . . ." "Away, away, away we go, what care we for any foe . . ." "Smashem, crashem, sink this rabble now . . . blow them loose with dynamite!" . . . "We'll never yield, but clear the field— and march to Victory!"

During one of the celebrations of a West Point victory, Cadet

Eisenhower, while riding the Army mule, fell off and injured his kneecap again. The jubilant mule kicked Ike and left him behind him on the ground. He limped around for many weeks, but solemnly declared, "It was worth it!"

It has long been the custom when the Army returns from a victory over the Navy to meet the team at the West Point station with a horse-drawn carriage, or an old stage coach, and later a "Victory Wagon." The Corps turns out en masse, unhitches the horses from the coach, substitutes a rope for traces, and amid shouts, songs, and yells, pulls the team up the hill. You could generally find Ike either in the coach or as one of the "horses."

Cadet Eisenhower's keen interest in world events is recalled by his classmates. Throughout his four years at West Point he kept pace with his times. Even during his hours in the gymnasium or on the field (where Sergeant "Marty" Martin Maher, the old Army war horse who takes care of the grounds, says, "He was first on the field and the last off"), Ike debated the events of the day.

His adventurous spirit was thrilled by Amundsen's discovery of the South Pole. He followed the latest news from the war between Italy and Turkey. The Agadir crisis and the differences between France and Germany in Morocco intrigued him. When China became a republic he predicted a rebirth of the Far East. The serious outbreaks along the Mexican borders, where he was soon to be in service, were main topics of conversation. The opening of the Panama Canal, a triumph in engineering by an old West Pointer, was to him the beginning of a new era in commerce.

But the greatest excitement came during Ike's last year at West Point, when World War I swept over Europe. He believed that ultimately the United States would be drawn into the conflict and eagerly expressed his own desire to get into action.

Ike's athletic career was terminated by a broken knee. It almost ended his military career as well. Over a period of years the medical boards which gave him his annual physical examination stretched their official consciences to keep him in active service. Here, at least, was one instance in which such spiritual elasticity returned rich dividends to the Army and the country.

Gaily and gregariously Ike carried on through his last two years. He did his share of the grousing, enough to show that he was a thoroughly normal cadet. To his classmates he remained always a leader, a man whose views and decisions on any important matter were to be considered fully, and usually to be accepted. His position in his class was something quite unrelated to chevrons. He did not need them.

For four years "Ike" maintained a fairly uniform academic average which finally graduated him at the top of the middle third of his class. His best showing in any subject was in English. Even now his former instructors recall his trenchant and frequently unorthodox style, a characteristic which has grown more pronounced with the years. He has never wasted words, nor left any doubts of the meaning of what he had to say.

Except for a brief emergence as a high-ranking corporal at the outset of his yearling year, this future commander of our armed forces in Britain was not overburdened with chevrons. Frankly, he was not interested. True, in the final year he re-emerged as a color sergeant. Perfect physique and a bit of dash are called for in the proper handling of the colors at ceremonies. Ike had both.

Graduation Day, on June 12, 1915, meant to Dwight Eisenhower only one thing—getting immediately into the service of his country. The sabers and gold bars were but symbols of new responsibilities and new opportunities in the days ahead. All he had learned was now to be tested in practical experience—a chance to command and be commanded.

The battalions marched onto the plain to the tune of "Stars and Stripes Forever." Immaculate in his uniform, erect and soldierly, Ike stood in line. The first classmen formed for "front and center" to the tune of "Army Blue." Marching forward to form the graduates' reviewing line, the Corps passed in salute. The stirring music of the Army band echoed through the hills along the Hudson.

The class of 1915 was the largest ever graduated from West Point up to that time. Cadet Eisenhower became Second Lieutenant Eisenhower with 163 classmates before the Battle Monument, viewed by one of the largest crowds ever to witness the impressive ceremonies. Among them were members of his own family who had come from the West "to see Ike graduate."

The Battle Monument, erected in memory of battle heroes of the Regular Army who were killed in action or died of wounds during four years of Civil War, gleamed in the brilliant June sunlight. Heavy cannon on Trophy Point, captured in the various wars in which Americans have been engaged, stood grim, silent witnesses.

Secretary of War Lindley M. Garrison, of President Woodrow Wilson's cabinet, addressed the graduates. His words were prophetic. "To be honorable, valorous, truthful, fair and just in your dealings with all others, to be ready to sacrifice all for your country . . . you have undertaken a great responsibility. You may be called upon at any time to demonstrate your worth . . . upon your conduct may depend issues of vital moment to your country. . . .

"Unless you look upon yourselves as men who have actually, not only in word, pledged all that is in you for your country's safety, you have not imbibed the proper traditions and you cannot worthily hand them on. . . . I congratulate the nation to whose service the lives of you young men are consecrated."

Every graduate got a rousing cheer as he stepped forward to

receive his diploma. The athletic stars were greeted with up-roarious applause. When Second Lieutenant Eisenhower, with sheepskin in hand, stood at salute, the crowd broke into a grand ovation.

Many stories about Ike are told by West Pointers. Highest tributes are paid to him as a soldier and as a man.

"I was a first classman when Eisenhower came in," Colonel O. J. Gatchell, professor in the Department of Mechanics, says. "The impenetrable wall between upper classmen and plebes did not allow me to get into fellowship with him. But Army life brought us into intimate contact in later years. I found him a strong character. It was a pleasure to work with him. He was one of the most considerate men I have ever met. A good listener, he was quick to grasp suggestions, analyze them, and adopt them if he considered them sound. He was always sympathetic and ready to help. He overlooked mistakes if he believed them honest, but he will not tolerate blunders. He rarely loses his temper: when he does it is for a good cause."

This picture of General Eisenhower is given by Lieutenant Colonel Meade Wildrick, Public Relations Officer at West Point: "He is good natured, very human, easy to work with. He enjoys a good joke and laughs heartily. His geniality pervades everything—but when he does get mad he is mad through and through. He explodes like a bomb at incompetence."

"West Point has given the nation many great men," says Colonel Wildrick, "and General Eisenhower stands in the front rank as one of the world's greatest commanders."

A one-time ranking officer of the Department of Tactics in Eisenhower's day recently summed up what may be accepted as the official prediction for his career, dated June 12, 1915, Ike's graduation day.

"We saw in Eisenhower a not uncommon type," he remarked, "a man who would thoroughly enjoy his Army life, giving both to duty and recreation their fair values. We did not see in him a man who would throw himself into his job so completely that nothing else would matter."

It was not the first time that higher authority has misjudged a youth. It is not beside the point that no one in West Point in the days of U. S. Grant's cadetship, not even one of his classmates, foresaw anything beyond an inconspicuous career for that future leader of the Union armies. What officialdom often overlooks is the fact that a military neophyte may be absorbing the solid values of his training, letting the frills go by the board. How well Ike had mastered the substance became apparent within three years after his graduation, when he proved himself an outstanding trainer in that newfangled infant of World War I, the Tank Corps. The substance appeared again in 1927 when Eisenhower easily led a class of two hundred selected student officers in the Command and General Staff School's grim course of map and terrain problems.

Ike's philosophy of life as a cadet found ample support among his classmates. Of the thirty general officers produced by United States Military Academy's class of 1915 to April 1, 1944, it is noteworthy that a high proportion never were seriously weighed down by cadet chevrons. Among them are the names of Lieutenant General J. T. McNarney, and Major Generals George E. Stratemeyer and Hubert R. Harmon of the Army Air Forces who sailed gaily through four years of West Point as "clean sleeves." Lieutenant General Omar N. Bradley achieved a junior lieutenancy, sergeant's chevrons fell to the lot of Major General H. S. Aurand, Commanding General of the Sixth Service Command, and Major General H. W. Waldron, crippled by a Jap sniper in the Southwest Pacific. On all of them the West Point system left its clearcut imprint, to be disclosed ultimately on the field of battle rather than on the parade ground.

International News Photo

An American tank rolls inland, bound for the fighting, after American "end run" by sea around the Nazi flank in Italy. Part of the invasion fleet which carried the fighters can be seen off the beach

International News Photo

United States parachutists float earthward from troop-carrying planes, as an effective means of landing behind enemy lines

· 14 ·

Lieutenant Eisenhower starts on road to fame

"Good-by and good luck!" exclaimed Ike's comrades as they grasped his extended hand at West Point on that June day in 1915. "We'll meet again somewhere at the ends of the earth."

The young Second Lieutenant's face was wreathed in a smile. He broke into hearty laughter. His voice boomed with geniality, but underneath he now carried the grave demeanor of a soldier. Under the firm discipline of West Point, he had been transformed from a "gale out of the West" into a strict disciplinarian. He came to the institution as an exuberant boy; he was leaving it as a man of strong resolution.

Let us stop here to pass in rapid review the long line of great men who had preceded this Kansas lad to the nation's military academy, looking both into the past and into the future, and recite with him the reverent stanza of "The Corps":

> The Corps! Bareheaded salute it,
>> With eyes up, thanking our God,
> That we of the Corps are treading
>> Where they of the Corps have trod.
>
> They are here in ghostly assemblage,
>> The men of the Corps long dead;
> And our hearts are standing attention,
>> While we wait for their passing tread.

151

Grip hands with us now, though we see not,
    Grip hands with us, strengthen our hearts,
As the long line stiffens and straightens
    With the thrill that your presence imparts.

Grip hands, though it be from the shadows,
    While we swear as you did of yore,
Or living, or dying, to honor
    The Corps, and the Corps, and the Corps!

We grip hands first in the shadows with Grant, who saved the Union; the great Lee who fought nobly for what he believed to be right; "Stonewall" Jackson, who died at Chancellorsville for his principles; Sherman, Bragg, Sumner, Hooker, Beauregarde, McClellan—all soldiers of the Corps who led their forces in the nation's crisis of Civil War.

In the lines of the Union we see 800 West Point officers in Blue—and in the lines of the Confederacy we see 296 officers in the Gray uniform. And "our hearts are standing attention" as the great Lee, former superintendent of the Academy, surrenders to the victorious Grant. In the shadows stands Jefferson Davis, the West Pointer who became President of the Confederacy. This is the most tragic spectacle in the annals of the historic Academy, the only time in history that the Corps has been divided on opposite sides in battle.

We hear the tramp of the Corps through the Mexican War, the Indian wars, the Spanish-American War, as it fades into the past—and, as we stand beside young Lieutenant Eisenhower on his last day at West Point, we catch glimpses into the future. World War I, which started while he was a cadet on the hill, was to bring many West Pointers to the front: General John J. Pershing, class of 1886, as Commander in Chief of the American Expeditionary Forces in France; General Peyton C. March, class of 1888, as Chief of Staff at Washington. All the armies commanded by West Pointers—Generals Liggett, Bullard, and Dickman. Out of thirty-eight corps and division commanders, thirty-four were from the Academy, among them Generals Summeral and MacArthur. A grand total of 3,445 officers from the Point fought in World War I.

A generation ahead, beyond the penetration of vision, young lieutenants grown older were to be commanding armies in World War II. On the battlefields with General Ike were to be his friends and comrades: Generals Spaatz, Patton, Clark, Brady, Keyes (fullback on the football team with Ike at West Point), fighting in North Africa, Italy, on the Second Front in the Invasion of Europe; General Devers in the European theatre; General Buckner in Alaska—carrying on the old traditions of the Corps.

And far across the Pacific the West Pointers were to lead great armies: General Douglas MacArthur (on whose staff Eisenhower was to serve in Washington and later for five years in the Philippines) in command in the Southwest Pacific; and with him Generals Eichelberger, Harmon, Patch and Griswold; and General Wainwright in the last heroic stand at Bataan and Corregidor; General "Vinegar Joe" Stilwell in command of the forces in China—8,337 West Point officers serving on all fronts.

We project ourselves for a few minutes into this world of 1944. We are at West Point, while the war is raging, talking about this same Lieutenant Eisenhower, who has become the great General Eisenhower, the first American ever to lead Allied Forces in an invasion of Europe.

Major General Francis B. Wilby, Superintendent of the United States Military Academy, analyzing what he calls "West Point in the War," says, "Our job is to train professional soldiers . . . training young men to become the military specialists, the planners, organizers, trainers, managers, and leaders of a greater, even more potent, army should it be needed ten, twenty, thirty years from now. . . . After we win this war, we hope also to win a peace that will allow us to share in a community of nations, each one of which may seek its own destiny, unhindered by threat of force from without.

"The soldier must know more than weapons," General Wilby declares. "He must be a citizen as well as a soldier. He has a stake in his nation as well as the man who follows any other profession. He must assume the responsibilities of citizenship, in the direction of his nation's destiny as well as protecting it from attack. . . . No one wants war less than soldiers, because they know best what it costs. But," he adds warningly, "they must be maintained by any nation which would preserve its freedom until the blessed day when men have found a better way of settling their disputes and achieving their ambitions."

Colonel Meade Wildrik, discussing the qualities of character which make Eisenhower a great general, gives this analysis: "The young men of America come to West Point because they intend to make the Army their career. . . . Through 140-odd years, West Point has played a leading part in shaping and preserving our country. Never has it failed to produce the man for the hour. In times of peaceful expansion it has given us the makers of canals, harbors, and railways. In times of war it has always produced military leaders.

"I hope that while you are on the trail of our great Eisenhower, you will not entirely by-pass the constructive achievements of his fellow alumni," suggests Colonel Wildrick. "We make great engineers here as well as great soldiers."

Colonel T. D. Stamps remarks, "A classmate of General Eisenhower's built the greatest earth dam in the world. The Fort Peck Dam near Glasgow, Montana, was built by Thomas B. Larkin of the class of 1915. And a man who was at West Point while Eisenhower was here built one of the greatest concrete dams in our country and one of the most important power projects: the Bonneville Dam near Portland, Oregon, was constructed by Charles F. Williams of the class of 1913.

"Another friend of Eisenhower's, who was with him here in cadet days, organized and completed the bulk of the work in the gigantic $10,000,000,000 Army construction program for World War II, Brehon Somervell, class of 1914. While Works Progress Administrator for the City of New York, Somervell also built the La Guardia airport. The greatest of all the world's engineering achievements was completed in the year Eisenhower entered West Point—the building of the Panama Canal, separating the continents and joining the Atlantic and Pacific Oceans, by Major General George W. Goethals of the class of 1880."

Colonel Stamps, in recalling these triumphs in engineering, listed them in martial array: The Wilson Dam in Alabama, one of the greatest structures in the country, carried to completion by George R. Spalding of the class of 1901. The great locks and dams on the Illinois Waterway, near Chicago, carried to completion by Daniel I. Sultan, class of 1907. The series of locks and dams on the Ohio River and the Great Mississippi Flood Control Project constructed by staffs of West Pointers. Highways stretching across the continents; bridges spanning rivers and canyons; tunnels burrowing through mountains.

Forty-six years before the first Eisenhowers migrated to the West, Benjamin Bonneville, class of 1815, started out "to explore the Great West and the Pacific." He had been a secretary to General Lafayette in France. When he was missing for three years his name was stricken from the Army lists. After "coming back to civilization," relating his story of perilous adventure, he was reinstated by President Andrew Jackson.

When Dwight David Eisenhower was born in Texas, his father was a railroad man. The gigantic task of building the railroads across the continent was led by West Pointers. They were the topographical engineers and surveyors who later made the work of Dodge possible. Charles W. Raymond, class of 1865, traveled up the Yukon, making astronomical calculations; Fred-

erick Schwalka, class of 1871, explored the Alaskan wastes;
Henry T. Allen, class of 1882, explored the Yukon to the Arctic
Circle.

While the pioneer Eisenhowers were holding their family
lines in the hills of Pennsylvania, West Pointers were opening
up the country for future migrations. Andrew Talcott, class of
1818, determined the northern boundary of their neighboring
state, Ohio, inventing the zenith telescope and methods for making latitude determination. Cyrus Comstock, class of 1855, surveyed the Great Lakes and the St. Lawrence River.

Young Dwight Eisenhower, product of what may be definitely
called the first scientific school in the United States, followed in
the footsteps of a long line of builders. Washington Monument
in our nation's Capital was completed by Thomas Lincoln Casey,
class of 1852. Construction of the dome and the wings of the
National Capitol was superintended by Montgomery C. Meigs,
class of 1832. The use of asphalt in paving and municipal engineering was developed by Francis Vinton Greene, class of
1870, who later became Police Commissioner of the City of
New York. The designer of Central Park was Egbert L. Viele,
class of 1847. The builder of the Croton water supply for America's largest city was George S. Greene, class of 1823. One of
the country's greatest water supply experts was William Lud-
low, class of 1864. The founder of General Electric, marking
the gigantic electrical development of the nation, was Edwin
Griffin, class of 1875.

We left the towering Administration Building at West Point,
the tallest stone masonry building in the world, and followed
the path which Cadet Eisenhower so often walked to the ancient
library, an old-world abbey, flanked at the door by two cannons
—one fired the first shot in the Civil War, the other the last shot
at Appomattox. An original portrait of George Washington,
painted by Gilbert Stuart, faces us as we enter. Here scholarly

Colonel W. J. Morton laid the records before us. Ike, coming out of the West from a pioneer family, must have been at home here. Explorers and adventurers have been going out from West Point from it earliest days. With the Long Expedition in the exploration of the West were John R. Bell, class of 1812, James D. Graham, class of 1817, William H. Swift, class of 1819, who also built the country's first iron lighthouse. George Wheeler, class of 1866, surveyed the United States west of the one hundredth meridian at the low cost of $1.48 per square mile.

The genius of West Point laid the foundations for the building of a new world. George W. Whistler, a member of the class of 1819, and father of the famous painter who later was a cadet at the Academy, went to England with other engineers and brought back some English locomotives which were assembled at the West Point foundry. He later went to Russia and built the St. Petersburg-Moscow railroad at the Czar's invitation. He was succeeded in Russia by Thompson Brown, class of 1825. The surveys for the Pan-American highway were started by Samuel Reber, class of 1886. The survey for the Nicaraguan Canal was directed by Daniel Sultan, class of 1907. The first railroad in Cuba was built by Benjamin Wright, class of 1922.

As we sat with the records before us Colonel Morton gave us this summary. The sons of West Point have served as leaders in five foreign wars, one civil war, and in the long-drawn Indian conflicts that blazed the trails for the settlement of the nation. In civil life they have held almost every office of honor and trust in the gift of their fellow countrymen.

Here is the formidable record: President of the United States, 1; President of the Confederate States, 1; presidential candidates, 3; vice-presidential candidates, 2; members of the cabinet, 4; private secretaries to presidents of United States, 3; ambassadors, 2; ministers to foreign courts, 15; chargé d'affaires, 3; United States consuls-general and consuls, 17; members of United

States Congress, 26; United States civil officers of various grades, 189; presidential electors, 8.

Governors of States and Territories, 20; governors of Panama Canal, 6; lieutenant-governors of States, 2; presiding officers of State legislatures, 8; members of State legislatures, 94; members of State constitutional conventions, 17; adjutants, inspectors, quartermasters-general and chief engineers of States and Territories, 66; State officers of various grades, 91; officers of State militia, 231; country officers of various grades, 58; mayors of cities, 20; city officers of various grades, 133.

Presidents of universities and colleges, 35; principals of academies and schools, 71; regents and chancellors of educational institutions, 17; professors and teachers, 240; superintendent of coast survey, 1; surveyors-general of States and Territories, 2.

Presidents of railroads and other corporations, 258; vice-presidents of railroads and other corporations, 243; chief engineers of railroads and public works, etc., 93; superintendents of railroads, public works, etc., 185; treasurers and receivers of railroads and other corporations, 158; bishop, 1; superior-general of clerical order, 1; clergymen, 22; engineers, civil, electrical, mining, consulting (not military), 367.

Judges of courts, 22; attorneys and counsellors at law, 264; physicians, 16; merchants, 158; manufacturers, 115; bankers and brokers, 62; bank presidents, 25; bank officers, 74; geologists, 5; chemists, 2; inventors, 25; publishers, 19; editors, 57; auditors, 276; contractors, 33; real estate and insurance, 132; engineers of foreign governments, 6; officers of foreign armies, 21; artists, 8; architects, 14; farmers and planters, 310.

Among the twenty-two West Pointers who entered holy orders were "Fighting Bishop" Leonidas Polk of Civil War fame; Clark, the Jesuit; Father Deshon, who became a Catholic priest and founder of the Order of Paulists after a career in the Ordnance Department; Culbertson, who became a Presbyterian missionary to China; Garth, who became a missionary in Japan.

The most famous artist to attend West Point was James A. McNeill Whistler, whose father also was a cadet. Many of his masterpieces bear the influence of instruction he received under Professor Weir at the Academy. Among authors are Edgar Allan Poe, who was a cadet for a brief time during his tragic career; Charles King, who, after being seriously wounded in Indian warfare, became famous for his books about soldiers and soldiering; Ethan Allen Hitchcock, assistant to Secretary of War Stanton in Lincoln's cabinet, who wrote several learned volumes. Among the other authors are Richard S. Savage, Arthur S. Hardy, and Oliver Lyman Spaulding.

The most celebrated of the diplomats was General Horace Porter, who made a notable record as Ambassador to France when Ike was but seven years old. He followed another West Pointer, Robert M. McLane, ambassador to France after representing the United States diplomatically in China and in Mexico. Serving as a minister in the court of the Hapsburgs in Austria-Hungary was Alexander R. Lawton, who was succeeded by Frederick Dent Grant, son of General U. S. Grant, father and son both West Pointers. After being wounded in the Civil War, Judson Kilpatrick rigged for himself an apparatus enabling him to sit on his horse despite wounds and later became minister to Chile. Three modern graduates distinguished themselves on the field of diplomacy as well as war: General Tasker H. Bliss, with President Woodrow Wilson at the Versailles Peace Conference after World War I; General John J. Pershing in the Tacna-Arica dispute; and General Frank R. McCoy in the Far East and in Central and South America.

And thus we have reviewed the long gray line, as Dwight Eisenhower starts on his great career—on the road to fame. Again we can hear the chant of the Corps:

We, sons of today, salute you,
　　You sons of an earlier day;
We follow, close order behind you
　　Where you have pointed the way.

The long gray line of us stretches
　　Through the years of a century told,
And the last man feels to his marrow
　　The grip of your far-off hold.

· 15 ·

Young Eisenhower in World War I—
organizes first tank corps

SECOND LIEUTENANT EISENHOWER, twenty-four years old, stepped
from West Point into World War I. Here he was to show his
genius in the new age of mechanized warfare as the organizer of
the first American tank corps to enter battle.

America was preparing for the inevitable day when it would
be drawn into the vortex. Thirty-six days before Ike graduated
from West Point German submarines had sunk the transatlantic
passenger ship *Lusitania* (May 7, 1915), with a loss of 1,195
lives, of whom 124 were Americans. Protests only brought defiance from the Germans. Ruthless submarine warfare came
home to ships flying the American flag.

We find young Ike first assigned to the 19th Infantry at Fort
Sam Houston, in San Antonio, Texas, on September 13, 1915,
a few miles from his birthplace in Denison. Here again he was
under the shadow of the historic Alamo. Six months later when
Pancho Villa began his raids over the Mexican border, burning
American homes, Second Lieutenant Eisenhower was made In-
spector-Instructor of Militia on the Mexican border. This was
his job from August 1, 1916, to April 1, 1917. Punitive forces
under General John J. Pershing were chasing the bandit into

the Mexican mountains. Some years later, after Pershing had won fame leading the American Expeditionary Forces in France, Villa was ambushed and killed in Durango.

Daniel S. Miller, now a military policeman at the Brooklyn Navy Yard, tells of his being the first orderly of Eisenhower at Fort Sam Houston in the fall of 1915, Ike's first assignment after being graduated from West Point.

"One day a young second lieutenant came to the Fort and joined our company," says Mr. Miller. "His name was Eisenhower. I was his first orderly. He was a strapping youth and seemed to know his way around. I reported at his bachelor quarters in the infantry post and looked after his trunks, etc., all being tagged 'Abilene, Kansas.' I was Eisenhower's orderly for some two months and then was assigned to the infantry band where I played cornet.

"One evening I had a date at San Antonio and needed a pair of civilian shoes so I sneaked a pair of the lieutenant's without being caught. The next morning I arose early to replace them under his bed. As I was cleaning his room that morning the lieutenant quietly remarked, 'If you want a pair of shoes don't be bashful, ask me for them—don't sneak them out!' I was so embarrassed that I couldn't say anything. I was dumbfounded when he added, 'You can use those shoes any time—they are yours.'

"I thought I would be fired from my job. But he never again mentioned the incident and we became real friends. As I look back on those days I am thrilled to see him the greatest general we ever had, God bless him!"

Young Eisenhower received his promotion to first lieutenant while stationed at Fort Sam Houston on July 1, 1916, and on that day was married to the charming Mamie Geneva Doud in Denver, Colorado. The soldier groom was twenty-five years old and his bride was nineteen. The story of this romance is related in another chapter.

Tense excitement swept the United States on April 6, 1917. Savage submarine attacks on American shipping forced us to enter World War I. Thirty-nine days after we entered the war First Lieutenant Eisenhower became Captain Eisenhower, on May 15. Captain Eisenhower was sent to Camp Wilson to train the National Guard of Illinois, and later became Assistant Mustering Officer of the Southern Department. He was now rereiving his first experience in the making of an army.

The first American troops landed in France on June 5, 1917. Captain Eisenhower was at this time the Regimental Supply Officer, with the 57th Infantry at Leon Springs, Texas, from April 1 to September 20. Across the seas battles were raging along the Somme, along the Ypres-Menin Road, at Verdun, at "Dead Man's Hill" and Hill 304, and at Cambrai.

Captain Eisenhower was making a reputation as one of the ablest young officers in American training camps. He was sent to Fort Oglethorpe, in Georgia, as instructor at the Officers' Training Camp from September 20 to December 1.

It was during this period that Eisenhower's war bride, back in Texas, presented him with his first son, christened Doud Dwight Eisenhower, born on September 24, 1917, at Fort Sam Houston in San Antonio.

We find the young father at Fort Leavenworth in Kansas, near his old boyhood home at Abilene, as Instructor of Provisional Officers at the Army Service Schools from December 1, 1917, to March 1, 1918; then organizing the 65th Battalion Engineers at Camp Meade, in Maryland, and finally commander at Camp Colt, the old Gettysburg battlefield in Pennsylvania, not far from the birthplace of his father, from March 24 to November 18, 1918.

There is a story told about Ike at Gettysburg. He had a junior officer who always agreed with him. Turning to the "yes man" he exclaimed, "I want you to figure out some things which are wrong with this camp. You make me uncomfortable by always agreeing with me. I feel that you either don't say what you think, or that you are as big a fool as I am!"

Ike handled privates with the same tact he uses with presidents. While stationed at a camp as C. O. he heard of a pair of privates who were constantly battling with one another. He solved the difficulty by assigning the two to a window cleaning detail. They were ordered to work on the same pane at the same time, one doing the outside, the other the inside. At the beginning of the task the two had nothing but scowls and growls for each other. They could not keep up their enmity for long as the humor of the situation began to dawn on them. Soon they burst out laughing. Harmony was restored through Ike's clever tact.

Ike, like his forefathers, was now a pioneer. The age of mechanized warfare was beginning. Fortifications on wheels, known as tanks, were to revolutionize land battles. He saw in these weird moving forts, leading the way for infantry charges, a great future and began to master their intricacies and develop strategy and maneuvers with amazing skill. He was training and sending his Tank Corps to France where they were making notable records in battle.

The attention of the General Staff at Washington, under its Chief, General Peyton C. March, and the War Department under Secretary Newton B. Baker, was directed to this young captain and made him major of infantry on June 17, 1918, while at Gettysburg. Four months later he was promoted to lieutenant colonel (temporary) of Tank Corps on October 14.

Young Lieutenant Colonel Eisenhower was in command of 6,000 men at Camp Colt. It became the best organized camp in the United States and netted its commander the Distinguished Service Medal at the end of the war. The citation read, "For displaying unusual zeal, foresight, and marked administrative ability in the organization, training, and preparation for overseas service of technical troops of the Tank Corps."

This youthful commander displayed considerable omniscience when he wrote to the *Infantry Journal:* "The tank is in its infancy and the great strides already made in its mechanical improvement only point to the greater ones still to come. The clumsy, awkward, and snail-like progress of the old tanks must be forgotten and in their place we must picture a speedy, reliable, and efficient engine of destruction." He also became a staunch supporter of air power, visioned its future, and wanted to apply for the Air Corps in 1917, stopping only because of his young bride's objections.

During these months while young Eisenhower was sending his trained tankmen to the battlegrounds of France, our American forces under General Pershing were helping turn the tide of the war against the Germans. They were winning the battle at Cantigny and at Bois de Belleau. On the day that Eisenhower, back at Gettysburg, became a major, they were fighting on the front between Soissons and Chateau-Thierry, their lines advancing until they ran from the Ourcq to the Marne. They were engaged in terrific combats in the Argonne and on the roads leading to Verdun. On the day that Eisenhower was made a lieutenant colonel, American troops were taking Grandpré and advancing along the Meuse.

Lieutenant Colonel Eisenhower appealed to Washington to go overseas and get into action with his men. But Washington insisted that the work he was doing in training soldiers at home was of equal importance—without these trained Tank Corps men the battles in France could not be won. Therefore a part of the credit for these victories belonged to Eisenhower.

General Pershing, his old commander on the Mexican border, was making history in France. General Douglas MacArthur, with whom Eisenhower was later to be connected, was gaining fame. Young Lieutenant Colonel Eisenhower was pulling on the leash—his bulldog spirit was longing to get into the thick of the fight.

He heard with pride the stories that came back home about the Tank Corps in active combat—the famous 301st Battalion which was the only American heavy tank unit on the Western Front. He had trained Number four, of Chicago, at Camp Colt in Gettysburg. They were making a great record for themselves in the Second Somme Offensive.

The *Stars and Stripes*, the doughboys' official organ in France, featured them in headlines: "Tanks Stood Gaff from Belgium to Argonne Battle—American Machines Few in Number but Active All the Time—Personnel Losses Heavy—Enemy Felt Shock of Their Assault on Hindenburg Line and Kriemhilde-Stellung."

"The dangers which they confronted and the splendid spirit of heroism," says this record, "was even greater than those encountered by the men of other branches of the service on the battlefront."

It relates how tanks fought with several American Divisions, while others fought with the British and the Australians, and graphically describes some of the battles. The "Tankdrome" of the 301st Battalion was located at Manaucourt, about fifteen kilometers behind the front line. The battalion started from there on the night of September 27-28 and went to Villers-Faucon, where the supply dump had been placed. Thence they moved for the front, distant about eight kilometers, on the night of September 28-29.

"The constant and terrible peril was the fire of the German artillery and anti-tank rifles. The moment a tank came into view, it was made the center of a concentration of artillery fire, and many machines were demolished or compelled to retire from action by direct hits. The tank command had not been notified of the existence of a mine field, and two American and several British tanks were blown up. Nevertheless, a number of the tanks on this flank went through the Hindenburg line, in spite of all the mines and trenches and the artillery and anti-tank rifle fire, and ambled about behind it, carrying terror and destruction among the German infantry and machine gunners with the fusillade of their Hotchkiss guns and six-pounders.

"At the end of the day's heroic work, the casualties among the personnel of the thirty tanks of the 301st Battalion which had been in action amounted to one hundred and twelve, of whom three officers and twenty enlisted men were killed, seven officers and fifty-five enlisted men severely wounded, eight officers and fifteen enlisted men slightly wounded, and one officer and six enlisted men missing. Of the tanks engaged, nor more than twenty-five per cent escaped without more or less serious injury, but they had accomplished a great deal of damage to the enemy, not merely in a material sense, but in breaking the morale of his troops.

"The First American Army had in the Meuse-Argonne offensive the First American Tank Brigade, under Lieutenant Colonel Patton, who was wounded early the first day and was succeeded in command by Major Sereno E. Brett, and the 13th and 14th Battalions of the 505th French Tank Regiment. The wary Germans, fully aware now of the tank strength in front of them, had developed very strong defense methods against this form of attack; the tanks suffered the heaviest casualties of any single day during the offensive, 41 officers and men being killed or wounded among the personnel of the 83 American and 12 French tanks in action.

"About 5:30 on the morning of October 1, the enemy made a violent counterattack on the 28th Division just north of Apremont. The Americans themselves were preparing to jump an attack over at six o'clock; eight tanks were in position to assist.

Their fire into the closely massed ranks of the assaulting Germans produced terrible execution. The First Army Corps Headquarters declared officially after the action that "prisoners of the II Landwehr Division state that in the counterattack north of Apremont they were completely demoralized by our tanks, as most of the soldiers as well as most of the officers had never seen tanks before. During all the fighting of the day, the tanks themselves suffered only sixteen casualties, of whom none were killed.

"On October 4 came the second general attack along the whole front of the First American Army. By repair and salvage work on disabled machines, eighty-nine tanks had been made ready for action again; one company was assigned to the 28th Division and two companies were assigned to the First Division, which had relieved the 35th. The remaining tanks stayed in brigade reserve. The tank commanders with the First Division found excellent support from the infantry, whom they assisted against bitter resistance in the capture of Hill 240, north of Exermont, while those with the 28th Division pressed the fighting along the edges of the Argonne.

"The most direct testimony to the severity of the work which they all underwent is found in the figures. Thirty tanks were ready for action on October 5 out of the eighty-nine which had been fit the day before. The rest had been destroyed or disabled; twenty-eight officers and enlisted men had been killed or wounded. Moreover, mechanical difficulties, due to long and terribly severe usage, were daily becoming more troublesome, while an epidemic of influenza had caused many men to be evacuated. Major Brett said in his report: 'The nightly gassing on the positions around Charpentry has caused a little sickness and inconvenience. Nevertheless,' he added, 'the men and officers are in good spirits.'

"During the course of the Meuse-Argonne battles, the tank units of the First Brigade had lost three officers and sixteen enlisted men killed; twenty-one officers and one hundred thirty-one enlisted men wounded. These losses were suffered in eighteen separate engagements, in many of which some of the French tanks also participated, supporting eight different divisions, including, besides those already mentioned, the 77th and 82nd, and the 91st."

Eighteen of the 141 American tanks were totally demolished by enemy fire. One tank disappeared entirely and was never found, the theory being that it was either disabled and captured by the enemy or that it fell into the Aire river and was completely submerged. The dangers of tank service were many and among them, oddly enough, that of drowning was not negligible.

Stories from the front aroused a determination in Ike to get overseas with the tank boys. He sent persistent appeals to Washington and at last they were to be rewarded. Ike was going to France. He was with his new tank unit aboard the transport ready to sail on November 11—when the news came. World War I had come to its sudden end. The Germans, facing defeat, had run up the white flag with the cry of "Kamerad" rather than continuing the war on German soil. The bugles sounded "cease firing" eleven o'clock on the morning of November 11, 1918, when an armistice was declared.

The ship's captain knew of young Eisenhower's eagerness to get into action. He also knew of his explosive nature if and when his plans were thwarted. Approaching him guardedly, he remarked:

"Sorry, Colonel, sailing orders cancelled—*it's all over over there!*"

Ike's reply is said to have been "classic." His command of vocabulary went into immediate action; he fought a battle of words on the deck of that ship with bombardments that might have sunk it. When the smoke from the burning declamations cleared away, he sat down.

Lieutenant Colonel Eisenhower, ready to sail with his tank unit, was silent. As a soldier he must take orders. But his friends state that he believed it was a grievous mistake not to force the Germans to fight it out to a decisive battle on German soil. He had dreamed of roaring with his tanks on to Berlin. He believed the Germans would interpret the armistice as a tactical victory, saving them from disaster, and begin preparations for another war in years to come.

"The Germans must be beaten on their own ground. Their own fatherland must be conquered and their military spirit broken before they will settle down as a peaceful people," was Ike's conviction. Time proved him to be correct.

The world accepted the armistice as a relief from the four years of war. Armistice Night throughout the United States, which had been in the war nineteen months, was a scene of great rejoicing. Throngs gathered in the streets in wild celebration. Bells rang. The air was filled with a tumult of horns and shouts. Crowds broke into song. Ike caught the spirit of victory and joined in the jubilation.

World War I had mobilized a grand total of 65,638,810 men in its armies and navies, the Allies creating a strength of 42,188,810 against the Central Powers' 22,850,000.

The grand total of casualties of all belligerents in World War I reached 37,508,686, of which those killed or died were 8,538,315, the wounded 21,219,452, the prisoners and missing 7,750,919. Of these the Allies' total casualties were 22,104,209 (52.3%) against 15,404,477 (57.6%) in the Central Powers.

During this conflict America mobilized 4,800,000 men and performed the first of its "modern miracles" by sending across the Atlantic 2,084,000 soldiers from the United States, something that Germany considered "impossible." One million three hundred ninety thousand American soldiers fought in the front lines. Twenty-nine active American divisions were engaged with the enemy, holding a battle front 101 miles long. Against the most desperate resistance their total advances were 485 miles.

The total American battle losses of the war were 37,271 killed in action, 12,934 died of wounds, 236,000 wounded. The Navy lost in action, dead and wounded, 893; the Marine Corps 10,178. These figures do not include losses from disease. The cost of the war in money to all nations involved exceeded $186,000,000,000.

This vast expenditure in men and money was to be but the prelude to World War II in which gargantuan forces were to fight at a staggering cost to finish the job, as Eisenhower predicted. And the young Lieutenant Colonel who trained the Tank Corps for the First World War was to be the General commanding the Allied Forces in the invasion of Europe in the Second World War.

We will now talk with some of the veterans of the Tank Corps who served in World War I. They have organized a World War Tank Corps Association and among its famous members are General "Iron Ike" Eisenhower and General "Blood and Guts" Patton. Former Secretary of War Harry H. Wooding was a second lieutenant in the Tank Corps. Professor Carl O. Brigham, of Princeton University, was a first lieutenant. Hon. Melvin Jones, War Food Administrator, was a sergeant. United States Senator Henry Cabot Lodge, Jr., was a young tank man, as were James Gleason and Hoot Gibson, the motion-picture stars.

Meet their National Historian, Claude J. Harris, in Los Angeles, California, and listen to his reminiscences: "The Tank Corps, U.S.A., was organized at Camp Colt, Gettysburg, Pennsylvania, in March, 1918, on the site of the old battlefield, over which our barracks, tents and training area extended, under direction of Colonel William H. Clopton, of the War Department, Washington, D. C. (he now resides in Gulf Post, Mississippi). Eisenhower came to the Tank Corps as a captain of infantry, early in April, 1918, undoubtedly being ordered there for the express purpose of assuming organization command of the forces, inasmuch as he relieved a major in his duties. At the time I was regimental sergeant major in his headquarters, and continued in that capacity until commissioned later that year.

"Eisenhower was a strict disciplinarian," says his sergeant major, "an inborn soldier, but most human, considerate, and his decisions affecting the welfare of his officers and men were always well tempered. Despite his youth, he possessed a high understanding of organization, the ability to place an estimate on a man and fit him into a position where he would 'click.' In the event his judgment proved erroneous the man would be called in, his errors pointed out, and adjustments made to suit the situation. This principle built for him high admiration and loyalty from his officers perhaps unequaled by few commanding officers.

"On the job Eisenhower was strictly military, therefore I had few words with him other than officially, perhaps more due to the fact that we were working under strain most of the time. Seldom did one see a paper on his desk. Mail and papers for his attention were immediately attended to—his desk cleared. No accumulated matters were inside his desk out of sight. He was always available to confer with his officers on either military or personal problems, but disliked being interviewed by non-military people. He just shied at publicity, preferring to remain in the background."

Harris explains, "Due to the mechanical requirements of personnel to operate the tanks, our own recruiting force was organized and dispatched into larger cities of the country to recruit the necessary manpower, and these men were soon rolling in to start training. Some three hundred second lieutenants, just previously graduated from officer training schools, comprised the initial commissioned personnel in the main. Our own officer training school was organized, affording our promising enlisted personnel opportunity to win commissions.

"The highly publicized accomplishments of the British Tank Corps on the battlefields created special appeal to many high caliber men to enlist—and they did. Perhaps no branch of the military service had a higher I.Q. rating among the enlisted personnel than the Tank Corps. Captain Norman Randolph, also a West Point graduate, proved an able aid to the C.O., and was responsible directly for the efficiency of the operation of the officer training schools.

"Eisenhower (stopped on the transport on Armistice Day as he was sailing for France) deeply regretted he did not get overseas. His disappointment can well be expressed in a statement he made in conversing with a young officer who had been overseas and complained that no promotions had been made over there. Eisenhower replied, 'Well, you got overseas—that should be promotion enough!' "

Following the Armistice, the Tank Corps personnel was transferred to Camp Dix, New Jersey, where soon the troops who had not got overseas were mustered out, with the exception of seven hundred and fifty enlisted men and thirty-five officers. The remaining men were soon removed to Camp Benning, Georgia, where they remained until March, 1919, when ordered to Camp Meade, Maryland. Soon Tank Corps troops from overseas arrived at that station for demobilization, which gives Eisenhower a most unique distinction of not only organizing those fighting forces, but also mustering them out.

In speaking of Patton, Harris says, "Patton was assigned to the tanks overseas and did not train with our forces on this side. However, I presume he and Eisenhower enjoyed personal acquaintanceship from West Point days. Patton was a colorful officer, loved by his men, but, like Eisenhower, a strict disciplinarian. In acknowledging a medal our Association voted him the past year, he wrote, 'Due to circumstances beyond my control I have acquired a few medals, but none for which I have a higher consideration than that of the old Tank Corps, and you men who fought in the last war should have nothing but pride for the magnificent valor and unhesitating devotion of your descendants in this war.'

"During the passing years I have heard from Eisenhower occasionally," remarks his former sergeant major. "When he was assigned as Commander of the European area, I wrote him a letter of congratulations and well wishes. He replied, 'Many thanks for your nice letter. I could ask nothing more of my present command than that they give me the same loyalty and devotion to duty displayed by the old "Tank Corps!" I truly appreciate your good wishes and your renewed expressions of confidence and friendship. Best of luck.'"

Recollections of these old tank days in World War I are related by National Adjutant "Salutin' Demon" Ed J. Price, in Chicago, Illinois, in what he calls "Tank Actions," recording the stories of the battles and heroism of the men. Mr. John J. Noll, assistant editor of the *American Legion Magazine*, in New York, also extended valuable assistance in directing us to sources for the stories we have related.

Ex-tankman H. O. Vernon, of Los Angeles, gave us his personal memories. "I first knew General Eisenhower when he was a captain. I did not get to see him again until our battalion returned from France, at which time Eisenhower had been promoted to a colonel. He was always very approachable and democratic and liked by both the officers and enlisted personnel. I was in Company C, 301st Battalion, American Heavy Tanks. I received my commission at Louisville, Kentucky, in what was known as the 65th Engineers, which was the beginning of the Tank Corps. We were sent to Camp Meade, Maryland, where we became the First Battalion, American Heavy Tanks. Later we were sent to England for training where we took over "J" Battalion from the British and were later designated as the 301st Battalion, American Heavy Tanks.

"The 301st was the only Battalion of Heavies that the U. S. ever had in action in World War I. We were on the Somme most of the time, around Bapaume, Cambrai, San Quentin, Le Cateau and then north to the Belgium border. Each tank crew had to go out into the fringe of 'No Man's Land,' pick out a tank which could be salvaged by the crew itself, take parts from other tanks as replacements, patch up shell holes, and go into action knowing that the spark plugs would all have to be taken out and cleaned every few miles even while in action.

"Our training in South England under the British was very thorough. One thing that impressed us was the fact that while learning tank driving we had to be on the *qui vive* to keep from running over the random graves of Roman soldiers who had fallen in their invasion of England in 75 or 79 A.D. I first met General Patton when he was a colonel in France. He was in charge of the light tanks. I also visited him on the desert, east of Indio, California, just before his outfit shoved off for North Africa. I have always held him in high regard, although I never served under him."

An interesting story is related by National Commander ("Treat 'em Rough") Eugene N. Edwards about Camp Roberts in California. "The Infantry-Field Artillery Replacement Center was named in honor of Corporal Harold W. Roberts, Co. A, 344th Battalion, Tank Corps, who participated in St. Mihiel and Meuse-Argonne Offensives. His heroic and self-sacrificing conduct on October 4, 1918, in the Montrebeau Woods, France, won him the Congressional Medal of Honor, the French Croix de Guerre with palms, the French Military Medal, and the Italian War Cross. The citation accompanying the award of the

Congressional Medal of Honor, which was presented to his father, John A. Roberts, San Francisco, reads as follows: 'Corporal Roberts, a tank driver, was moving his tank into a clump of bushes to afford protection to another tank which had become disabled. The tank slid into a shell hole, ten feet deep, filled with water, and was immediately submerged. Knowing that only one of the two men in the tank could escape, Corporal Roberts said to the gunner, "Well, only one of us can get out, and out you go," whereupon he pushed his companion through the back door of the tank and was himself drowned.' "

While General Eisenhower was commanding the European theater in World War II, his fellow tankmen back home, who had been trained by him in the original Tank Corps units at Gettysburg, sent him a medal from Battalion Number Four, of Chicago, with resolutions of highest tribute. National Adjutant Price, as the resolutions were "thunderingly voted," even proclaiming "Eisenhower for president," exclaimed to the tankmen, "Now one of the outstanding men in the world carries in his wallet the same membership card you carry." He dispatched the resolutions to Comrade Ike with the medal. This is the letter General Eisenhower immediately sent back:

Dear Mr. Price:

I am honored and touched by the action of Battalion Number Four of the "Treat 'em Roughs" for sending me the Tank Corps Medal.

To be remembered by old friends and comrades-in-arms is the kind of an honor that means the most to any man, especially to me. You couldn't have sent anything more pleasing.

I hope this letter reflects something of my depth of feeling, which might be better expressed if I had the opportunity personally to thank each one of you.

Again, the best of luck and thanks for pulling for all of us.

National Adjutant Price remarks, "The fine letter from our very own General Eisenhower speaks for itself and shows his feeling for the men whom he trained at Gettysburg in 1918. He will get plenty of other decorations but none I'll venture that comes from men who think more of him than do fellows such as Harris who was his sergeant major and those who compose our outfit. Frankly, we 'lugs' of the old Tank Corps can't be blamed for throwing out our chests—just a mite anyway—when such men as Generals Eisenhower and Patton still lead the league in hitting, and they are Tank Corps men also. I know there isn't a man who wore the Tank Corps colors but will take pride in this letter and the fact that he served under such a leader. Our hopes, our prayers are going to him and to the men he now leads. In the fierce light in which he now stands General Eisenhower will not be found wanting."

Ike has never forgiven World War I for ending before he could take his tanks rattling down *Unter der Linden* into Berlin. As a veteran he carries his membership card in the Anthony and Grover Shook Post, No. 3279, Veterans Foreign Wars, in Abilene, Kansas. When his old comrades were asked how they would describe Ike in the fewest words, they replied:

"American as pumpkin pie or corn on the cob!"

· 16 ·

Eisenhower with MacArthur in Washington and Philippines

THE STRANGE INTERLUDE between two wars, which might ironically be called the tragedy of peace, was to find Eisenhower preparing for "Der Tag" when Germany would strike again.

An obscure young corporal, Adolph Hitler, a transient house painter, was to rise out of World War I, usurp power over the German people, set up his dictatorship, and plunge the world into the greatest catastrophe in history. One Benito Mussolini, a young firebrand agitator, was to seize control of Italy and drench it in blood as the partner of Adolph. And Eisenhower from America was to lead the Allied Armies against these despots.

Six days after the armistice ending World War I, signed in Marshal Foch's railroad coach in the Forest of Compiègne, Eisenhower was commanding Tank Corps troops at Camp Dix, New Jersey, from November 18 to December 22, 1918, with the 57th Infantry. Thence he went to Fort Benning, Georgia, until March 15, 1919, when he was ordered to Fort Meade, Maryland, to serve as executive officer and command various tank battalions for the next three years.

He was in Maryland when the peace treaty was signed at Versailles between the Allied powers and Germany on June 28,

1919, after five months of deliberation, with President Woodrow Wilson as the head of the American delegation. Ike carefully scrutinized every provision in this treaty. It embodied for the first time in history a plan for adjudicating disputes in a League of Nations—the first step ever taken toward the abolishment of the age-old war system. Lincoln emancipated 3,000,000 slaves in the American Civil War; Wilson attempted to emancipate the entire human race, 2,000,000,000 human beings, from the scourge of war.

Wilson, while President of Princeton University, had become deeply interested in a draft for a Constitution of the United Nations, published in the *Journal of American History* (1908), edited by the author of this book. He had taken with him on the ship to France copies of this draft which he carefully analyzed as basic suggestions for his proposed League of Nations.

Ike saw in Wilson a great humanitarian and scholar to whom political intrigues and machinations were not within his understanding. His political opponents back home were organizing to defeat him while he was at Versailles. If he had taken with him a coalition delegation, comprising both major political factions, he probably would have succeeded.

Leaving his political enemies behind him created a cabal waiting upon his return to destroy him. And these opponents in the United States Senate refused to ratify the Versailles Treaty with its League of Nations provisions. It was rejected on November 19, 1919—and that date marks the beginning of World War II.

The League of Nations, repudiated by the United States, the home of its progenitor, was set up in Geneva and functioned with success on nearly a thousand disputes, but when a great issue arose it was shorn of its power because of the refusal of American cooperation. If the United States had been an active participant and asserted its power when Mussolini, Hitler, Hirohito started their first invasions they could have been instantly stopped.

Without the United States the League was defied and the seeds sown for World War II. World Courts and treaties, excellent within themselves, required power and organization to enforce their agreements. Thus in destroying Wilson the peace of the world was destroyed, and the United States was forced to fight again in the greatest war in the annals of mankind. Wilson, rejected, died a martyr to the greatest cause in human history.

During these discussions Eisenhower was the observer on a transcontinental journey with a motor-truck train from July 2 to September 1, 1919. He was graduated from Infantry Tank School, 1921, and became commander of the famous 301st Tank Battalion. He heard these political disputes from both sides; as a military man he could not engage in them. But his later utterances, while commanding Allied forces, demonstrate that he is a firm believer in world cooperation to protect the peace—in some form of unity and organization between nations to stop war at its inception.

While at Camp Meade, Lieutenant Colonel Eisenhower's temporary war rank reverted to his permanent rank as captain on June 30, 1920, but he was promoted two days later to major, the designation that he was to bear for the next sixteen years. While at Camp Meade he lost his son, little three-year-old Doud Dwight Eisenhower, who died on January 2, 1921.

We find him sailing for the Panama Canal Zone on January 8, 1922, where he remained as executive officer of the 20th Infantry Battalion at Camp Gaillard until September 19, 1924. Eisenhower had been recommended to Major General Fox Connor by the then Colonel Patton, the tank commander who in future years was to serve under Eisenhower.

General Connor took young Major Eisenhower to Panama with him. On the ship they discussed the "next war." General

Connor, a farsighted man, declared, "Another war is inevitable within the next twenty years." As Ike said later, "He hit the estimate right on the nose."

A fellow officer tells this anecdote about Ike at Panama. One afternoon Ike casually remarked, "This is a fine day to have your appendix removed." Asked whether that organ had been troubling him, he replied, "No, I don't even know I have an appendix, but it might rear up and put me out of action sometime when things aren't so quiet."

General Connor, his boss in Panama, said of him, "The work of the day was always first with him, but every spare moment was devoted to higher studies. His grasp of the lessons of the World War was superb. It was evident that he would go far."

Ike, always keeping a weather eye on the world, was convinced things were going to happen fast. And they did. The Russian giant, having thrown off its centuries of czardom, had established the Union of Soviet Republics; the Irish Free State had been established; Turkey had become a republic; Greece had become a republic.

Germany was a republic, but there trouble was brewing again; a group of political incendiaries were gathering in a beer hall in Munich and plotting putsches to overthrow the Government. They contrived what was to be known as Nazism.

And in Italy, young Benito Mussolini, the vagrant, had marched on Rome and set up his Fascistic Government which was to become the bastard brother of Nazism.

Eisenhower, in America, always vitally interested in history, was watching these developments with forebodings. In 1924, the year of the death of Woodrow Wilson, he returned to the States from Panama. And we find him a recreation officer in the headquarters of the Third Corps Area at Baltimore, October 1 to December 8, 1924, where he is encouraging sports and coaching the football team, his old love in his West Point years.

He leaves Maryland and goes to Colorado where he becomes recruiting officer at Fort Logan from December 15, 1924, to August 19, 1925. It was here in Colorado, where he had married Mamie Doud seven years before, that another son was born to them to succeed the little fellow who had died in Maryland. His wife had come home from Panama and the second son was born in Denver on August 3, 1923, and christened after his mother's father, John Doud. This lad was to live to follow in his father's footsteps, graduating from West Point during World War II.

This seemed to be an era of "stopgaps" between nations. Conferences were held to delay impending conflicts. The Washington Arms Conference, under President Harding, "scrapped navies" as a gesture toward peace; the Dawes-Young Plan for reparations from Germany was agreed upon; and later the Locarno Treaties were ratified.

While these stratagems against war were being developed, Major Eisenhower was completing a course at the Command and General Staff School at Fort Leavenworth, Kansas, where he was graduated with honors in June, 1926. He was assigned to Fort Benning, Georgia, as assistant post executive and commander of the Second Battalion, 24th Infantry, from August 15, 1926 to January 7, 1927.

Throughout these years of military preparation young Eisenhower started, when he was a second lieutenant, to keep a set of notebooks, which he still continues. These private notebooks are rich mines of observation and comment.

Always vitally interested in military history, he was assigned to Washington and detailed to the American Battle Monuments Commission, under General Pershing, where he served from January 18 to August 15, 1927. He pursued his studies in the Army War College at Washington, and was graduated on June 20, 1928, leaving immediately for France, where until September

Acme Photo

"Somewhere in England," General Eisenhower fires a Browning light machine gun, sans mount, from his hip

International News Photo

An excellent camera study of General Eisenhower viewing target practice in England. 1. He is tense as tank fires at target. 2. He is pleased with the result. 3. He points out to target and results. 4. He makes suggestions

15, 1929, he was again on duty with the Battle Monuments Commission in Paris.

During fifteen months we find Major Eisenhower journeying over the battlegrounds of World War I in France, jotting down notes and making maps for an official "Guide to American Battlefields in Europe." This was published by the Government; its thoroughness and keen observations were highly commended. General Pershing—who was devoting his time to the preservation of these shrines in France, especially the supervision of military cemeteries where thousands of his boys lay under little white crosses with the American flag waving over them—was deeply impressed by Eisenhower's profound interest and affection for these sacred landmarks.

While Eisenhower was living in Paris, the Kellogg-Briand Anti-War Treaty was being created. Ike met the leading military figures and statesmen of the time. He attended sessions of the treaty conference, of the Chamber of Deputies and the French Senate, went to Geneva to observe the League of Nations in operation, and became an ardent student of international relations and world affairs.

He studied with penetrating analysis the Kellogg-Briand Treaty proclaimed by President Hoover on July 24, 1929, in which sixty-two leading powers pledged themselves to renounce war as an instrument of national policy. Great as was this document, it was based largely on moral obligations without effective provisions to enforce them by power if necessary. Its moral intention was magnificent; its dependence on character and integrity without due consideration for the greed and avarice of scheming politicians left loopholes for its repudiation.

Eisenhower was receiving his first insight into both diplomacy and human nature. He was assigned to the War Department, in Washington, where as assistant executive in the office of the Assistant Secretary of War, he gained his first knowledge of the necessity of preparedness to preserve peace and enforce it in case of emergency. Here he remained from November 8, 1929, to February 20, 1933—more than three years of intensive study and work. It was at this time that he was awarded the Distinguished Service Medal. Here again his insight and sound judgment attracted the attention of his superiors. Here again they predicted, "He will go far."

He was in the War Department during the last days of the Hoover Administration. The great depression, which was sweeping the nation and the world, was developing into a crisis. This depression, it should be recorded in justice to President Hoover, was not of his making; it was in the making before he took office, and was the direct result of the inflated prosperity which was ready to burst like a balloon. This inflation, in turn, was the direct result of the war, which had cost the nations of the world nearly two hundred billion dollars. Instead of preparing a readjustment of world economy, writing off this stupendous loss, and laying foundations for a healthy restoration of peace, human greed had entered into an orgy of profit. Tremendous personal fortunes were created from nothing as long as it lasted.

This was the age of profligacy which President Hoover inherited and which was to be bequeathed to President Roosevelt. Neither of these statesmen was responsible for the depression; both were victims of it.

General Douglas MacArthur was Chief of Staff of the United States Army, at Washington, during these critical days of 1930–35. He, too, was visioning perils ahead and working indefatigably to arouse the nation to the necessity of preparedness. Hitler was rising to power in Germany, which also was in the throes of economic depression; by pressure, intimidation and threats he was made Chancellor by the aged President-General von Hindenberg.

These were the conditions when we find Major Eisenhower

serving General MacArthur as special assistant to the Chief of
Staff from February 20, 1933, to September 24, 1935—through
more than two and one half years of crisis.

Eisenhower had just been graduated from the Army Industrial
College and was now one of the best equipped military men in
Washington. MacArthur was exerting his energies to arouse
both Congress and the American people to the immediate necessity of establishing a mechanized army. His vigorous appeals for
appropriations for American defense occupied thousands of
pages in the records of Congress. If they had been heeded, we
would not have been caught unprotected in the Philippines and
the Pacific when the Japs were to make their vicious attack. It
should be stated also that during the Hoover Administration,
while Honorable Henry L. Stimson was Secretary of State,
heroic efforts were made to stop the Japanese on their first invasion of Manchuria; again if we had heeded Stimson's advice the
coming World War could have been averted.

Working unceasingly, Eisenhower was collecting the materials and evidence for General MacArthur's reports to Congress.
After reading the documents placed before him, MacArthur appointed Eisenhower as his aide. Eisenhower's office was placed
next to MacArthur's and for two years they collaborated in
developing and presenting their practical ideas for American
defense.

In the meantime, Japan was at war with China. Hitler, in
Germany, began surreptitiously to build a powerful army. The
Reichstag, now under his control, voted him absolute power.
He began his reign of intrigue, persecutions, executions, as his
storm troopers and Gestapo started on their nefarious cam-
paigns.

Mussolini, in Italy, defiant of all pledges to maintain peace,
started on his invasion of Ethiopia to create a new Italian Empire, and after ruthless warfare, during which Emperor Haile

Selassie and his family were forced to flee from Addis Ababa to England, Mussolini decreed Victor Emmanuel Emperor of Ethiopia. Hitler, in Germany, repudiated the Versailles Treaty and ordered conscription, openly defying the world.

These were the ominous rumblings as General MacArthur received an urgent appeal from the Philippines to come to their defense. President Manuel Quezon, observing the Japanese thrusts into China, realized that the warlords were plotting to invade his country as the key to their conquest of the Pacific. He could read the handwriting on the wall.

General MacArthur answered the call, retired from the General Staff at Washington, and sailed for the Philippines. And in September, 1935, Major Dwight D. Eisenhower was crossing the Pacific to become assistant military advisor to General MacArthur. Stationed at Manila, from October 26, 1935, to December 13, 1939, he was promoted to lieutenant colonel (July 1, 1936). Here they began the heroic effort against time to build up the defenses of the islands. History has recorded these five years of tremendous labors to avert the approaching tragedy. MacArthur's achievements with his limited resources and manpower are notable military records.

Eisenhower was placed in charge of the organization of the Philippine Air Force. He designed the fields and outlined training plans. He helped establish the Philippine Military Academy and wrote the Commonwealth Defense Act which used the Swiss universal military principles for a model. His knowledge of military principles and his skill in organization were now being applied.

As it was necessary for him to fly around the islands in mapping out strategy, he decided it would be a good idea to add flying to his many talents. A firm believer in the future of air power as one of the decisive factors in warfare, he studied aeronautics and became an expert pilot at the age of forty-seven years, with more than three hundred hours to his credit in the Philippines.

"There's exaltation being up there in the blue all by yourself," Ike said. "No muddy roads, no detours, no signs. If you want to take a look at something, you dive down and take a look at it. If you don't like it, you soar up and find something else. You can do any damned thing you like."

"The Lieutenant Colonel is a 'natural,'" exclaimed his instructors. "He is crazy about flying. We never saw a more enthusiastic pilot. And what he knows about maneuvers in the air will some day make history."

He played a major role with MacArthur in planning the defenses of the islands which were destined to give the Japanese armies such stubborn resistance in the Second World War. It was Eisenhower who devised the hidden airfields there. He flew constantly back and forth to Corregidor, and over the jungles of Bataan, and was a familiar figure on the streets of Manila. The native Filipinos were very fond of him because of his spirit of brotherhood.

Colonel Thomas Jefferson Davis, once aide-de-camp to MacArthur and later Eisenhower's adjutant general, gives this contrast between the two Generals:

"They complement each other perfectly. MacArthur was the statesman and the man in the public eye. Eisenhower, who dislikes personal attention, stayed behind the scenes doing the planning and seeing that essential details were carried out. If they have anything in common it is their ability to inspire their men with unshaking loyalty and their apparent ability to do big things."

"Der Tag," which MacArthur and Eisenhower had predicted, came on September 3, 1939, on the other side of the globe. World War II flamed into action. MacArthur and Eisenhower listened over the radio as the news came to them and examined the official dispatches laid before them. Hitler's troops had invaded Poland, and had thrust into Pomerania, Silesia, and East Prussia, to the city of Danzig. Prime Minister Chamberlain announced in Parliament that a state of war existed between Great Britain and Germany; Australia and New Zealand followed with their declarations; France declared a state of war; Canada came into line. The United States proclaimed neutrality. In the ensuing days Russia invaded Poland and Finland.

Lieutenant Colonel Eisenhower was ordered back to the United States. When he left the Philippines on December 13, 1939, General MacArthur grasped his hand and wished him great success in the days to come. President Quezon personally conferred upon Eisenhower the Distinguished Service Cross of the Philippines and offered to insure his life for $100,000. Eisenhower smilingly declined.

Quezon considers MacArthur and Eisenhower as the two greatest men he has ever worked with. Unbounded was his pride, as the war developed, when he could point at the two men from the Philippines who were leading the mighty Allied Forces —one in the Pacific and the other in the invasion of Europe.

In speaking of Eisenhower, the President of the Philippines says, "Among all his outstanding qualities, the quality I regard most highly is this: Whenever I asked Ike for an opinion I got an answer. It may not have been what I wanted to hear, it may have displeased me, but it was always a straightforward and honest answer."

We find Ike aboard ship, crossing the Pacific, on December 13, 1939, en route to the United States. On January 16, 1940, he reported at the Presidio in San Francisco and remained on temporary duty at headquarters with the 9th Coast Artillery until February 2. He joined the 15th Infantry at Fort Ord, California, and accompanied this regiment to Fort Lewis, Washington, as regimental executive officer until November 30, 1940.

His movements were rapid as defenses were set up along the

Pacific Coast. We find him chief of staff of the Third Division at Fort Lewis from November 30, 1940, to March 1, 1941, when he became chief of staff of the Ninth Army Corps. On March 11 he was appointed full colonel. It was at this time that his father, David J. Eisenhower, died in his eightieth year back home in Abilene, Kansas.

Colonel Eisenhower was back at San Antonio, Texas, as chief of staff of the Third Army, on June 24, 1941. During the fall months he was conducting war maneuvers in Louisiana, under General Krueger with 220,000 men. His side won through brilliant strategy and the use of armored forces. General Krueger declared Eisenhower's command to have been superb. At the end of maneuvers, Eisenhower was promoted to the temporary rank of brigadier general on September 29, 1941.

"Keep your eyes on Ike," Army men prophesied. "He will be a major general in six months."

Their predictions were to come true. Ike was called to Washington and made chief of the War Plans Division on the War Department general staff on February 16, 1942. In April he got his two stars when President Roosevelt nominated and the Senate confirmed him as a major general. He was designated as Assistant Chief of Staff in charge of the Operations Division, Office of the Chief of Staff, on April 2 and was headed for higher honors within the next few weeks.

During these first months while Eisenhower was helping build an army, Hitler's blitzkriegs in Europe were sweeping everything before them. The Germans overran Denmark and Norway, invaded Holland, Belgium and Luxembourg, and conquered France. They marched into Paris and took possession. Italy with its ten-year alliance had joined the Axis. The Battle of Britain was being fought in the air, with London undergoing terrific aerial bombardments. Yugoslavia and Greece had been invaded. The Axis forces in Libya were driving toward Egypt.

Eisenhower was in Texas when the Japs struck at Pearl Harbor and the Philippines on the fateful December 7, 1941. The Japs began sweeping everything before them in the Pacific. He heard the declaration of war as it came over the radio from Washington on the following day—the answer to the infamy and perfidy of Japan, Germany and Italy. The United States, despite its efforts to "keep out of war," had been stabbed in the back. And the obstructionists who had been holding America back were responsible for the disaster. Against all the warnings of President Roosevelt they had attempted to block every move for preparedness. The price must now be paid in human lives.

Aroused to outbursts of indignation at the subversive groups that were giving "aid and comfort to the enemy" at a time of our nation's peril, Ike's scathing remarks would scorch this paper. He had no tolerance for the "damned deaf, dumb and blind fools" who could not see what was sure to happen if we failed to heed the warnings. The Axis was out to conquer the world and enslave humanity. Nazism and Fascism must be crushed if human freedom was to be saved.

The tragic news from the Philippines of the heroic stand of his old comrades at Bataan and Corregidor weighed heavily on his shoulders. The Japanese had struck at them on that fateful December 7, 1941, while Eisenhower back in America was carrying out the largest concentration of troops ever assembled on the American continent. He had hoped to go back to the Philippines with a powerful army and rejoin his friend MacArthur. After a gallant stand MacArthur had left General Wainwright in charge and gone to Australia to organize the forces for the liberation of the Philippines.

When the news of the Jap attack came through, Eisenhower was with his Blue Third Army in Texas. Worn out after a terrific day's work, he had left word that he was going to take a nap and must not be disturbed. His orderly, startled by the news coming over the radio, hesitated in awakening him.

"He'll murder us if we don't wake him," one orderly exclaimed.

Eisenhower had become known as "Alarmist Ike" because of his constant predictions. He was convinced that the United States must enter World War II, but he thought that the first attack would come from Europe. His orderlies finally mustered up courage, knocked on his door, and delivered the message.

Ike sat up and listened, his face tense as he looked straight ahead. His only remark was, "Well, boys, it's come!"

· 17 ·

America enters World War II—Ike becomes a General

WHETHER THE EVENT makes the man, or the man makes the event, is the conjecture of historians. With General Douglas MacArthur fighting to hold off the Japs swarming into the Philippines and the islands of the Pacific, the question arose, Who will lead the forces against the Axis hordes who have conquered Europe and now threaten to invade both North and South America?

There were many able generals in Washington, many of them having won renown in World War I. The nation faced the emergency of building a great army in the quickest possible time. How the miracle was performed under General George C. Marshall, Chief of Staff, the farm boy from Pennsylvania who had come out of the Virginia Military Institute (Stonewall Jackson's old institution across the campus from General Robert E. Lee's famous Washington and Lee University in Lexington, Virginia) is a book for future historians.

The Army's revitalization program needed a man. Five days after Pearl Harbor, General Marshall, a keen analyzer of potentialities in soldiers, sent for Eisenhower. He was informed that he was to take over the War Plans Division, as its chief, and was to formulate the grand strategy for all theaters of operation.

His only comment as he left General Marshall's office was, "Yes, they've given me a new job. I guess somebody must have told General Marshall I was a hot shot."

With a shrug of his shoulders he went away—to go to work. Sitting at his new post in Washington, the world became a huge chessboard before him. Watching every move, he sent strategic orders to American commanders in both hemispheres. His penetrating vision gained immediate respect. They knew a master hand was playing the game.

President Roosevelt, recognizing Eisenhower's skill, nominated him for the rank of major general. The Senate immediately confirmed it. Six days later the War Plans Division was renamed the Operations Division, and General Eisenhower was now at the head of what the War Department described as "the controlling nerve center of the Army."

The War Department, the General Staff, and the White House were in conference day and night. Finally the momentous decision was reached—this was the man. He measured up to all the qualifications of modern warfare, had a genius in organization, was an expert with tanks, a firm believer in air power, and the coordination of land, sea and air forces. He was a natural-born leader of men.

The General Marshall called Major General Eisenhower to his office and said, "You're going over to command the European divisions. When can you start?"

Eisenhower, taken by surprise, swallowed quickly and replied, "Tomorrow morning!"

It is said that he received this appointment because of two reasons: First, his amazing record in getting things done; second, his strong advocacy of a Second Front. Convinced of this necessity, he had worked out "practical plans" which were so plausible and brilliant that they commanded the attention of the War Department.

Ike "talked it out" with Mamie, his wife, at their home in Washington. The responsibilities of the new job were discussed. He was willing to undertake anything in the service of his country. His wife had full confidence in his ability to carry out his plans; she had lived with him twenty-six years; she knew the Eisenhower character and determination. Their son, John D. Eisenhower, was a cadet at West Point. The General's mother, Ida Elizabeth Stover Eisenhower, whom we met in earlier chapters, was celebrating her eightieth birthday back in Abilene, Kansas. His father had been dead a year; he never lived to see his son a general.

This is the General Dwight D. Eisenhower who, at fifty-two years of age, was taking not only the destiny of his nation on his shoulders but the future of the world. Eisenhower was a name almost unknown to the American people. It was now to become one of the great names of history.

General Staff officers in Washington give this word picture of Ike's last meeting with them. Snappily laying his plans before them, he said: "This is what it is. . . . This is what we're going to do. . . . This is what we need. . . . We're counting on you to see that we get it. Good-by!"

The General is death on long-winded reports. He calls them "transatlantic essay contests."

We find him a few days later in England in secret conferences with Prime Minister Churchill and the great military leaders on the British staff. His mission ostensibly was to help prepare a merger of United States and British Air Forces to carry out bombing raids on the European continent. He was reported in London with General Mark W. Clark, on May 25, but was back in the United States on June 3 at a discussion of military and supply problems which was also attended by Lord Louis Mountbatten.

Out of these and succeeding conferences came the first news that our nation was soon to throw its power against Hitler's mighty forces for the liberation of the conquered countries of Europe—the armies of freedom were soon to meet in decisive combats the armies of despotism. The official proclamation on June 25, 1942, read:

"The War Department today announced the formal establishment of a European Theater of Operations for United States forces. Major General Dwight David Eisenhower, formerly assistant chief of staff of the Operations Division of the General Staff, has been designated Commanding General, European Theater of Operations, with headquarters in London, England."

As Ike was leaving to return to England on the most challenging mission ever intrusted to an American soldier, he turned to General Marshall and said simply, "General Marshall, I haven't tried to thank you yet."

"Don't try to thank me," General Marshall replied. "You go over and do the job and we'll have cause to thank you."

Thus began the road that was to lead to North Africa, to Sicily, to Italy, into Hitler's Fortress Europe, and finally to the Second Front invasion of the continent from the shores of Great Britain. General Eisenhower was already on the way.

Before the General left for Europe, his friend, President Manuel Quezon, President of the Philippines, wanted to present him with an annuity policy made out to his wife. "I want to show my gratitude," exclaimed the President. "This is a decoration. You can accept a decoration, can't you? Well, this is a kind of decoration. I want to be sure that Mamie will always be taken care of."

The General replied to the effect that he would rather take care of that matter himself, so he was finally awarded the Distinguished Service Cross of the Philippines.

Indicative of the determination and ability of America to meet the challenges of sinister forces that were endangering the world, was the astounding fact that a considerable force of United States soldiers had already arrived in England and Ireland—the beginning of the mighty forces that were to prove the indomitable will of American democracy in action, with its gigantic resources and manpower to back them up.

General Eisenhower, at his headquarters in London, issued his first official statement:

"I have been assigned to command the European Theater of Operations for United States forces. The formal establishment of the European Theater is a logical step in coordinating the efforts of Great Britain and the United States. Six months ago the Prime Minister of Great Britain and President Franklin Delano Roosevelt heartened the people of the United Nations by moving swiftly to merge the military and economic strengths of Britain and the United States for a common effort. At that Washington conference, they set a more effective pattern for unqualified partnership than has ever been envisaged by Allied Nations in pursuit of a common purpose. Only recently they have met again to bring combined action into even closer coordination. The presence in the British Isles of American soldiers and pilots in rapidly increasing numbers is evidence that we are hewing to the line of that pattern."

The General made his first inspection of Major General Russel P. Hartle's troops in Ireland and reported on July 2 in the following statement:

"I am highly pleased with what I have seen, especially General Hartle's staff and the way they have carried out their jobs. I feel that they are doing their jobs like Americans, and nothing more could be asked."

General Eisenhower had three major problems facing him in establishing the European Theater of Operations. The first was the training of United States troops; second, the establishment of close cooperation between the personnel of British and American armed and civilian services; third, preparations for future actions.

He discovered that his first job in England was to defeat defeatism. The courage and resolve of the British remained strong through the perils which they had faced alone. Their little island would stand to the last man against invasion by Axis hordes. The terrific bombing of London and coastal towns had only aroused their spirit and determination. The Battle of Britain with its suffering and devastation had only strengthened their resolution. Rumors that they and the Americans were now to invade Germany and fight Hitler on his own ground seemed to confront them as a colossal undertaking. They were thrilled by the arrival of the Americans and would fight with them to the ends of the earth if necessary. The question, however, was, "Is this the right time? Are we strong enough yet to undertake the gigantic job of invading Germany and fighting Hitler to a finish on his own ground?"

This question, too, was in the minds of the Americans. The tremendous successes of the Axis on the continent and its striking power had created the myth of the invincibility of Hitler.

General Eisenhower, addressing his own soldiers, declared, "Pessimism and defeatism will not be tolerated. Any officer or soldier who cannot rise above the recognized obstacles and bitter prospects that lie in store for us has no recourse but to ask for instant release from this theater. And if he shows such an attitude and doesn't ask for release he will go home anyway."

His Western fighting spirit aroused the morale of his boys. They went through the grueling weeks of training with a "do or die" determination.

"We'll go where Ike goes," they declared. "We'll follow him into hell if necessary. He's got guts and we'll show the world that we can both take it and give it."

"That's the way men act!" is said to have been Ike's reply. "That's the stuff that makes a nation great."

The British officers found in General Eisenhower a man they could work with. Brilliant military men, old warriors who had been through many campaigns, recognized in this man who had never fought a battle a great military strategist with inspiring leadership. The task of coordinating the Americans and the British into an unconquerable fighting force was to be the greatest achievement in the annals of warfare.

The Nazis taunted the Allies in radio broadcasts: "You've had to find a German named Eisenhower to do it." But they did not have to be told the ominous meaning of his name—"striker of iron."

Iron Ike laughed at the jibes. It was three hundred years since the Eisenhowers fled from Germany to escape the same oppressions and persecutions the Nazis were inflicting on conquered peoples today. The righteous vengeance of his forefathers was in his blood. Through centuries of intermarriage with Scotch-Irish, Holland Dutch, Swiss, English, many strains had entered into his veins.

In assembling a competent staff, General Eisenhower, who was advanced to the rank of lieutenant general on July 9, had under him three old friends in whom he placed implicit confidence: Lieutenant General Andrew Spaatz as his air chief; the then Major General Mark W. Clark as head of ground operations; Major General John C. H. Lee as supervisor of supply.

"Ike," a doughboy at heart, insisted that his troops be kept happy. They were arriving with unprecedented speed; their spirits must be maintained as they became acclimated to a new world while being rigorously trained for the battles ahead of them; they must be given relaxations and recreations.

The General demanded that they be given as many of the

"comforts of home" as the conditions would allow. His love for his soldiers always was foremost. They in return demonstrated their love for Ike, declaring him to be "a regular fellow, just like the rest of us. He is like our own fathers back home and treats us as if we were his own sons."

While solving the problems of these soldier boys with human devotion and practical common sense, he overlooked nothing that he felt would make them happy. He knew neither race nor creed; they were all somebody's sons. There were a large number of Negro troops stationed in England whose social opportunities were severely limited by the lack of women of their race. General Eisenhower remedied the situation by informing Colonel Oveta Culp Hobby, head of the WAAC, and steps were taken to have a large number of Negro WAAC's assigned to Great Britain.

"We are giving Negro troops equal status in the military field," the General stated. "We must give them the same consideration in their personal relationships. We are all giving our lives to our country together."

General Eisenhower's first victory was to win the hearts of his own soldiers and the British soldiers and people. He established his headquarters in an old renovated London apartment building which was quickly dubbed "Eisenhower Flat."

His simplicity and his devotion to his fellow men, his intimate touch with the common man, gave him somewhat the character of Lincoln. One Britisher remarked, "We all call him 'Ike,' but there's a lot of 'Abe' in him." It was, in fact, the Eisenhower in him, the same integrity, frankness, simplicity, we have seen in his forefathers.

This was demonstrated when he broadcast his message to war workers back home in American industries, thanking them for the great support they were giving him with munitions and supplies for the war. "We pledge you that we will use them effectively. I will leave it to our enemies to guess when and where and how we will use the supplies you send. I understand their suspicions have been aroused of late. We shall politely continue to leave them in the dark."

The maintenance of good-will with the British Allies the General considered of paramount importance. When rumors were maliciously circulated to the effect that there was trouble between the Royal Air Force and the United States Air Forces, the General called in reporters and declared, "Time is short and United States soldiers must be trained to stand the most rigorous operations. I am not asking you to take what I say because I might be wrong and I might even lie to you, but I want you to go around and see for yourself whether there is any friction between the R. A. F. and our Air Force. If there is one place where cooperation and collaboration is perfect, it is between the R. A. F. and the United States Air Force."

With tremendous responsibilities on his shoulders, working day and night with indefatigable energy, dealing with his hundreds and thousands of problems, he found time to act as a diplomat to both his troops and to the British. We find him at Buckingham Palace on July 8 in conference with King George, and again on August 18, autographing a drum for a proud American private.

His personal attendants had nothing but praise for him during this trying period of preparation. His Irish girl chauffeur, twenty-three-year-old Kay Summersby, who knew all the bomb-pits in London, said, "If the General likes his chauffeur as much as I like the job I'll have it a long time. When the war's over I'd like to see the United States. Who wouldn't?"

The speed and efficiency with which Eisenhower works and acts was demonstrated to correspondents who complained about military censorship in England. The General asked for specific complaints and found that there were only two censors who were working twenty-four hour stretches. After hearing the complaint late in the afternoon, correspondents found he had remedied the situation when they discovered four censors at work the next morning.

In England Eisenhower soon became a pleasant legend and was known as the "best liked and least social of American officers." A British officer said of him, "He knows he is fighting a foe who sneers at the rules and he is not above teaching the Nazis a few tricks he has thought up all by himself."

His treatment of military men is unique and informal. Correspondents one day overheard the following conversation.

"Hello. . . . Yes, this is Ike. . . . Hello, Betty. How are you, Betty? . . . Will I have lunch with you? . . . Why, there's none in Britain I'd rather have lunch with than you. . . . Sure, Betty, I'll see you at one." He then faced the bewildered correspondents and said, "Great fellow, Betty."

This was too much for Leonard Lyons, who exclaimed, "Great fellow? What kind of man's name is Betty?"

Eisenhower replied, "Since Admiral Stark graduated from the Naval Academy his nickname has been Betty. All his friends call him Betty, and I'm one of his friends. We lunch a lot. Get a lot of things done that way. His office is just across the hall, you know. We're always in and out of each other's offices. Great fellow, Betty."

Since the beginning of his command in Europe, the General eschewed all social gatherings for the duration of the war. This policy was decided upon when, at a London party, he found himself at the handshaking end of a receiving line of twenty-six hundred persons.

War needs all his time, the General believes, and as a result he prefers the quick interview to the formal conference. He hates dawdling and unnecessary respect. When a junior officer hesitated before entering his office, Ike growled, "Look here, dammit, if you have anything, bring it in. Don't act like this was a boudoir."

General Eisenhower in London was a very busy man. One day, when asked to a luncheon, he bowed politely and said, "Hell, I can't. I've got a date in Berlin!"

The General, however, accepted an invitation to lunch with Ambassador Winant and shook hands with about twenty-five hundred people. This was his last social venture.

He ate at "home" while he was in London because a standing rule forbids smoking in British club dining-rooms. Not knowing of this regulation he once lit up in a club after a meat course and was immediately corrected by his host and some waiters. After this experience he ate in the hotel suite that was his London home, where he had the added comfort of being able to discuss plans with guests in private.

"Eisenhower Flat" was guarded by U. S. Marines. On the top floor, the General's offices were located. The exact situation of the General Headquarters was kept a semi-secret, for a bomb dropped judiciously by the Germans would have netted them a fine plum.

General Eisenhower's suite was composed of a living-room, a bathroom, and two bedrooms. He chose the place because the pretentiousness of the lobby of his previous quarters was too much for him.

"It made me feel as though I were living in sin," he said.

He has a reputation for being a rough, tough, square shooter with the British. A British officer remarked that "Ike" was the next best thing to having a general from the Russian army. "He is our 'Eisen' and this is our hour," he said.

The General lived in London with his close personal friend and naval aide, Lieutenant Commander Harry C. Butcher.

The two men closest to General Eisenhower are Butcher and "Mickey" McKeogh, the General's orderly. "Butch," now forty-three, is a village boy from Springville, Iowa. While working his way through the University of Iowa he became interested in radio. He is credited with inventing the phrase "Fireside Chat," when he thus described President Roosevelt's first radio speech to the American people.

"Butch" was rising rapidly in the radio world. He was general manager of the Columbia Broadcasting System's first Washington station and then became vice-president of the company. His wife and General Eisenhower's wife were intimate friends and lived together in Washington after their husbands left for the war.

It is said that when General Eisenhower was assigned to command the European war theater, the General's wife called Butcher over the phone and broke the news to him.

"I'm going with him!" Butcher replied. He immediately resolved to get himself assigned to his friend's staff. His little daughter, Beverly, aged nine years, became very excited over the prospect. Butcher gets what he goes after, and thus we find him aide to General Eisenhower.

Sergeant "Mickey" McKeogh, the General's orderly, hails from Corona, in the Queens. Mickey was a bellboy at the Plaza Hotel in New York when war broke out. Entering the service of Uncle Sam, he was sent to Texas. Eisenhower, then conducting maneuvers, spotted Mickey as a lad with "the right stuff in him."

When it was discovered that Mickey was a whiz at the wheel of an automobile, he was assigned as Ike's chauffeur. They were soon to be separated, however. The "boss" was called to Washington and made a major general, and Mickey was left behind at Fort Sam Houston in Texas. But Major General Eisenhower did not forget him. He sent for Mickey to come to the nation's capital.

"Mickey," exclaimed the Major General, "how would you like to go to London with me?"

Mickey says he was "flabbergasted." "Sure," he said. "I'll go anywhere you go, General."

"All right," Eisenhower replied. "Go home and get your mother's permission."

Let proud Mother McKeogh, back home in the Corona, tell the rest of this story. "My permission? Why nothing on earth could keep Mickey from going to the ends of the earth if the General said so!"

And so it was that in London General Eisenhower pinned the chevrons of a staff sergeant on Mickey McKeogh. The bellboy from the Plaza was chauffeuring a general to Buckingham Palace, to 10 Downing Street, and the most renowned addresses in England. Sergeant Mickey writes many letters to his mother, telling her of his great adventures, generally closing with the sentence, "The General is well and very busy," for Mickey never divulges any war information.

General Eisenhower also shared his quarters with a Scotty puppy, an acquisition of the General's after he stamped into his office one day and asked whether there was any regulation forbidding his keeping a pet. Informed that there wasn't, he said, "I want a dog. I need somebody to talk to. And I want someone who can't ask questions about the war and cannot repeat what I say if I say anything."

The staff chipped in and purchased the puppy, which was named "Telek" and was housebroken by the staff.

The General's fondness for dogs is traceable to his Kansas boyhood, where his mother always kept a dog "to keep the boys busy." Once Dwight found a small terrier with a broken leg which he nursed back to health and became one of his favorite boyhood companions. Army life had prevented his keeping a pet in the meantime, so the General was delighted with "Telek." Eisenhower gave the pup this name because he was occupying a former telegraph signaling post at the time of the pup's acquisition. "Telek" accompanied Eisenhower on foot, ship, plane, and every other conceivable type of military and civilian conveyance.

General Eisenhower never neglected details which might weld unity between the Allies. When United States forces offered to help British war orphans, he commented, "I am delighted to hear that the Stars and Stripes is presenting to American Forces the opportunity for aiding orphan children of our Allies. You may be assured that the officers and men of my command are heartily in accord with this undertaking."

D-day drew closer; reports and rumors from E. T. O. flew thick and fast, while preparations continued deliberately. The largest United States convoy of troops yet to arrive in England, winning their first battle against the submarines in the Battle of the Atlantic, came safely into port on August 23. On September 19 it was announced that Lieutenant Colonel Edson D. Raff was training paratroops in England.

At the end of October, a story was "planted" in the newspapers to the effect that General Eisenhower had been recalled to the United States for a series of discussions. This rumor accounted for his absence, an absence later explained by the fact that the General went to Gibraltar. He was given command of the fortress.

"Never in my wildest dreams in my West Point days," he said, "did I ever think that I—an American General—would ever command the British fortress of Gibraltar."

His headquarters were under fourteen hundred feet of solid rock and constituted forty rooms. The only exercise the General and his staff was able to get consisted of running to their offices through a dripping tunnel. Many a private was startled at the sight of his commander and his staff sprinting through the narrow passageway.

To outwit Hitler and divert German attention, General Eisenhower had ordered that units of American forces be outfitted for the Arctic. The Eisenhower strategy worked perfectly. The Germans were reported to be bolstering their defenses in Norway.

All through the night of November 7, General Eisenhower worked in his cavern headquarters. Great events were impending; great chances were being taken. The die was being cast. In his hand he held a decoded message. It was from General Marshall, back in Washington, and read:

"You and your command sailed with the hopes and prayers of America. For months you have planned, trained, and conditioned yourselves for the great task ahead. Godspeed to your success. I have complete confidence in your leadership and in the aggressive fighting quality of your troops."

General Eisenhower, his features tense and lined by tremendous strain, read dispatches, issued orders, and waited. . . .

Through the night hours the hands of the clock were ticking the fate of thousands of men on the greatest adventure in their lives. The genius of General Ike was now to be tested for the first time.

On the morning of November 8, 1942, the world was startled by the news: *"The Americans have landed in North Africa."*

The greatest armada in the world's history, up to that time— 850 ships—had brought the first American army to the battlefront. They had landed during the night hours and at daybreak were engaged in a gigantic pincer movement. Within seventy-six hours they had won 1,300 miles of the coasts of North and West Africa, advancing from Algiers and Morocco.

Eisenhower, with the aid of the British, had outwitted Hitle and Mussolini.

· 18 ·

With General Eisenhower on battlefronts in North Africa

"THE YANKS ARE HERE!"

The joyous tidings swept across Africa. The British in Cairo, three thousand miles away, lifted their glasses and toasted: "Here's to the Americans! Here's to Ike! By the way, who is this Eisenhower?"

The turbaned Moroccans, the Algerians, the embattled Libyans, all asked the same question. Out in the sandstorms on the Sahara white-robed horsemen were asking the question—and grim-visaged, bronzed men on camel caravans.

"It's a long way to America," they said. "These Americans must be miracle workers, magicians, to get such an army across the Atlantic and land it in Africa. It must be a great people and a great country."

There was jubilation in beseiged England, where they had waited long for the "The Day" when the Americans would get into action. There they had met Eisenhower and liked him. "Ike did it!" they said. "He's a jolly good fellow. We wish him luck!"

Hope came to the hearts of the enslaved Norwegians, the Danes, the Hollanders, the Belgians, and the French, who never lost confidence that the Americans would come to help liberate them. In bleeding Poland and Czechoslovakia, suffering under the iron heel of the conquerors, the first glimmer of joy passed over their tragic faces. In Jugoslavia they smiled with grim determination. In Greece, where they had never lost faith in America, they thanked God for their coming deliverance. The Russians, who were heroically driving the Axis from their soil, nodded their heads in affirmation. "At last they are here! Now we can fight on with renewed courage."

But it was in Egypt that they breathed the deepest sighs of relief. Rommel's forces had knocked at their gates, only seventy miles from Cairo. Montgomery with his British Army had saved them. If the enemy had broken through into Egypt he could have driven on into Iraq and Iran and India, and joined the Japs in the conquest of Asia; nearly three-quarters of the world would then fall under their power. With the might of America coming into the war, the tide would turn. With the British Empire, Russia, China, and America *united*, no power on earth could stand against them.

These were the thoughts in the nations of the world when the news reached them of the American landing on the soil of Africa.

General Eisenhower's only comment as he left Gibraltar to advance his headquarters to North Africa was, "The only thing I was disappointed in was the resistance of the French Navy, particularly the coast batteries. We don't want to fight the French and they are opposing us, holding up the job and expending effort which might well be used against the common enemy—Germany. The way the Navy delivered the goods at the right time and the right place was marvelous. The way the naval staff planned the giant convoys with exact timing was nothing short of wonderful."

General Eisenhower's mission was to liberate the French from their Nazi captives, not to engage in warfare against them. Appealing to them in his name this message was broadcast:

"Frenchmen of North Africa, the forces which I have the honor of commanding, come to you as friends to make war against your enemies. This is a military operation directed against the Italian-German military forces in North Africa. Our only objective is to defeat the enemy and to free France. I need not tell you that we have no designs either on North Africa or on any part of the French Empire. We count on your friendship, and we ask your aid.

"I have given formal orders that no offensive action be undertaken against you on condition that you for your part take the same attitude. To avoid any possible misunderstanding, make the following signals: Fly the French tricolor and the American flag, by day, one above the other. I repeat, by day, fly the French tricolor and the American flag, one above the other, or two—I repeat, two tricolors, one above the other. By night, turn on a searchlight and direct it vertically toward the sky. I repeat, by night, turn on a searchlight and direct it vertically toward the sky.

"We come, I repeat, as friends not as enemies. We shall not be the first to fire. Follow exactly the orders which I have just given you. Thus you will avoid any possibility of a conflict, which could only be useful to our enemies. We summon you as comrades to the common fight against the invaders of France. The war has entered the phase of liberation."

The voice over the radio, speaking in General Eisenhower's name, rang out over land, sea and air. "The President of the United States has asked me as commanding officer of the American Expeditionary Forces to convey to all the people in Morocco and in North Africa the following message:

"No nation is more closely bound by historic ties and deep affection to the people of France and their friends than the United States of America. Americans are striving not only for their own safe future, but also for the restoration of the ideals, the liberties, and the democracy of all those who have lived under the Tricolor.

"We come among you to save you from conquerors who would remove forever your rights of self-government, your rights to religious freedom, and your rights to live your own lives in peace. We come among you solely to destroy your enemies and not to harm you. We come among you with the assurance that we will leave just as soon as the menace of Germany and Italy is removed from you. I am appealing to your sense of realism, self-interest and ideals. Do not obstruct this great purpose. Help us and the day of a world of peace will be hastened.

"Frenchmen of North Africa: Faithful to the traditional and age-old friendship of the government and people of the United States for France and French North Africa, a great American army is landing on your soil. The purpose of the mission is to protect the people of French North Africa from the threat of Italo-German invasion. Our principal aim is the same as in 1917, that is to say, the annihilation of the enemy and the complete liberation of invaded France. The day when the Italo-German threat no longer menaces French territory we will leave your soil. The sovereignty of France over French territory remains complete. We know we can count on your support to open the road which leads to victory and peace. All together we shall triumph."

Within two days an armistice was reached—the French ceased firing and Algiers and French Morroco surrendered on November 9, 1942.

It is not our intention to record the history of the war in North Africa; neither shall we attempt to present all the members of Eisenhower's great staff who assisted him in this epoch-making campaign. We shall confine ourselves largely to Eisenhower, himself, to keep you standing by his side as he directs these battles, and issues his orders, to observe his reactions as a man as well as a soldier—the human Eisenhower.

We see him first as a diplomat as he sits in conference with his American advisers, his British colleagues, and French leaders.

When, on November 10, 1942, he approved the French General Giraud as leader of the French Forces in North Africa, to organize the French Army again to take up the fight on the side of the Allies, he remarked, "He (Giraud) and I understand each other perfectly, I am sure of this. There is no doubt about the complete unison of both sides to work together to establish a sound basis for the conduct of affairs in this country."

In the meantime Americans were battling for Oran, the capitulation of which was the equivalent of the duration of French resistance. Eisenhower sent word to Major General Lloyd R. Fredendall to "clean it up." Upon the completion of the taking of Oran, General 'Ike' said, "He started in and made a job of it. Everybody did a fine job. I'm sure proud of my boys. Remember, they hadn't had any sleep since Friday night. After their long sea voyage there was no question of the hardihood of our soldiers. The air, navy, and ground forces cooperated beautifully."

When his intelligence officers informed General Eisenhower that Hitler was plotting to seize the French fleet, he broadcast this message: "I invite the French fleet to join the United Nations in the fight for freedom, and so to hasten the day of France's liberation. Hitler has taken your country and now he wants your ships. Do not let him take them. The enemy is close upon you, sail at once for Gibraltar and join us."

With the fall of Casablanca, on November 11, Eisenhower faced the choice of driving on into Tunisia or going into Lybia. He decided to make the gamble to "grab Tunis" and bottle up the Axis along the coastline while General Montgomery with the British forces were driving across North Africa to join him.

Another crucial decision confronted Eisenhower. Who should be intrusted with the political administration of the French territory now under his command in North Africa? The French were politically divided into two groups.

Admiral Jean Francois Darlan declared himself High Commissioner in French North Africa and West Africa. To meet the critical emergency General Eisenhower, and his Government behind him, decided to support the situation on the grounds of military necessity. He considered the move essential in the light of the military crisis, because it would swing units of the French fleet to the United Nations and bring substantial French forces to his support.

President Roosevelt deemed the appointment justified as merely a temporary measure. Other military men, such as General Smuts of South Africa, who called Eisenhower "a first-rate general," were solidly behind the move. It was revealed that Admiral Darlan has assured General Eisenhower that "my sole purpose is to save French Africa, help to free France, and then retire to private life with the hope that future leaders of France may be selected by the French people themselves and by no one else."

When the agreement was reached, on November 15, General Eisenhower said specifically, "Now the working arrangement is very satisfactory," indicating the temporary nature of the move. Within two weeks units of the French fleet as well as Dakar surrendered and joined the Allies, sparing thousands of American lives and strengthening our naval power.

Political factions in America, England, and France attacked the Darlan agreement, but the General's only remark to friends is said to have been, "I am not a politician. My job is to help win this war. I shall do whatever in my judgment will help to end the war victoriously in the quickest possible time."

It was during this time that General Eisenhower held a family reunion. His brother, Milton Eisenhower, arrived from America just before the Christmas holidays. This, to Ike, was like a visit back home. He eagerly inquired about his aged mother in Kansas, his wife in Washington, his son at West Point, and his brothers in the States.

The mission of Milton Eisenhower, however, was official. He had come in the capacity of assistant director of the Office of War Information to discuss problems of censorship and work out a plan for the freer flow of news from the battlefronts. As a trained journalist, his visit was in the nature of "ambassador plenipotentiary" for the American press and radio.

General Eisenhower, a firm believer in the freedom of the press, agreed with his brother that the dissemination of news to the families of the soldiers back home is the greatest possible morale-builder. He considered the press and radio the army on the Home Front. The problem was to protect military information which might be of aid to the enemy and thus endanger the lives of his boys, and the disturbance of lines of communication. Results of this conference were seen almost immediately in an increased flow of news.

Milton Eisenhower, upon his return to America, said, "I found the General in grand health. This despite the fact that he is rising before dawn each day and working late into the night. He's getting less than five and a half hours of sleep—most of the time less—but doesn't show the strain."

On Christmas Eve a revolver shot decided the Darlan issue. Admiral Darlan, sixty-one years old, was shot to death at his headquarters in the city of Algiers. A twenty-year-old lad, member of a French patriotic youth organization, was the assassin. Two days later the ardent young crusader was tried by court martial and sent to his death before a firing squad.

General Eisenhower was with his troops in the front lines at the hour of the assassination. American and British forces were engaged in heavy fighting on Christmas Eve and Christmas Day on the road to Medjez-el-Bab. The General was just issuing this greeting: "I extend Christmas and New Year Greetings to all members of Allied forces in North Africa. My admiration for your accomplishments in the last six weeks is equaled only by my complete confidence that you will meet every test in the future with the same fortitude and determination. My profound thanks and best wishes go to all the ranks of the Army, Navy, and Nurses Corps as well as to all civilian organizations aiding our campaign in North Africa. Good luck to every one of you."

General Ike was sitting at the officers' front-line mess, dining with members of his staff, when the message of Darlan's death was delivered to him. His aide and friend, Lieutenant Commander Harry G. Butcher of the Navy, was at his side. Leaving their Christmas Eve dinners on the table, they stepped into their car and started for Algiers.

All night long they drove at high speed over the roads through the darkness, the General taking turns at the wheel with Butcher. Long lines of trucks bound for the battlefront passed them. Airplanes were zooming over their heads, bombers going to and coming from their missions of death.

Christmas morning dawned over the desert. About noon Ike and Butch stopped by the roadside, and standing beside their parked car ate British field rations for their Christmas dinner. It was Christmas night when they arrived in the ancient capital of Algiers. Here the details which could not be transmitted over the telephone were related.

The night was spent locked in consultations. After a few hours sleep, General Eisenhower went to Darlan's home and offered his condolences to the Admiral's widow. He then attended the military funeral at the cathedral and returned to consultations. On the following day it was announced that the successor of

U. S. Army Official Photo from Acme

General Eisenhower and Lieut. Gen. Mark W. Clark conferring on invasion plans
in Italy

International News Photo

Upper photo shows German labor corps hastily building wall of defense on the Mediterranean coast of France. Lower, a Nazi chieftain inspecting what is supposed to be the "perfect defense" against invasion

International News Photo

ON BATTLEFRONTS OF NORTH AFRICA 215

Darlan would be General Giraud. This appointment, too, was confirmed over political protests for "military reasons."

The Eisenhower strategy was proving itself day by day. Through these early weeks the French port of Dakar, which Hitler had planned to use as a springboard across the South Atlantic to South America, was turned over to the use of the United Nations. American ground forces reached Dakar. American forces were battling at Tobourba. Allied planes were bombing Bizerte in Tunisia. United States and British forces were inflicting severe casualties on the enemy.

General Ike's only complaint was, "Hell, I'm not seeing enough of this darn war."

New Year's Day, 1943, found the Allied forces driving hard wedges into the Axis strongholds. There was a constant succession of blows and counter blows as the Americans advanced, were driven back, and then drove forward again in terrific onslaughts.

Eisenhower called his headquarters "Grand Central Station" because of the crowd constantly passing through. There he sat and sweated in the daytime and nearly froze at night as he issued orders and listened to complaints.

"General Ike is the man to take your troubles to," exclaimed an officer. "Ike can grin at anyone and make him feel good. When you see what he is up against more than half your troubles disappear."

His informality, with his sound advice or admonition, was a compelling force in itself. At the beginning of the campaign he sent this message to General Patton.

"Dear Georgie: Algiers has been ours for two days. Oran defenses crumbling rapidly with Navy shore batteries surrendering. Only tough nut left to crack is in your hand. Crack it open quickly. (Signed) Ike."

Even when forced to fight two wars at the same time, one on

the military front and the other on the political front, General Ike remained cool. His great working capacity, his vast memory and extraordinary organizing ability, commanded respect of friend or foe.

His regular working day lasted between sixteen and eighteen hours. He remarked that this was better than to keep everybody else awake by snoring. If he could wedge in a few minutes for exercise he went out with a handball and "had a catch" with some of the officers. Originally he had planned to exercise with a medicine ball, but he lost it overboard in transit.

General Ike dislikes formality of all sorts and avoids it scrupulously, never wearing medals and seldom ribbons. When working around headquarters he generally wore an old air-force jacket. At one time, when receiving distinguished guests for dinner, he asked, "I'm not much on etiquette. Do you think I should wear a tunic for dinner? Or is it more proper to wear a field jacket?"

He was a picturesque figure as he traveled back and forth to the battlefronts by plane or jeep. Generally he wore what he called his "goop suit," his nickname for the tankman's "zoot suit." This consisted of a pair of pants which came up the armpits with the bottoms buttoned around his shoes. For a coat he wore a heavy battle jacket; instead of the regulation military cap, a heavy knitted helmet covered his head.

We can see him as he holds important conferences under the wings of Flying Fortresses or in scanty field headquarters, or standing in a jeep, traveling over two hundred miles a day. And he covered a lot of territory; no soldier worked harder than the General.

He once left his headquarters at 3:00 A.M. and arranged to meet various commanders along the way, working until midnight. Then he lay down for three hours of sleep and began again until he returned at noon the following day to headquarters. There he held conferences until dinnertime, and then set about studying maps and plans until 11 P.M.

While he traveled he allowed himself no privileges and ate the ordinary C or K rations of the troops. These consisted of hard biscuits, chocolate, coffee, canned vegetables, and stew. This he ate cold. Rather than to take the time to heat the coffee, he drank water from his canteen.

The General did not escape his share of danger. Once his jeep was pushed into a ditch while it was threading its way along a road between two long motor convoys in a blackout; he suffered a badly bruised back. Another time he and his party were under heavy machine-gun fire. On another occasion he slept in a town which was heavily bombed a few minutes after his departure. He could see the antiaircraft guns go into action as he drew away in his jeep.

The news was secretly guarded that President Franklin D. Roosevelt had arrived in North Africa, the first time a president of the United States had ever left his country in wartime—and the first time a president had ever crossed the Atlantic in an airplane. He grasped the hand of General Eisenhower as he landed in Casablanca, in French Morocco.

He had come to discuss strategic plans for the invasion of Europe from its "under belly." For ten days (January 14–24, 1943) in a white villa, near the shores of the Atlantic, the conferences which were to make history were held. Prime Minister Winston Churchill sat beside him. General George C. Marshall, Chief of Staff, surrounded by advisers from the Army and Navy, was seated near General Eisenhower. Around the conference table were the British Chiefs of Staff with General Henri Honoré Giraud and General Charles de Gaulle, representing the French.

With military maps and plans spread before them they laid the plans for the "coming invasion," working from early morning until midnight. American infantry stood guard with fixed bayonets on all roads leading to the villa. The peaceful-looking villa, under the waving palms and covered with bougainvillaea in full bloom, was surrounded by emplacement guns and barbed-wire barricades. Here the future was being molded.

At the end of these epoch-making conferences President Roosevelt made a tour of inspection of General Eisenhower's troops in Morocco. Riding in the car with the General, he wore a gray suit, with a white pullover sweater and an old gray felt hat. As they passed down the line of soldiers a mile long, standing at attention in front of their artillery and tanks, the President and General Eisenhower gazed upon them with pride, shaking hands with more than fifty who were decorated with Silver Stars and Purple Hearts for their bravery in action.

The President and the General, with their staffs, sat down in folding chairs before twenty mess tables for "a bite to eat," and then went on to the scene of the toughest fighting in the invasion of Africa, the Port of Lyautey on the coast, where a fierce hand-to-hand combat had raged for three days. They visited the little white crosses behind the gates bearing the inscription "U. S. Military Cemetery" in English, French and Arabic, and laid a wreath at the foot of the flagpole, over which the Stars and Stripes floated in the African sunlight.

When President Roosevelt and General Eisenhower parted, the destiny of nations had been decided. The ten days' conference at Casablanca set up the "Unconditional Surrender" proclamation to the armies of the Axis. The "beginning of the end of the Axis" was strategically laid out.

President Roosevelt returned by airplane to America. General Eisenhower went back to his headquarters to put these plans into operation—to drive the Axis out of Africa, to invade Italy, to sound the doom of Mussolini.

· 19 ·

First great Allied victory—Fall of Tunisia

GENERAL EISENHOWER at the conference at Casablanca was intrusted with one of the biggest jobs in the war. He was selected by the British and American Governments and their combined staffs to drive the Axis out of North Africa.

Again President Roosevelt and General Marshall, in full agreement with Prime Minister Churchill and the great British war lords, had said, "This is the man."

While they were closeted in conference Montgomery's British Army was administering heavy punishment to Rommel's forces in retreat across the deserts of North Africa. They captured ancient Tripoli and left the city burning. The Axis fled in panic across the Tunisian border. The day was near when the British and the Americans would join forces in the final conquest of Africa.

Rommel was digging in along the Mareth Line for a last desperate stand. Tunis and Bizerte were under continuous bombardment by Allied air forces. The Americans were battering at Axis strongholds barring the roads to Tunisia from Algeria.

News was now to come which marked the end of Axis power on the African continent. Eisenhower was placed in supreme command of all Allied Forces in North Africa on February 6, 1943. For the first time in history the British and Americans were united into a consolidated fighting force under an American commander.

The "Big Four" were announced as General Eisenhower, commander in chief, with three great British warriors on his General Staff: General Alexander (direct superior of the indefatigable Montgomery); Air Marshal Tedder with his Royal Air Force; and Admiral Cunningham, with his powerful navy. Eisenhower, although outranked by all three, was their chief.

Prime Minister Churchill in making this unprecedented announcement said, "In General Eisenhower and in General Alexander you have two men remarkable for their selflessness of character and their disdain of purely personal advancement. Let them alone, give them a chance, and it is quite probable that one of these fine days the bells will have to be rung again."

Admiral Cunningham, with the gallantry for which the British Navy is famous, declared, "I am General Eisenhower's naval commander and I want to emphasize that I am very content to serve under him. He has welded together some of the most diverse ideas. Our British Staff ideas differ from the American's in various ways, but nevertheless General Eisenhower has joined the staff into a happy family. It does not really matter whether you are British or American; in fact he never thinks of it that way. Very few men could have done this. It is a tremendous achievement, holding great promise for the future."

President Roosevelt on February 11 proposed General Eisenhower as a "four-star" full general to the Senate. Suspending all rules, they approved the appointment that afternoon. Eisenhower now joined General MacArthur and General Marshall as the third full general in active service.

Secretary of War Stimson said, "He has done a fine piece of work thus far, in which he has apparently won the confidence of all with whom he has come in contact. I don't think he would wish me to say any more until the campaign is over."

General Eisenhower was advised of his appointment by his wife in a cablegram which she quickly dispatched when she heard of it in Washington, but she was anticipated by a naval officer who heard the news over a ship's radio. The official confirmation was received by the General just as he received an enterprising French jeweler who was delivering twelve handmade silver stars.

At his first press conference as supreme commander, General Eisenhower said, "The British have given their best, their stars, and I'm honored. We've got some stars of our own. But we're all working together to beat the Axis. And I mean *together*. Men are going to forget their nationality in getting the job done."

Eisenhower planned his staff on a "business basis" and called himself "Chairman of the Board." Under him were Admiral Cunningham (British) as Mediterranean naval chief, with Vice Admiral Henry K. Hewitt (American) as deputy; Air Marshal Tedder (British) was chief of strategy with General "Tooey" Spaatz (American) as tactical leader and Major General "Jimmy" Doolittle (American) as the bomber boss. General Alexander (British) was deputy Allied commander and the leaders in the field were General Montgomery (British), General Clark (American), General Anderson (British), and the General George Patton (American).

The Allied Headquarters grew to tremendous size, twelve hundred officers and sixteen thousand enlisted men, housed in fifteen hundred requisitioned buildings in Algiers. In preparation for the Sicilian invasion General Eisenhower issued a combat order which exceeded one hundred thousand words, and yet, despite the huge preparations, the General had the satisfaction to say, after the attack at Gela, "By golly, we surprised them!"

Passing the buck is out with Ike Eisenhower. He assumes all blame for whatever goes wrong. When the Yanks took their greatest licking at Faid Pass, the American and British units became hopelessly entangled. The General issued this statement: "Any blame for the mixing up of units belongs to me. We saw a chance to grab all of Tunisia before the Germans could reinforce. We threw up every combat unit we had, regardless. It was a long gamble, but we almost got away with it. After you mix up your units, even on a good gamble like that, it takes time to sort them out."

Another time, when supply lines were particularly long, French troops under Giraud were guarding supply routes and DeGaulle chose this critical moment to present a demand that all Vichyites be purged from the French army. General Eisenhower settled the matter by explaining the military exigencies and the problem was solved diplomatically.

"I'll cooperate with you fellows and I want you to cooperate with me," Ike told war correspondents. In his dealings with the press, he is friendly and honest, but expects strict secrecy when he asks it. He sent home a correspondent who had revealed a military secret in an article extremely complimentary to himself. He does not like guesswork on the part of the press, because it can have no beneficial results. He says a right guess informs the enemy and a wrong guess makes everybody look foolish, but he is quick to confide in newspapermen. He revealed his plans for the Sicilian invasion thirty days in advance. Later he praised the correspondents for the way they kept the secret. He calls his staff his "all-star team." Although he is the man in charge, he always wants headquarters referred to as "Allied Force Headquarters" and not as "Eisenhower's Headquarters."

Supreme Commander Eisenhower remained the same smiling Ike, genial, simple, easy to talk with, but firm in his determination and strong in decision. About the only concession he made to his former habits was to leave his "goop suit" behind him and wear a uniform which his distinguished staff would consider more dignified. He looked every inch a soldier but refused to put on any frills.

He lived with his friend and naval aide, Lieutenant Commander Butcher, in a small house adjoining Admiral Cunningham's, and chose the servants' quarters for his own when he entertained visitors. His little Scotty, Telek, brought with him from London, was always at his heels, a faithful worshipper of his master. At the sound of his master's voice Telek's tail wagged vociferously. The General called it his "sign language," a code which he clearly deciphered, like the wigwag of the signal corps.

Telek, too, was a soldier and airman. When flying with the General the Scotty wore a special-made canine parachute so that he could follow his master "in case of emergency." This parachute was a gift from General Spaatz, also a lover of "man's best friend."

When Lieutenant Commander Butcher returned from an important mission to the United States, he also brought a present to Telek. It was a little Scotty mate which flew back with him over the Atlantic. The gift was from the Commander's little daughter in Washington who had named the lively little lady, "Caacie" (initials of the Canine Auxiliary Air Corps). This romance resulted in "marriage"; Telek and Caacie became the proud father and mother of two heirs—Telek, Junior and Sister Rubie, named in honor of Mrs. Butcher.

Wherever the General went, Telek was sure to go. During the Tunisian campaign he barely escaped being a war casualty. While stretching himself too far out of the window to observe the lines of soldiers moving toward the front, he fell out. A four-star general's car drew up to the roadside; an orderly hopped out, rescued the missing Telek, and hurried on to restore him to his master.

"You'd better keep on guard," the General warned Telek,

"or you may be taken prisoner. You won't get treated as well in the German Army as we treat you in the American Army."

It was during these North African campaigns that General Ike received a new nickname from his intimate associates—*Ikeus Africanus*. This classical tribute was in recognition of his vast store of human knowledge.

"There was nothing about Africa or the entire world that Ikeus Africanus didn't seem to know," one of his staff confides. "When we asked him about Hannibal's march to Italy he gave us a forty-minute extemporaneous lecture. Later I went and checked on his dates and facts. You know, he hadn't made a single mistake.

"And," remarked the staff officer, confidentially, "Ikeus Africanus is one of the world's experts in the strategy of poker. He doesn't play during the war, because he says he doesn't want to win from his own staff. He can maneuver the game like a Grand Marshal. He knows every move and all the percentages. And how he can read human nature! He can see right through his adversaries. That may be what gives him the skill to out-bluff Hitler. He says he learned the game with the Kansas cowboys."

Ike is happiest when with his soldiers at the front, where he is well known and liked by his men. He speaks the language of the troops.

"Hell, we'll change that!" he exclaims, instead of the more pompous version of what soldiers call "brass hats." They like his straightforwardness. It makes them feel he is one of them, just another doughboy. While he can swear like a tough sergeant if the occasion demands, he prefers plain homespun American.

Soldiers like the air of the unexpected that clings to the General. He will do strange things in a most matter-of-fact way that lends interest to his personality. Once, for instance, a cook was surprised when the General, on a tour of inspection around a kitchen, saw a delectable piece of raw beef lying on the table. He picked it up and took a good chew, without a single comment.

"My God!" the startled cook exclaimed. "That must be a tough guy. Eats raw meat!"

In an effort to unify the soldiers, Eisenhower told both British and American troops that if they could not get along together they would go home "on a slow boat, unescorted." He is tough, and yet understanding and tactful. He nipped all conflicts in the bud. When a British officer reportedly disparaged American troops, the General, as soon as he was informed, consulted the officer's superior, who was already on his way to clear the matter up. Before the day was over the matter had been settled and unity and mutual respect ran higher than before.

Things looked dark when the Germans were rushing supplies into Africa from Italy. The Allied air forces were paralyzed by bad weather; armies were bogged down in torrents of rain. They had been beset by supply difficulties, transportation by sea, and a thousand-and-one problems. Eisenhower was quick to place any American troops needed at the disposal of the British. It was then that the actual joining of the armies began, and not until after the British Eighth Army had taken Tripoli and won the supply race did Eisenhower relax.

This critical period welded the Americans and Britons together both in the field and at headquarters. Together, sharing the glory, they went on to victory. Eisenhower used his genius for coordination also in working with the French. Seeing the French fight without proper equipment or clothing, he quickly allocated some of his material to them and gave them a chance to participate in the Tunisian victory. By his great tact and by placing credit and responsibility with the right men he gained their respect as chief in name and action. His frankness and intelligence carried him through until he could make changes and give commands which the British Imperial General Staff approved without question.

Every morning at 9:50 a conference was held which lasted usually for about half an hour—an informal exchange of viewpoints in which Britons and Americans got together, calling each other by first names and nicknames, and discussed the day's business.

There is no pretense or affectation in Ike—just plain Texas-Kansas. When an argument becomes too confused he interrupts it by remarking, "Maybe I'm dumb, but I didn't get that. Repeat it, please."

There is a story told about the time General Marshall, coming from America, visited the North African front. He was appalled by the number of hours on Eisenhower's schedule and the enormous amount of work he was doing. Marshall entrusted an aide with the task of imposing a more leisurely schedule on Eisenhower.

Ike accepted the orders from his boss in Washington by coming to work the next day at 9:30 in the morning. His habit was to rise about sunrise and start to work. On the new schedule Ike took a long lunch instead of a snack; he left his office at five o'clock in the evening instead of working into the night. This new routine lasted exactly one day. The next morning Eisenhower was at hand about daybreak to "make up for the lost time."

The aide who had been instructed by General Marshall to see that Eisenhower abided by the new rules, was worried. He went to Marshall's aide and reported his failure.

"Hell," exclaimed Marshall's aide, "that's all right. Marshall never follows his own routine, anyhow."

Strenuous labors are a stimulant to Ike. He says, like Thomas Edison, that five hours sleep is enough for any man. He gets up at dawn with keen intelligence, ready to tackle any problem on the minute.

"The General's mind doesn't need much rest," his staff members report. "He is a human dynamo. He opens his eyes and turns on the power, two thousand revolutions a minute."

General Eisenhower never complains of being tired—sometimes he looks it, but he never admits it. When he can find a few minutes' relaxation he plays handball or tennis (in which he is a star player); he occasionally jumps on a horse and takes a fast ride as a reminder of his years as an expert horseman on the Western plains.

He approaches every problem with homey common sense. An expert on almost every phase of military operations—infantry, tanks, air, strategy, supplies—he discusses them with his commanders, asks their advice, and listens attentively. A skillful coordinator of minds, he places full confidence in his staff and stands back of them.

General Eisenhower now definitely established himself as a front-line general. He conducted an extensive tour of the front, which had been cut short at Christmas by the assassination of Admiral Darlan. Meeting many narrow escapes, he came very close to being captured by German armored forces. The Germans were conducting a push from Faid. General Eisenhower, traveling by jeep, was inspecting forward positions at Sidi bau Zid, a dozen miles from Faid, an hour and a half before the Germans attacked with their strong 21st Armored Division. He lingered long enough to hear the battle and missed capture by ninety minutes.

"Things were getting hot," as Ike called it, all along the line. The Axis was fighting desperately at great cost of lives and supplies. They broke through American artillery positions west of Faid Pass, imperiling the Allied positions at Gafsa. American forces under heavy assaults withdrew to the hills in the Tebessa region on the Algerian border. Montgomery's British Eighth Army was only 165 miles away after fighting its way across North Africa.

The battles at Kasserine Pass were being waged with terrific onslaughts from both sides. The first battle lasted two days and ended in defeat for the Americans and French, who were forced back into Algeria. It was a death struggle to take this mountain gateway to Tunis. The Germans, spirited by their temporary victory, advanced rapidly towards Thala.

General Eisenhower was at the front witnessing the battle. Standing beside him were General Alexander, General Giraud, and General Patton. They watched the American forces as they rallied a few days later with a powerful attack. Through brilliant strategy the Germans were caught between the sheer, cliffed walls in the mountain pass—a modern Thermopylae. Waves of American bombers poured death from the skies. Panic-stricken, the Germans tried to escape the flaming tomb, but the American ground forces drove through with devastating power. The Battle of Kasserine Pass was won (February 24, 1943), and the remnants of the Germans retreated toward Gafsa. And Gafsa, with General Eisenhower witnessing the battle, was captured in terrific combat by American infantry on March 17, St. Patrick's Day.

The strength of the Allies was being matched against the so-called invincibility of the Axis. The Americans captured El Guettar. The German Mareth Line began to crack under Allied bombing and a major battle was brewing. General "Monty" Montgomery was making rapid progress coming from the east and sent the following message to his chief on March 21:

"We are all looking forward to joining the United States of America forces very shortly and after that we will finish off this business very quickly between us."

The British forced Rommel from his Mareth Line (March 29) into Southern Tunisia towards Gabes, which was under heavy naval shelling. They captured El Hamma and Gabes (March 30). Rommel was pushed farther and farther into the coffin corner, until he joined with von Arnim's forces in Northwest Tunisia. Here he had decided to make one more desperate stand. But the fates were to be against him. The Axis armies were being beaten all along the line—driven into death traps.

The long-awaited day arrived. It was April 7 when the message came to Eisenhower that Monty's battle-scarred British veterans, who had fought their way two thousand miles across the African deserts, had joined the Americans in Tunisia, south of De Djebel Chemsi on the Gafsa-Gabes road. Monty's gallant Eighth and Patton's Second U. S. Corps were fighting together against the common enemy. In the meantime, other American forces had accomplished a major thrust by pushing twenty miles and taking Fondouk in Central Tunisia.

The combined force swept forward. The total Axis prisoners of the two armies counted 12,000 as Axis forces abandoned Mahares and retreated towards Sfax on April 9. Sfax was captured the next day and on the eleventh they were twenty-seven miles north at La Hencha while American troops stormed and swept through Faid Pass. Kairouan was taken on April 12, and the armies swept on, capturing thousands of Axis troops, 30,000 by April 15.

On April 18, 1943, our Paul Reveres of the air were on midnight rides dropping bombs on Tunis and Bizerte and the Axis-held islands in the Mediterranean—the roads of escape back to Italy. American forces were twelve miles from Mateur, while the French advanced from Djebel Monseur and the British swept on towards Tebourba.

General Eisenhower visited the Eastern front and returned with respect for the German Rommel but with confidence of Allied victory.

"He (Rommel) is a great general but no superman," Eisenhower said to his officers. "Your enemy is tough, resourceful, and battlewise. Your duty to yourself, to your men, and to your country is to be tougher, more resourceful, and better trained than the enemy in every phase of battle activity."

Rommel was being beaten at his own game. He had only the sea behind him. He must fight to the last ditch or attempt a German "Dunkirk" with what was left of his shattered army. In North Tunisia American troops, in total darkness, captured all the Djebel Tahent, Hill 609. American troops captured Mateur, nineteen miles southwest of Bizerte, after a fifteen-mile advance through the German position of Jefna to the west.

On the coast the French drove to within fifteen miles of Bizerte. Mateur was taken after the Germans were forced out by constant American attacks. With Bizerte under shelling and aerial bombardment, the French swept to within thirteen miles of Bizerte overnight. Meanwhile the British advanced towards Tunis. All Axis territory was under the merciless attack of the Allies, who had complete domination of the air.

Eisenhower's road had not been strewn with flowers—it was strewn with the bodies of men, friend and foe, who had fallen in battle. The General visited the hospitals to cheer up the wounded; he visited the camps to give courage to the soldiers. They were going through hellfire in these North African deserts and mountains. Torrential rains and mud up to their knees had frequently bogged them down. They had met defeat, barely escaped disaster, and rallied heroically to victories. Many had been left behind under little white crosses.

The Axis in Africa had come to the end of the trail. On a glorious May day (May 7, 1943) at 4:15 in the afternoon Bizerte was captured by the U. S. Second Corps aided by the French. Tunis was captured by the British First Army after advancing twenty-three miles in thirty-six hours. United States armored forces were advancing toward the Gulf of Tunis to cut off the retreating Axis troops. The British pushed along the coast to stop the enemy from withdrawing into the hills of the Cape Bon Peninsula.

Bombers were pouring death and destruction on the fleeing armies of Rommel. His desperate attempt to escape to the sea had failed. There was but one thing left for him—to escape to Italy by air and leave his bedraggled army behind him.

May 9 was a dismal day to the "all-powerful" Axis. Germans and Italians began surrendering unconditionally *en masse*. Six great German commanders, headed by the proud Major General Willibard Borowietz, surrendered to the American General Bradley of the Second Corps. The 15th German Armored Division surrendered to the British Seventh Armored Division.

The death rattle was gurgling in the throats of the mighty Axis. A few hours later, on May 10, British forces were advancing up both sides of Cape Bon peninsula to strangle Hitler's "supermen" with a last powerful grip. Germans by tens of thousands threw down their arms and threw up their hands in abject defeat.

General Eisenhower, at his headquarters, issued this statement on May 12: "Organized resistance, except in isolated pockets of the enemy, has ceased. General von Armin, commander of the Axis forces in Tunisia, has been captured."

Rommel had fled, but Eisenhower was to meet him again in Europe. The North African campaign had cost the Axis 291,000 captured, 30,000 killed, 27,000 wounded. The British casualties were more than 35,000 in captured, missing, wounded and dead. The American losses were 2,184 killed, 9,437 wounded, 8,973 prisoners and missing.

The myth of the "invincibility" of Hitler had exploded in his face. The forces of democracy, under General Eisenhower and his Allied commanders, had won their first great victory in World War II.

Messages of congratulations began to pour into General Eisenhower's headquarters from all parts of the world, giving him credit for commanding "the greatest combined operation in history." President Roosevelt, Prime Minister Churchill, General Marshall, and Secretary of War Stimson heaped tributes upon him. King George V of England sent him this message: "Throughout the six months during which you have been in command of Allied forces in North Africa I have watched with admiration the progress of operations. . . . Under your leadership, forces diverse in nationality and race have been knit into one united and successful whole. . . . On behalf of all my people I express to you our heartfelt congratulations on your victory."

Admiral William F. Halsey from the Pacific: "The South Pacific forces salute you and your fighting winners. We hope to beat you to the next punch."

Ho Ying Chin, Chinese war minister, announced, "We have the highest respect and admiration for General Eisenhower."

President Roosevelt's message read, "My warm personal congratulations on the great success of the recent operations in North Africa."

General Eisenhower was decorated by King George V and made a Knight of the Bath "in recognition of most valuable services in command of troops of the Allied Nations."

Later in the year General Eisenhower was chosen "Number One Father of the United States." Upon this occasion he commented, "I am honored to be nominated Number One father of the year. As we look back on the campaign in Tunisia, the fathers of the United States may indeed be proud of the conduct of their sons in the field, and the sons at home who have fathers here may be justly proud of what they have done."

Ikeus Africanus (he prefers to be called plain Ike, or the Kansas Cowboy) was now world-famous. But he insisted on giving the credit to his brilliant staff and the soldiers in the Allied forces.

"They did it!" he said. "The honors belong to them."

· 20 ·

With General Eisenhower in fall of Sicily

WITH NORTH AFRICA safely in his possession, General Eisenhower cast his eyes toward Europe. The Axis, driven from Africa, must now be forced to fight on its own ground.

Working indefatigably for five weeks, Ike and his staff planned every detail of the job. When he was questioned about his chances for success, he pointed toward Sicily and remarked, "We'll be in there going well in a month."

Day and night his bombers were creating havoc over the islands of the Mediterranean and far into Italy. The island of Pantelleria, after twenty days of incessant bombing and coordinated bombardment by naval forces, was reduced to shambles. The garrison of 10,000 troops surrendered without an Allied loss on June 11, 1943. The island of Lampedusa surrendered on the following day—and then Linosa.

General Eisenhower sat at his headquarters, with his staff, working out the details in accordance with a general plan which had been decided upon at the Casablanca conference. Through long hours of ceaseless discussion the strategists surveyed charts, blueprints, and maps involving every problem. The minutest details were analyzed. Tedder, Cunningham, and Alexander were given the responsibility for strategy and supply.

At the oblong council table, with Eisenhower sitting at the

233

head, they shot questions back and forth in verbal volleys. When a technical problem arose they called in experts and other generals to advise with them. After the day's session, Ike would remain working alone until far into the night. He was now rising at four o'clock in the morning and staying on the job till midnight.

While the campaign was being organized, Anthony Eden, back in London, affirmed his complete confidence in them. "Not enough has been said about the invaluable work of General Eisenhower in North Africa. Literally there is no parallel for it in history. It is not a joint Allied staff that he has created, but one single staff working toward one objective. What can be done in North Africa in war can be done elsewhere in peace."

It was General Eisenhower's idea that they should attempt to land first on the southeastern corner of Sicily to give General Alexander a chance to anchor both flanks on the sea. He also suggested several feints and diversions to distract Axis warships and air power from Sicily to the eastern and western Mediterranean, despite obstacles of fog and bad weather.

When asked about fighter plane support, Ike retorted, "What the hell do you think we took Pantelleria for?"

On July 4 Ike made an Independence Day speech. "The Declaration of Independence was made 167 years ago, after a long and bitter battle," he said. "The three nations involved are now represented here. Unhappily they were not on the same side in that war. But today we are marching side by side to defeat an enemy which is trying to defeat everything our Declaration of Independence stands for."

The invasion of Sicily on the night of July 9 was now but a matter of hours. The warships and transports had sailed. General Eisenhower watched the departure of an Allied air fleet and then went to his headquarters. He spent the night tracing the course of the invasion on charts in his office and in the Fighter

Command room which had charge of the air umbrella covering the action.

A few hours before the Sicilian invasion a terrific wind swept over the Mediterranean. Ike watched and gauged it with his weather-trained plainsman's eye. He went to headquarters and found a message from General Marshall:

"Is it on or off and what do you think?"

"It's on!" Eisenhower wired back. "There's a high wind but I think we'll be able to report success in the morning."

Throughout the work of the night, Ike sustained himself by sipping tea. Turning to an aide he smacked his lips and remarked, "The English know what they're doing. This tea habit is not so bad!"

It was revealed at this time that Ike always carried seven good-luck pieces in his pocket. They were old coins which he rubs when in a particularly ticklish action. The officers, watching him with his hand in his pocket, nodded and said, "We'll win—Ike's rubbing his good-luck pieces."

At 1:30 Ike was convinced from the reports coming to him that the "boys are doing a good job." While he waited he lay down and took cat naps until 4:30 when an orderly announced, "General, the invasion is a success. The boys have landed in Sicily."

"By golly!" shouted Ike. "They've done it again!"

Immediately he began to broadcast his messages to the beseiged peoples.

Sicilians listened enthralled as the proclamation of their American liberator came to them over the radio in their own language. They scrambled in the street to pick up the messages falling like glistening petals of flowers in the sunlight from planes out of sight in the clouds.

Always thinking far ahead of his enemies, and knowing that Hitler would use the invasion of Sicily to excite fear in France that they, too, were about to be invaded, Eisenhower sent this message to the French people and listened in the broadcasting room as it went out over the air:

"Anglo-American armed forces have today launched an offensive against Sicily. It is the first stage in the liberation of the European continent. There will be others.

"I call on the French people to remain calm, not to allow themselves to be deceived by the false rumors which the enemy might circulate. The Allied radio will keep you informed on military developments.

"By remaining calm and by not exposing yourselves to reprisals through premature action, you will be helping us effectively. When the hour of action strikes we will let you know. Till then, help us by following our instructions; that is to say, keep calm, conserve your strength."

Back in the United States the War Department issued this brief communique: "Anglo-American-Canadian forces, under the command of General Eisenhower, began landing troops in Sicily early this morning. Landings were preceded by an air attack. Naval forces escorted the assault forces and bombarded the coast defenses during the assault."

The news swept through the country. "Ike's done it again!" was heard on the streets in villages and cities. "He's landed his troops in Sicily and started on the invasion of Europe."

When told about the excitement created when the news press dispatches and radio began to sing his praises, Ike grunted, "What are we in this war for but to beat fascism and autocracy!"

On the night of July 12, 1943, a group of officers gathered in the darkness on the wharf of a North African port.

General Eisenhower stood looking out into the foggy night. There was a barge rocking in the surge of the tides. Ike turned to Admiral Cunningham and remarked, "I'd trade you a lot for this."

"Wait until your dinner starts going up and down," the Admiral replied.

A few minutes later the General and his staff were aboard a destroyer, waiting in the heavy seas. As Ike climbed to the deck he chuckled. "I never know what to do when they pipe me on."

Every general and all the officers and men carried full combat equipment, but Ike was in dress uniform. Apologizing for their helmets, they explained, "General Patton won't let us ashore without one."

The next morning the ship approached its destination. Daylight revealed a frantic scuttling about in the harbor, while in the distance landings were still in progress and big guns boomed. The ship was crowded with generals, admirals, and lesser officers. German planes flew in low to strafe and machine-gun landing forces. General Eisenhower was having breakfast with General Patton. Ike was writing a message to all ships: "Best wishes and good luck."

Fifteen minutes later—at 9:45—the command "Action Stations!" sounded. The crew began to fire. Germans hidden on the beach were bombarding General Eisenhower's ship. When advised to take cover in a place of safety, he quickly waved his advisers aside.

"This is war," he said, "and I'm in it!"

Somebody brought the General a helmet. He tried to put it on but the strap reached only to a point just below his nose.

"If I use this I'll need two men to hold it on," Ike chuckled.

Pushing them aside, Ike went to work—passing cotton around to the crew to stuff their ears.

"It seems I'm the bird in the gilded cage," Ike remarked. "The last time I was shelled near Pantelleria the shots fell three hundred yards away, but now they're missing by four hundred. I guess we're doing better."

One of the officers aboard ship told later how the General

paced the deck, smacking his fist into the palm of his hand. A sailor, looking at him with admiration, exclaimed, "Geez! I bet the Old Man would give his four stars to be the first man ashore."

At 10:24 on this eventful morning General Eisenhower, accompanied by his aide, Lieutenant Commander Butcher, and John Gunther, war correspondent, stepped ashore on a sheltered cape on the southeastern tip of Sicily—the first three Americans to set foot on the island. They had come from ship to shore by "duck," an amphibious truck, and then jumped out onto the beach. He carried little to identify him as the great Eisenhower, Commander in Chief of all the forces along the Mediterranean.

"I want to talk to the senior Canadian officer of this beachhead," the General explained to a soldier on guard.

"This is a Canadian beachhead, sir, but headquarters is some distance inland."

"I don't care if it's a second lieutenant," the General said. "I want to talk to some Canadian officer. I want to welcome Canada to the Allied command."

Determined not to be stopped, Ike jumped into a jeep (as his party was coming ashore by "duck") and started out over bomb-pitted roads. Finally a Canadian officer was sighted.

"Good morning!" remarked Ike cordially. "I'm General Eisenhower."

The Canadian Colonel looked at him in astonishment. He was seeing the great Eisenhower! The General's party soon followed.

Thus Eisenhower set foot on European soil for the first time.

The General had come to Sicily to meet the men who were conquering the island, to congratulate the British and Canadians who had made the initial thrust, to meet the soldiers face-to-face.

He talked with them about their "fine coordination" and "great courage." He commended them for the skillful operations in carrying out the invasion. All his praise was for them alone and no one could imagine from his conversation that he had any part in it. The British were charmed by his humility and graciousness.

"He's a great man," they said. "Greater than even they say he is!"

The conquest of Sicily was now to be pushed with increasing force to drive the Axis from their island stronghold. Reinforcements and supplies streamed across the Mediterranean from North Africa. The Allied plans were working with precision on clocklike schedule.

Syracuse fell eighteen hours after the first landing. Pozzallo surrendered to naval forces after intense shelling on the following day. The battle of Gela came to a victorious conclusion a day later, after American troops had twice been driven from the town. General Patton jumped into the surf and led his men in storming the beaches. British troops landed near Catania in sight of the volcano, Mount Etna. Ragusa fell under the American, British and Canadian onslaughts.

The battle of Catania was the greatest in the Sicilian campaign. Allied bombers dropped destruction on the city. British paratroops landed and cleared a strategic bridge for the arrival of advance units. Resistance was strong, but on July 19 the British were within three miles of the city. The Axis contested every foot of the way.

American forces, marching across Sicily, captured Palermo on July 23 and continued to advance. Catania was still holding out. The British attempted to enlarge their bridgehead across the Dittaino River, while naval forces shelled enemy positions from the sea.

The Battle of Catania was won on August 5, when the British entered the ruined citadel after a twenty-six-day drive. American forces took Troina without opposition and swept on. The British had now reached the foot of Mount Etna. Desperate fighting slowed down the Allied advances until on August 9 American troops landed behind the Axis lines at Cape Orlando, Randazzo, Brolo, and other Sicilian villages.

The power of the Axis was broken. They were forced into a pocket of one hundred square miles. Again they were in retreat, as thousands were killed, wounded, and forced to surrender, while their comrades fled in ships across the Straits of Messina to the Italian mainland.

The Americans entered Messina on August 17. The scenes which greeted them were memorable. Sicilians fell on their knees and prayed; they threw flowers in the path of their liberators from America. Italian mothers who had sons in America threw their arms around the soldiers and kissed them. Italian fathers grasped them by the hands, while their daughters and children broke into songs of rejoicing.

The war was over for the Sicilians. It was something they had never wanted but which was imposed upon them. Their devotion to the conquering Army was unbounded. The young "Gods of Democracy," as the Sicilians called them, had liberated them from the despots. The forces of Eisenhower had conquered Sicily in thirty-eight days.

General Eisenhower sat in his headquarters and read the messages that were now bombarding him with high praise. Pondering over one of the dispatches in his hand, he bowed gratefully and put it down on the table. It read:

"All of us are thrilled over the Sicilian campaign now successfully concluded in accordance with the timing and planning of the Allies. This is especially true when we realize that the enemy force in Sicily amounted to 405,000 men.

"Events of the last thirty-eight days show what can be done by teamwork based on preparation, training and timing, and above all gallantry, on the sea and in the air.

"From the ancient citadel of Quebec I send you my warm

congratulations and to the officers and men under your command—British, Canadian, French and American—my thanks and
enthusiastic approbations. Tell them all, well done."

Franklin Delano Roosevelt

The President at this time was in conference with Prime Minister Churchill and British-Canadian-American staffs in Quebec,
Canada. The Prime Minister and the other officials also sent
their congratulations to General Eisenhower.

The General felt the warm grasp of these "hands across the
seas." He read the cordial tribute from General Marshall. He
had "made good" with the Chief. Then he lingered over the
message from Secretary of War Stimson: "To you and your
men I extend my heartiest congratulations and my admiration
for the skill and fortitude with which you carried through
the conquest of Sicily. The power of your Army and its magnificent spirit give assurance that it is poised to an even greater
success."

Among the messages piling high on his desk was this from the
Chief of the British Imperial Staff, General Sir Alan Brooke:
"Hearty congratulations on the brilliant Sicilian success and
good luck for the future."

General Ike, turning to his staff, said reflectively, "It was a
real victory. Our troops have done everything that the best
troops in the world could have done. And that includes the three
services."

This was the message he sent to his soldiers, again giving *them*
the full credit. This was the *real* Eisenhower, humble in victory
and great in his devotion to his men.

Eisenhower had fought and won the campaign under the rank
of a temporary major general. He had entered the war as a
lieutenant colonel a scant two years previously. Upon the completion of the Sicilian campaign—his second great victory in the

war—President Roosevelt on August 31, 1943, announced his promotion to the permanent rank of major general and awarded him the Distinguished Service Medal, Oak Leaf Cluster.

The citation read as follows:

"As Commander in Chief of the Allied forces in North Africa General Eisenhower has, by skillful planning and direction, made an outstanding contribution to the war effort of the Allied nations. The organization and leadership of the expedition to occupy North Africa was a notable contribution.

"Thereafter, by his firmness and sound judgment, General Eisenhower was successful in the prompt establishment of a well-organized regime in North Africa.

"In the face of violent Axis resistance in Tunisia he successfully coordinated the British, American and French air, ground, and naval forces in a decisive campaign which destroyed the last elements of Axis resistance on the African continent. In a brilliant campaign of thirty-eight days General Eisenhower directed the combined operations leading to the conquest of Sicily and reduced Italy to a state of military impotence.

"Throughout the period of these operations, in preparation and execution, General Eisenhower has displayed conspicuous ability to secure complete unity of command and action of a great Allied force, with disastrous consequences to the enemy."

General Eisenhower had received the Distinguished Service Medal at the close of the last war, when he was a lieutenant colonel, for his direction of the Tank Training Center at Camp Colt at Gettysburg, Pennsylvania. When a soldier is cited a second time for this medal, he receives an Oak Leaf Cluster which is worn either on the ribbon bar designating the medal or on the ribbon from which the actual medal is suspended. However, the medals themselves are seldom worn.

President Roosevelt, in elaborating on the circumstances of the promotion, said that it was "in recognition of General Eisenhower's outstanding services as Commander in Chief of Allied Forces in North Africa.

"It was under his supervision," the President related, "that the successful landing in North Africa was made by combined British and American forces on November 8, 1942. More recently General Eisenhower has directed another critical amphibious operation resulting in the conquest of Sicily. The success of this campaign and the perfection of Allied teamwork, air, ground and naval, have undoubtedly had a decisive effect on the oppressed people of Europe and the course of the war."

The President, his face beaming with pride, exclaimed, "The fate of Italy lies in the balance as the continent of Europe trembles under the impact of the forward surge of massive Russian forces and the great aerial bombardment increases in fury with each succeeding week."

But Sicily to Eisenhower was but a stepping stone. He began to work harder than ever—there was no let-down. His eyes were now on the mainland of Italy, just across the strait, and the ultimate conquest of Europe. He set about making Sicily a great supply base for the next invasion. Shiploads of men, munitions, and supplies poured in from North Africa. Day and night the Allied bombers raided the Italian Coast from the tip of the boot to the outskirts of Rome.

"We're playing in the big leagues now," General Eisenhower exclaimed. "You can't hit a home run by bunting. You have to step up there and take your cut. The time has come to discontinue nibbling at islands and hit the Germans where it hurts. I don't believe in fighting battles to chase someone out of somewhere. Our object is to trap and smash the enemy."

A radiogram from the States requested the General to send a message to the folks back home. Ike replied promptly:

"No time for messages until we can say them with bombs and shells."

· 21 ·

Fall of Mussolini—driven from power by Eisenhower

Momentous events were brewing. The conquest of Sicily was but another move by Eisenhower on the chessboard of war and diplomacy. He was playing a masterhand with Kings, Queens, Bishops, Knights and Pawns. The stakes were the ultimate conquest of Europe.

While subduing Sicily, the Allies began an all-out air offensive against the Italian mainland which left that nation reeling. Over 425,000 pounds of high explosives were dropped on airdromes at Crotone and Vibo Valenia in Italy on July 13, 1943. On the fifteenth Messina took the full weight of 400,000 pounds. Allied air power had begun a demonstration of irresistible strength.

President Roosevelt and Prime Minister Churchill on July 16 sent this message to the Italian people: "The time has now come for you, the Italian people, to consult your own self-respect and your own interest and your own desire for a restoration of national dignity, security, and peace. The time has come for you to decide whether Italians shall die for Mussolini and Hitler—or live for Italy and civilization."

The appeal was punctuated by the roar of Allied planes over Italy, but they did not carry bombs—they bombarded Italy with

244

this message in printed leaflets. The following day the heaviest Allied force ever to raid the Italian mainland smashed at Naples. Three days passed without any apparent reaction in Italy. On July 19 the Allies struck at the Italian capital at Rome.

General Eisenhower was demanding his answer. After six more days of terrific bombing, on July 25, 1943, the answer came, and it astounded the world.

Mussolini has fallen! His despotic rule is ended. He has been forced to abdicate.

Eisenhower had driven Mussolini from power after twenty-one years of ruthless dictatorship. An exultant world received the news. It was revealed that in a dramatic meeting with King Victor Emmanuel in Rome, Mussolini had been voted down by his own Fascist Grand Council through opposition led by his son-in-law, Count Ciano (who, later, upon the demand of his own father-in-law, was put to death before a firing squad in Germany). The fallen Dictator was held prisoner in protective custody.

Italy hailed "the end of the painful nightmare that has dominated our lives for the past twenty years." Demonstrations sprang up spontaneously everywhere, and anti-German sentiment ran high as crowds cried for a peace. Thousands of Italian workers stormed the plant of the Fascist "Popolo d'Italia," Mussolini's official newspaper, in Milan and laid it in ruins.

While the Italian people were celebrating the overthrow of Mussolini, General Eisenhower sent them this message on July 29:

"We commend the Italian people and the House of Savoy for ridding themselves of Mussolini, the man who involved them in the war as a tool of Hitler and brought them to the verge of disaster. The greatest obstacle which divided the Italian people from the United Nations has been removed by the Italians themselves. The only remaining obstacle on the road to peace is the German aggressor, who is still on the Italian soil.

"You want peace. You can have peace immediately and peace under honorable conditions which our Governments have already offered you. We are coming to you as liberators. Your part is to cease immediately any assistance to German military forces in your country. If you do this we will rid you of the Germans and deliver you from the horrors of war. As you have already seen in Sicily, our occupation will be mild and beneficent.

"Your men will return to their normal lives and to their productive avocations and, provided all British and Allied prisoners now in your hands are restored safely to us and not taken away to Germany, the hundreds of thousands of Italian prisoners captured by us in Tunisia and Sicily will return to the countless Italian homes who long for them. Ancient traditions and liberties of your country will be restored."

The fall of Mussolini caused the expectation of surrender to mount high. General Eisenhower granted Italy a reprieve from incessant bombing in order to give the new Badoglio Government an opportunity to surrender. Badoglio, for reasons of national pride and lack of military strength, did not take advantage of the opportunity. General Eisenhower put the issue squarely to the Italians on July 31:

"Italians! Tonight we send you a solemn warning. Listen carefully, and tell your friends to listen, for what we say affects the lives of every one of you.

"Six days have passed since the overthrow of Mussolini. In those six days the Italian people have achieved much. But while you are working for your liberation, the Germans, too, were busy. When they first heard the news of Mussolini's downfall, the Germans were stunned. They said to themselves, 'We Germans in Italy are caught like rats in a trap if Badoglio makes peace immediately.' But since then, day by day, they watched the inactivity of the Badoglio Government. You know better than we what has happened. There has been no sign of German

Acme Photo

General Eisenhower pointing out a bit of interesting action to Air Chief Marshal Sir Arthur Tedder, who in turn, finds something of similar interest to point out to General "Ike," during a pre-invasion show of an American armored unit in England

Acme Photo

Members of the Allied Supreme Command in conference in England. Left to right around the table are: Lt. Gen. Omar N. Bradley, Senior Commander of American Ground Forces; Admiral Sir Bertram Ramsay, Allied Naval Commander; Air Chief Marshal Sir Arthur Tedder, Deputy Supreme Commander; General Dwight D. Eisenhower, Supreme Commander; General Sir Bernard L. Montgomery, Commander in Chief of British Forces; Air Chief Marshal Sir Trafford Leigh Mallory, Air Commander in Chief; and Lieut. Gen. Walter Bedell Smith, Chief of Staff withdrawal. Day by day, the Germans regained their former insolent attitude towards Italians.

"Italians! You know that on July 25 we let up on the aerial bombardment of Italy. We hoped thereby to give Italy a breathing space wherein to unite for peace and freedom. But the Germans, too, have used that breathing space to strengthen their own position, and for that, full and sole responsibility rests with the new government in Rome. Had that government acted speedily, Germany by now would be in full retreat. But instead the new government temporized, it missed the opportunity. It permitted the Germans to recover.

"Italians! We cannot tolerate this, and we issue you this solemn warning; the breathing space has ended. Be prepared!"

Riots approaching revolution broke out in northern Italy. Soldiers joined civilians in demanding the immediate overthrow of Badoglio. They demanded peace. The center of the revolt lay in Milan, where rioting had been going on all week. Crowds marched, shouting, "*We want peace!* Badoglio, do something quickly. We don't want our cities bombed again."

Underground radio stations broadcast appeals to the people to refuse to cooperate with the Badoglio Government and begin organized resistance. Italy was in turmoil. Badoglio had to declare martial law and militarize the railroads and highways and communication lines. In Milan, the Cellari jail was stormed and two hundred prisoners of the Fascist Government were released.

The whereabouts of Mussolini was a mystery. President Roosevelt issued a warning to all neutral countries to the effect that anyone offering asylum to Hitler or Mussolini or the Japanese war criminals was committing an unfriendly act against the Allies.

Still the Badoglio Government held its silence. On August 1 Allied planes bombed the docks at Naples and other points. On the eighth Milan, Turin and Genoa were bombarded from the air and then, as the Axis was frantically evacuating troops by the Straits of Messina, Rome was bombarded.

Suddenly, the bombing raids quieted somewhat and it was apparent that something was about to happen. What was actually happening was revealed later. In two neutral countries Italian diplomats had approached British diplomats and informed them of the Italian desire to make peace; also of Italy's complete inability to cope with the Germans still within her borders. Of these moves the Germans were held completely in the dark.

General Eisenhower went to Lisbon during this period and attended a meeting presided over by Sir Ronald H. Campbell and the American Chargé d'Affaires. The representatives of the Badoglio Government parleyed. They wanted conciliatory terms. There was but one answer from General Eisenhower and the Allied delegates: "Unconditional surrender!"

The Italian representative, a general, left to go back to Rome for consultation. Because of the secrecy of his mission it took several days to reach the Eternal City. The Italian Government sent back a second general; and to prove their good faith, the one-armed British General, Carton Dewiar, who had been an Italian prisoner since early in the war, went with him.

The second Italian general went on to Eisenhower's African headquarters while the first returned to Lisbon with the reply that the Italian Government could not act as a free agent because of its ties with Germany; therefore the armistice could not be announced prior to Allied landings on the Italian mainland.

The Allied representatives ignored the protestations and demanded a definite yes or no within twenty-four hours. The answer came to Eisenhower's headquarters by a secret communications' route the next day, revealing that the Italians had accepted the Allied terms and that a representative would return to sign the armistice.

In the presence of General Eisenhower and General Sir Harold R. L. G. Alexander, the armistice was signed on September 3 by General Bedell Smith, representing Eisenhower, and General Castellano, representing Marshal Badoglio. Others at the signing were Robert Murphy, of the United States State Department, and Harold MacMillan, of the British Foreign Office.

With most of Italy in German hands, General Eisenhower decided to coincide the announcement of the Armistice with the landings of his Allied troops at Naples on September 3.

Hostilities between Italy and the United Nations ceased at 12:30 P.M. United States Eastern Wartime on September 8, 1943.

The radio again was made an instrument of war and peace when its voice proclaimed the glad tidings to the Italian people waiting anxiously in their homes.

"This is General Dwight D. Eisenhower, Commander in Chief of the Allied Forces. The Italian Government has surrendered its armed forces unconditionally. As Allied Commander in Chief I have granted a military armistice, the terms of which have been approved by the Governments of the United Nations. Thus I am acting in the interest of the United Nations.

"The Italian Government has bound itself to abide by these terms without reservation. The armistice is signed by my representative and the representative of Marshal Badoglio and it becomes effective this instant.

"Hostilities between the armed forces of the United Nations and those of Italy terminate at once. All Italians who now act to help eject the German aggressor from Italian soil will have the assistance and support of the United Nations."

The message of Badoglio followed: "The Italian Government, recognizing the impossibility of continuing the struggle against the overwhelming power of the enemy, with the object of avoiding further and more grievous harm to the nation, requested an armistice from General Eisenhower. This request has been granted. The Italian forces will, therefore, cease all acts of hostility against the Anglo-American forces wherever they may be met. They will, however, oppose attacks from any other quarter."

The terms which Eisenhower demanded were: Italy to cease hostilities at once and do its utmost to deny the Germans facilities for use against the United Nations; all United Nations prisoners or internes to be immediately turned over to the Allied Commander in Chief and protected; Italian warships and aircraft to be transferred to points designated by the Allied C. I. C.; Italian merchant shipping to be requisitioned as needed; Corsica and all islands to be surrendered for use by the Allies as operational bases; immediate use of Italian airfields and ports which are to be protected by the Italians until taken over; Italian forces to withdraw from participation in the war and the Government to guarantee to employ all available armed forces for compliance with the terms of the armistice; the Allied C. I. C. reserves the right to take any action deemed necessary to protect the interests of the Allied Forces in the prosecution of the war and the Italian Government binds itself to take any action the Allied C. I. C. might order; the C. I. C. will have the right to impose means for disarmament, demobilization, and demilitarization. Other conditions of a political, financial, or economic nature will be transmitted later."

Repercussions of the armistice occurred swiftly. The Italian fleet dashed out to sea and surrendered to the Allies. Italy declared war on Germany.

Eisenhower had won another epoch-making victory. Through a masterly combination of military strategy and most skillful diplomacy he had forced Italy out of the Axis—the partner of Nazism was now its enemy. Forty days after the war-weary Italian people had thrown off the yoke of Fascism by discarding their broken dictator—and after 1,181 days of war—the Italians were allied with Eisenhower's forces to drive the Germans out of their beloved homeland.

Hitler, in desperation, contrived a cunning coup to rescue his friend Mussolini, who was held by Badoglio under guard in prison. In a daring night raid the Italian guards were caught unaware. The emaciated and half-mad Mussolini was dragged from imprisonment by Axis agents, carried to a waiting airplane, taken to Germany, and delivered to Hitler.

This proclamation was issued on September 12: "Members of the armed SS Guards and Secret Security Service, aided by members of parachute troops, today carried out an undertaking for the liberation of the Duce. The coup de main was a success. Mussolini is at liberty and his delivery to the Anglo-American Allies, which was agreed to by the Badoglio Government, has been frustrated."

In Italy the seventy-one-year-old Marshal Badoglio was made premier by the king. Upon his new assumption of power he said, "The war continues. Italy, hard hit in her invaded provinces and in her destroyed cities, loyally keeps her given word (to the Allies) as the jealous custodians of her military traditions."

The trembling, almost senile voice of the fallen Mussolini was now heard over the radio appealing to the Italians to turn against the Allies under Eisenhower. Its bombast and bluster were gone; it faded away into almost incoherent mumbling—the end of a ruthless dictator.

Hitler, staggering under the collapse of Italy and the overpowering might of the Russians, who were driving steadily on toward their invasion of Germany, was besieged on two sides. He must fight off the Russian juggernaut moving upon him from the East; he must fight Eisenhower's victorious forces moving upon him from the South.

Eisenhower was poised for the next blow.

· 22 ·

Invasion of Italy—on road to Rome

THE FALL OF MUSSOLINI and the surrender of Italy were but the prologue to the great drama soon to be enacted on the stage of history. Seventeen days after the conquest of Sicily, and timed with the Italian surrender, the curtain rose for the next act.

The German invaders must now be driven from the Italian homeland. Eisenhower knew the Axis, now revolving on but one wheel in Europe, would throw all the forces it could rally against the Allies in an attempt to keep the battleground in Italy, rather than to fight on German soil. This has been the cunning strategy of Hitler since the beginning of the war—to fight on the ground of the conquered countries and keep his Fatherland from being drenched in blood.

But the war in the air upset his plan. Germany was being devastated by British and American bombers based on England. Berlin was already in ruins. Every large city in Germany was in shambles; millions were homeless. Hitler's "best laid plans" were turning to ashes as the flames lighted the night skies.

The invasion of Europe through Italy was begun. The veterans of the British Eighth Army, which had fought its way across the African deserts, stormed across the Straits of Messina into the toe of Italy on September 3, 1943. With them were the doughty Canadians. They landed on the west coast of the Prov-

252

ince of Calabria in the Marina di Gallico section under an air umbrella and pulverizing bombardments from air, sea, and land. Powerful aerial forces were softening up the attack along the Italian roads. American and British warships sent high explosives into key targets.

Eisenhower threw a stream of reinforcements and supplies across the Straits of Messina. American Commando troops established their footholds. Allied planes bombed Naples. The Battle for Salerno raged fiercely. General Mark Clark, American Commander of the Fifth Army, informed Eisenhower, "We have arrived at our initial objective—our beachhead is secure. Additional troops are landing every day, and we are here to stay. Not one foot of ground will be given up."

In the Fifth Army were many Italian-American boys whose fathers had come from the villages, towns, and cities they were now storming—Salerno, Taranto, Sorento. Fighting their way along the coastal road skirting Mount Vesuvius, and breaking through the mountainous barriers, led by British tanks, they entered Naples on October 1, shortly before dawn, twenty-two days after landing on the beachheads below Salerno.

The scene before them was one of desolation. The city had been devastated by fire and explosions and the population had fled into the mountains. The harbor was full of sunken ships. Deserted by the Nazis, who had left the wreckage behind them, the Neapolitans began to return to their city to greet the Americans and British as their liberators. Old Italian mothers threw their arms around our soldier boys and wept. Their sons, too, were in America, and some of them were in this very army.

The name of Eisenhower to these beleaguered people assumed a greatness equal to that of Garibaldi. There was singing once more in the streets of Naples and the sound of the guitars. These peace-loving folk, who had been victims of the machinations of Mussolini and Hitler, could laugh again. They greeted Americans, who had come to help drive the Nazis from their sacred soil, as brothers.

Eisenhower's boys looked up in wonderment at the grim Mt. Vesuvius growling and groaning in the distance. Huge clouds of smoke and flame poured from its crater. Here was an ageless war in which Mother Nature had been engaged from the beginning of time, thundering its power to the terror-stricken humanity at its feet. With overwhelming fire, deluges of burning lava, smothering gases, and violent earthquakes, it had destroyed the ancient cities of Herculaneum, Stabiae, and Pompeii. On these ruins our American boys were now standing.

The grumbling volcano, ruling through the aeons, seemed to resent mere humans engaged in warfare. Peasants prophecied that old Vesuvius would yet enter World War II, as a victor, and to a *Life* correspondent from America exclaimed, "First it was twenty years of *Fascismo*. Then it was the Germans. Then it was the Allied bombers. And now Vesuvius! *Mamma mia!* It is the end of the world!"

The forces of Eisenhower moved slowly forward until they were fighting along the banks of the Volturno, under heavy fire from German artillery and tanks. They were now on the Capua-Formia road to Rome, fighting their way village by village. Mud, rain and mountainous terrain challenged their advance. Floods turned the battle roads into almost impassable quagmires through which tanks could not pass.

American soldiers in Sicily and at their bases along the old battle routes in North Africa, and men aboard ships in the fleets of the Navy, stood inspired as the message of General Eisenhower, addressed to all the American military and civil personnel in the Mediterranean, was broadcast on November 5.

"We have reached the first anniversary of the initial British-American landings in this theater. You came here to take part in the crusade to eliminate ruthless aggression from the earth and to guarantee to yourselves and your children security against the threat of domination by arrogant despotism.

"During the year just past you have written a memorable chapter in the history of American arms, a chapter in which are recorded deeds of valor, of endurance and of unswerving loyalty.

"From my heart, I thank each of you for the services you have so well performed in the air, on the sea, in the front lines, and in our ports and bases.

"But we must now look forward, because for us there can be no thought of turning back until our task has been fully accomplished. With the gallant and powerful Russian Army pounding the European enemy on the east and with growing forces seeking out and penetrating the weak spots of his defenses from all other directions, his utter defeat—even if not yet definitely in sight—is certain.

"The heart of America supports our every endeavor. Reports of sporadic troubles on the home front are occasioned by the ill-considered actions of relatively few individuals. Let us always remember that our great nation of 130,000,000 people is ceaselessly working and sacrificing to provide us weapons, equipment and supplies and to send us an increasing flow of reinforcements.

"With high courage let us redouble our efforts and multiply the fury of our blows so we the more quickly may recross the seas to our homeland with the glorious word that the last enemy stronghold has fallen, and with the proud knowledge of having done in our time our duty to our beloved country."

The Allies were now holding one-third of the Italian peninsula, the British advancing up the east coast while the Americans were contesting every foot of the ground up the west coast—both driving along the roads toward Rome.

As stated, it is not our purpose to describe these battles and campaigns in detail, but to give side lights on General Eisenhower during these crucial days. While burdened with the tremendous responsibilities of these actions, we find him the same strong but genial Ike in his contacts with his generals and soldiers at the front and his staff back at headquarters. His human qualities never deserted him even in the greatest crises. The tumult of battle was constantly relieved by his simplicity in "the little things of life."

General Ike had witnessed the Battle of Salerno, arriving there by land, sea, and plane from his African headquarters. He left headquarters in a Flying Fortress and boarded a British ship which took him to Italy. There he went ashore in an American PT boat and then traveled around by jeep.

While with General Clark he found himself under direct fire. A German mortar shell whined over their heads and landed a short distance away. He was again under fire at the Battle of Volturna. His men were used to seeing him conferring with their chiefs at advance field headquarters amid the screaming of shells and roar of bursting bombs.

Throughout the Sicilian and Italian campaigns the General never forgot the welfare of his troops and no problem was too small for him. He visited an army show and commended the actors.

"You are entertaining soldiers. You are not fighting with machine guns, but your job is just as important as long as you are doing your job well. And you are doing it extremely well. You are rendering a service, and a great one, to your fellow soldiers and your country."

One of the performers in a show given at Sicily was a hillbilly one-man band. Part of his act was to greet friends from the footlights. He called out in turn, "Hi, Seth! Hi, Reuben!" And then, turning to the General's box, exclaimed, "Hi, Ike!" The General answered with a quick and genial smile.

When he heard of a proposed visit of the all-star baseball teams he wired, "I not only want those teams but I insist that they stay over for thirty days."

Neither did he lose touch with his family. A letter from home told him his brother Milton was offered the post as president of Kansas State College. He wrote back, "A large part of the kind of peace achieved after this war rests on the principles laid down in America's schools."

When the WAAC was changed to the WAC, Ike urged all the members to reenlist and said, "I am too simple a soldier to see the difference. A WAAC often does the job, in her particular sphere, of two men."

His WAC secretary was Staff Sergeant Nana Rae. "He is a very fast dictator and he knows some awful big words," she confided. "He sits at his desk when you come in, but that's the last you see of him sitting down. He paces around while he dictates and gets up speed."

Once the Sergeant had an exceptionally witty letter published in *Stars and Stripes,* and the General began his morning's dictation by saying, "In this morning's *Stars and Stripes—*" Then he smiled and added, "That was a delicious piece of humor you had in the paper this morning."

On the occasion of National Bible week he sent the following message back home: "It is truly gratifying to know that the people of the United States are setting aside a week to honor the book which is 'our daily bread,' the 'Word of God.' While the utterances of God as recorded in the Bible are ever the need of mankind, it is in war, and particularly in the present war with its issue of humanity and morality, that their essential presence is felt.

"On this front, I am happy to report, this thought is foremost among our men. Our objective is total victory, not only victory by arms, but victory also for America's ideals. With the help of God in this fight for right, which help our men are ever and devotedly seeking, this victory is assured."

General Eisenhower is a man who considers no task too small

if he feels he should do it. He received a letter in Italy from a small St. Louis boy who had been appointed by his classmates and teacher to write to the General. The lad told him how they were writing to fellow parishioners of the Assumption School on the battlefronts. The General immediately sent back this reply:

"Dear Alfred: I am more than delighted to take a few minutes off to answer your encouraging letter. The one thing our soldiers depend on more than any other is the knowledge that their work and risks and sacrifices are not only appreciated by the people at home but are supported in every way, every minute of the day.

"I am sure that in writing regularly to soldiers in the service you and your schoolmates are doing a very fine thing and one which you may be sure is definitely contributing towards the winning of this war. Thank you so much for the nice things you had to say and for your assurance that you continue to pray for the magnificent body of Americans that is now in North Africa."

Another epic in the warm-hearted personal approach of General Eisenhower is the story of Duckworth, a dog, and his two fighter-pilot masters. Lieutenant Harold Taff and Lieutenant Richard East had brought the dog to Africa with them, taking the little Spaniel on the long voyage across on a troopship.

One day Lieutenant East failed to return from a mission. His parents were duly notified that he was missing. They dispatched a letter to General Eisenhower, asking if the dog could be sent home to them. "If it is not inconsistent with general policy and it doesn't interfere with the war effort, Dick's mother would particularly appreciate it. If the dog could be placed on a plane or a freighter coming to New York Harbor, I could meet the dog and take him to our home."

The General commanded immediate compliance with the request. Just prior to the dog's departure he learned that the co-master, Lieutenant Taff, was alive and also wanted the dog. This information came to him in a letter from General Spaatz. Ike quickly sent the following letter to Lieutenant East's parents:

"It is learned that the dog, Duckworth, belonged jointly to Lieutenant East and his best friend, Lieutenant Taff. Lieutenant East was killed in action, April 4. His plane and grave were located after our forces moved into the Tunis area. The loss of his best friend deeply affected Taff. The commanding officer of the fighter group brought Taff with the dog to the airplane. Taff was heartbroken at the thought of losing his dog, and wanted to spend every possible minute with him until the plane took off. He placed him in the plane and carefully tied him. He left the plane just before the take-off. Colonel West had been waiting in his car to take Taff back to quarters, but Taff was seen to thank him and walk away from the car to an adjoining field.

"Under the circumstances, and in particular in view of the statement that the dog was jointly owned by your son and his best friend, and especially as Taff has shown strong affection for the dog, I believe you will agree with me it would be unwise to return the dog to you as requested.

"The friendship of a dog is precious. It becomes even more so if one is so far removed from home as we are in Africa. I have a Scotty. In him I find consolation and diversion. For me he is the one 'person' to whom I can talk without the conversation turning back to the war. Duckworth is performing a patriotic service. I respect the quality of warm friendship shown by Taff for the dog. I am confident you and Mrs. East will view the situation similarly despite your natural and understandable desire to have with you this close companion of your gallant son who died for his country on the field of battle."

After spending two months at his advance headquarters in

Sicily and Italy, General Eisenhower, surrounded by war correspondents, said he had something important to say. The newspapermen who risk their lives along the fighting fronts to get eye-witness accounts for the folk back home, were on the alert for a "big news break."

"I would like to speak to you people for about a minute," the General exclaimed. "It's my belief that you people aren't giving the footslogging soldier the credit he deserves."

The common soldier is "big news" to Ike. He isn't impressed over what they say about him, but he'll fight for headlines for his men.

"The foot soldier is not as spectacular as a tremendous raid on Berlin or Hamburg," Ike admitted, "or like the whole Italian fleet sailing in to surrender. We are too apt to forget him except in individual cases of heroism. But as an overall picture of infantry fighting—from El Alemein to where the Eighth Army is now and on the other side—those long bitter days of the British First Army and the American troops fighting their way up—just think of what has been accomplished by the foot fighter. Think of the days in the mud, in the cold, and the endurance exhibited.

"You know it's pretty hard," Ike continued, "after four or five weeks of lying out—I remember the First Unit of the British First Army without even a greatcoat—it's pretty hard to carry into battle a realization that you are fighting for the Four Freedoms.

"It comes down finally to just a sense of duty—one of the noblest virtues of the British and American soldiers. It has been high in our troops. One thing that I recommend to all of you, if you get a chance, is that you visit a front-line hospital—not the ones that you had the opportunity of seeing here where the men have become used to being well treated—see those men coming in there freshly wounded—see the courage exhibited by the Anglo-American in conditions of rain, mud, dust, and heat.

"I think that the overall story, the mass of those soldiers, is something that we could do well to glorify a bit. In both our countries the great portion of our fighting men go into those services."

The thoughts of the man from Kansas were straying back home. "We realize it in our own consciousness," he said, "but the postman in Abilene, Kansas, in some little village in England, does he realize just exactly what these boys are doing? How they are performing? Does he realize it as well as the feats of the big bombers or one of the destroyers carrying out a gallant mission to Taranto?"

Ike's love for the common soldier was uppermost in his mind as he came from the battlefronts in Sicily and Italy. "This is something I've felt for a long time," he said. "I don't know whether there is much to do about it, but it is from the heart."

These and many other stories are told about General Ike as the campaign was waged in Italy. Throughout the autumn days and early winter of 1943, while the Allied Armies were fighting their way toward Rome, against tempests and floods as well as a heavily barricaded and intrenched enemy, Ike never lost his intimate touch with his soldiers.

Steps were taken by General Eisenhower toward liberating Italian labor. Fascist labor syndicates have been abolished under a directive issued in Naples and fullest sanction had been given for free organization of workers into unions of their own choosing. Labor groups expressed their wish to cooperate with American and British workers in hastening the destruction of the Axis. Under Fascist rule, wages were near starvation level. Under Allied control plans were organized to restore to the Italian workers as rapidly as military developments permit all of the rights taken away from them more than twenty years ago.

Hitler was defiant. Even with his Armies meeting ignominous defeat as the Russians drove them back toward Germany, battering down his strongholds, killing and taking captive hundreds of thousands of his soldiers, Hitler decided to strongly resist the advance of Eisenhower's forces in Italy. He issued this defiance in Munich. "The war can last as long as they want and we will never capitulate. . . . Germany will lay down its arms only five minutes past victory."

It was during this time that two more epoch-making conferences were being held between the United Nations. President Roosevelt again had flown the Atlantic, and with Prime Minister Churchill and Generalissimo Chiang Kai-shek held a five-day conference at Cairo (November 22–27, 1943). Four days after this conference Roosevelt and Churchill were with Premier Stalin at Tehran, in Iran, shaping a common policy for the destruction of the German forces and a peace "which will banish the scourge and terror of war for many generations."

General Eisenhower was missing a few days from the scenes in Italy. He had gone to ancient Carthage on the African coast to meet President Roosevelt. For forty-eight hours they were closeted together in conference. Here, it was later revealed, the President informed the General about decisions which had been reached with Stalin and Churchill.

During this conference President Roosevelt conferred upon General Eisenhower the decoration of the Legion of Merit. The citation concisely recorded the General's notable achievements since the beginning of the war in a series of positions of great importance, stating:

"He planned for and supervised with marked ability and conspicuous success the planning and carrying out of the largest concentration of troops ever assembled on the American continent and their subsequent participation in large-scale maneuvers. . . . He played a major part in placing in effect the United States

Army's plans for war . . . he served with distinction during a most critical period in the history of the United States. . . . He rendered invaluable service by organizing the European Theater, establishing an effective supply system and training and preparing for battle the large American Ground and Air Forces which have since played such an important part in active operations from the United Kingdom, in Africa, and in Italy. His outstanding contribution to the Allied cause and to the successes now being realized by the Armed Forces of the United States are deserving of the highest praise and reflect great credit upon himself and the military service."

Upon his return to his staff, General Eisenhower made this cryptic statement: "I have just been in conference with the Commander in Chief. Your part is going to be a vital one—one that will require more and more work from us."

The Christmas season was approaching. The boys in Eisenhower's armies were waiting eagerly for the packages from home, the gifts of mothers and wives, sisters and sweethearts. had hoped to be able to celebrate Christmas in Rome, to Mass in the great cathedrals, kneeling in prayer before of the Prince of Peace who had been born in a manger at Bethlehem nearly two thousand years ago. This memorable time was to be denied them; they must celebrate the Christ along the battle roads.

On Christmas Eve, General Eisenhower was at the front visiting his troops when he received a message informing him that he had been officially named by President Roosevelt to direct the invasion on a new Western Front. This new duty was to require him to leave his generals who were now launching as the greatest ever conceived in even this te mark was, "Well, I'll celebrate by visiting Capri, something I have always wanted to do."

Two days later, on December 27, 1943, General Eisenhower delivered his farewell speech to his armies and naval forces in Italy and North Africa.

General Eisenhower said:

"Soon I leave this theater to assume other duties assigned me by the Allied Governments. I take my leave of you with feelings of personal regret that are equaled only by my pride in your brilliant accomplishments of the year just passed.

"Although tempted to review again the many advantages that have accrued to the Allied cause through your bravery and fortitude, I believe all these will come home to you if you will merely compare your present position and prospects in this great conflict with your position and outlook in the late fall of 1942.

"Then the Eighth Army was making its final preparations to attack the enemy who was standing only a short distance west of Cairo. Vast Allied armadas were approaching Northwest Africa to learn whether good fortune or complete disaster were awaiting them. No Allied ship could transit the length of the Mediterranean. Our fortunes appeared at a low ebb.

"All this was changed—by your skill, your determination an your devotion to duty. Enemy action against our convoys the Mediterranean is limited to harassing and submarine effo You have established yourself on the mainland of Europe. are still advancing. You, along with other Allied forces figh n many fronts, have already achieved the certainty that d every soldier, sailor and every airman, and every homelands continues incessantly to do his full du be ours.

her you comprise a mighty fighting machin

fenses and assist in bringing about his final collapse. United we meet again in the heart of the enemy's Continental stronghold. I send Godspeed and good luck to each of you along with the assurance of my lasting gratitude and admiration."

On the occasion of his farewell to British and American correspondents he pledged a 1944 victory in Europe "if everyone all the way from the front lines to the remotest hamlet does his full duty."

"My own personal job immediately, of course, will be to do what we have done here," he said. "That is to weld the directing team together in such a way that no real friction ever develops, that people trust each other, work in unison and go into this thing with their full weight."

The departure of General Eisenhower from the Mediterranean theater of war was the occasion of both regrets and high expec tations. He shook hands cordially with officers gathered about him at his headquarters, assuring them he would meet them in Berlin. As he left them this twenty-seventh day of December to take up his expanded duties, a soldier watching him board an airplane, exclaimed, "I've always thought a lot of the General, but now he's tops on my list of great greats!"

General Eisenhower mysteriously disappeared for twenty days. Nothing was heard or seen of him. On January 16, 1944, he appeared in England to take up his new command in preparation for the Second Front. It was then discovered that he had crossed the Atlantic by air, conferred with General Marshall, President Roosevelt, and Secretary of War Stimson in Washington, visited some of his wounded soldiers in the hospital, held reunion with his wife, flown up to West Point to meet his son, and then taken a bomber to Kansas to spend a night with his mother and brother. He had brought with him as a gift a little puppy, Telek, Junior, from across the seas. The family had kept the secret of this unexpected visit.

The General also had conferred with Prime Minister Churchill, who was stricken with pneumonia at the time, before returning to London.

The General's headquarters in England were ready when he arrived and the only travel casualty was his dog, Telek, Senior, who was detained in canine quarantine for six weeks. He held his first London press conference and took the opportunity to discuss the problem of news censorship which had troubled him in the past.

"Fundamentally, public opinion wins wars. I take it that you are just as anxious as I am to win this war and get it done so that we can all go fishing. In coming to this theater I could not fail to mention what has been done here in advance of my coming. I hail the grand work of the naval forces, particularly recently when they nailed the *Scharnhorst* and got those three destroyers in the Bay of Biscay.

"The work that the navies have been doing is evidenced by all the troops brought into England safely. We all salute the grand work of the Air Forces—what they have done by pounding Germany and reducing her military potential at great risk to themselves and with absolute courage. It's a wonderful story, even those parts of the effort which have not been published.

"We should not overlook the fine infantry training and preparing out on the cold moors and in the countryside in mud and rain. They are getting themselves toughened for any job."

The General sent this message to the United States in a War Bond appeal: "We are going to hit the enemy and hit him again and keep hitting him until the last measure of Nazi resistance is crushed to beaten earth. There is no other course. Military defeat is the only logic that a Nazi understands. I do not expect that the Nazis will accept it quickly or without fierce resistance."

General Eisenhower was now organizing his mighty forces for the liberation of Europe.

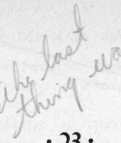
the last thing was

· 23 ·

Great invasion—Eisenhower in England directs mighty forces

ONE HUNDRED DAYS after Iron Ike reached England from Italy he was ready for the invasion of Europe from the West in the spring of 1944.

Ike was ready to strike! Again he was to meet his old adversary Rommel, whom he had driven out of Africa, in decisive battle at the gateways to Germany.

During these hundred days little was heard from Eisenhower except that he was following his usual pace, sleeping little, working from dawn to dark and longer, and applying his attention to every detail. Even the Nazis were impressed, as witness the story published by the Munich newspaper, *Neueste Nachrichten:* "The American General has an athletic appearance, full health and strength, a well formed jaw and head showing great will, and is a man whom his countrymen would call a 'he man.' He is a man who has great abilities as an organizer and who has demonstrated great good sense in leadership and tactics in Africa."

The British, too, heaped honors on the General. He was made a knight by King George, and was elected to the exclusive Athenaeum Club, a literary club of London, for "eminence in science, literature, or the arts, or for public services."

267

He was inspecting troops in England while across the Channel Field Marshal Rommel was conducting a detailed inspection tour of his defenses.

"I found the troops in good condition," General Eisenhower said, "intensively engaged in efficient training for the big job that lies ahead. If their fighting is as good as their training, God help the Nazis!"

General Eisenhower's tour was as informal as it was thorough. He insisted that no parades or formal inspections be arranged for him. Commanding officers were ordered to continue the regular training schedule when he arrived. He traveled in a special train which carried staff cars for trips through the countryside, and was in continuous radio communication with the Supreme Allied Command in London. A radio-equipped jeep followed the General on all tours in order to allow him to remain in touch with his headquarters. He worked nights on deskwork in a fully equipped office on wheels.

His first inspection at any camp was the kitchen. Next the General checked the health of the men and then their guns and equipment. Once in a while his passion for informality was frustrated. A long column of troops was marching down a road along which his car was moving. As the car approached, with its red plate bearing the four stars of a full general, cries of "Eyes right!" echoed down the column.

The General averted the threat of an impromptu review by jumping from his car, motioning two or three men out of formation, and asking, "How's your chow and your billets?"

During these Second Front preparations the General received the top Soviet award, the Order of Suvaroff, first class. To the Russians on the twenty-sixth anniversary of the Red Army, the General sent this message:

"In stopping the Nazi military machine the Red Army showed the world the most courageous exploit ever accomplished during a defensive war. I salute the officers and men of the Red Army. When we come to attack the troops of the Wehrmacht from the East, West, South, and North, the quality and valor of our forces will make final victory certain."

As General Eisenhower was inspecting American and British ground units, he stood on a cold windswept plain watching American tanks, guns, and infantry scramble across the country in a highly complicated maneuver. He watched tanks and field guns pound to bits a series of targets far across the rolling terrain.

An American soldier, recognizing the General, commented, "So, that's the boss! He looks like the guys you know at home."

One of his last speeches was at Sandhurst, the British West Point, when the General said, "Your nation and mine have found themselves partners in a great war. More than any other time in history we find the forces of evil ranged against those of decency and respect for the human mind. We stand on the side of decency, democracy, and liberty.

"Our great air forces by night and day are punishing our enemy, softening him up—but much remains to be done. Every one of us must not fail to do his duty."

American troops poured into Britain from across the seas. The Nazis worriedly fortified the invasion coasts. Invasion jitters grew stronger and stronger. Despite his tremendous burden, General Eisenhower found time for inspections and close contacts. He told American fighter pilots that their role in the great three-way invasion of Europe was a dawn-to-dusk death express against the Luftwaffe.

"Only a self-disciplined Army can win battles," he told his soldiers. "We must all work on the basis of mutual respect, consideration, and cooperation, dedicated to the single task of doing our duty in winning this war. We must see that justice prevails.

"Assurance of our success in battle and our chances to return home safely and speedily are directly affected by our success in establishing here a reputation as a first-class, disciplined fighting organization. . . . My deep appreciation to each of you for duty well performed in the past and with the best of luck in the future."

According to reports in England, General Eisenhower as Supreme Commander of the Allied Western Front will be invested with the greatest authority in history, greater than that of old Roman generals. Commanding all Allied land, sea, and air forces, the joint American-British Governments have agreed, it is said, to give him control never before placed in the hands of one man.

The Allied Armistice Plan providing for the end of the war is said to place the entire economic life of Europe under Eisenhower's control for whatever period is required to restore peace and trade after the war ends. All nations except Germany and her satellites will be allowed to choose their own governments. France, Norway, Holland, Belgium will be under Eisenhower's control until their safety and security is assured and they are able to resume self-government without Allied protection.

These authoritative sources further state that Eisenhower will have direct control over all parts of Germany occupied by Allied troops (except the Russians). German territory occupied by the Red Army will be controlled by a Soviet Military Government. General Eisenhower will set up a similar protectorate over Italy until it is purged of its enemies.

Iron Ike as he stands surrounded by his "Invasion Team" (his name for it) is the commanding figure in the greatest military adventure in the world's history. Eight old warriors—five Britons and three Americans—stand beside him, the key men in the final drive on Hitler's three thousand miles of fortifications on the western coast of Europe. This invasion team, comprising the best military brains and experience in America and Britain, is a masterpiece of organization.

Eisenhower is a genius in cooperation and coordination. He believes in teamwork and places responsibilities for each phase of the operations on the ablest man that can be found. Ike is not the type that must do everything himself. He builds a great staff around him, advises with them, allows them to work out their plans, and then commands the operations. Upon these commands rest the lives of the millions of men who do the fighting and hundreds of millions more in the nations involved.

Three years ago Eisenhower was a lieutenant colonel; today his record of successful generalship includes the conquests of North Africa, Sicily, and Italy. His formula is starkly simple: "Plan to the least detail, then strike like death itself."

Meet these men as they direct the invasion of Europe by air, sea, and land. Here is General Sir Arthur Tedder, Deputy Commander in Chief under General Eisenhower. He is a Scot, fifty-four years old, described as "small and soft-spoken." Son of a nobleman, he is in direct contrast to Ike. He was graduated from Cambridge and for a time played professional Rugby. A veteran of World War I, a flier in France and Egypt, he settled down for life with the RAF, where he became Air Chief Marshal. His record in World War II has made him one of the greatest airmen of all times. It was under him that the RAF gained command over the Mediterranean and in the Middle East.

His invincible aerial armada supported Montgomery in smashing the forces of Rommel in North Africa. The war has brought tragedy to his home: his wife was killed in a plane crash in Egypt; his eldest son lost his life while fighting off Hitler's raids over England. This accounts, somewhat, for his haggard appearance. When Tedder is not fighting he likes to paint pictures of the rugged hills of his native Scotland.

The keen-eyed, strong-featured man beside him is sixty-one-year-old Admiral Sir Bertram H. Ramsey, commanding the combined naval forces under General Eisenhower. Son of a general, married to a colonel's daughter, his life has been devoted to the navy since he was fifteen years old. The tremendous responsibility falls upon him to transport safely across the English Channel to the fortified coasts of Europe the huge armies engaged in the invasion. Known as "Dynamo" Ramsey, he brought about the miracle of Dunkirk, when he literally snatched from the jaws of death 335,000 British soldiers and brought them safely across the Channel back to England.

He commanded ships patrolling the English Channel in World War I when he was thirty-one years old. Later he was on duty in China. When Eisenhower made his landing in North Africa, it was Ramsey who helped plan the landings and shared in command of the great armada of warships. He also was with Eisenhower in the Mediterranean when Sicily and Italy were invaded. His invasion fleets undertake one of the most perilous tasks in history.

Salute the stern, strong face set with determination—Lieutenant General Carl A. Spaatz, known as "Tooey" Spaatz, commanding the American Strategic Air Forces on the Western European invasion. Born in Pennsylvania fifty-two years ago, he was at West Point with Eisenhower, graduating in 1914, one year before Ike. "Tooey" commanded the Northwestern African Air Force under Eisenhower, which became known as the Anglo-American "Spaatzwaffe" because of its two-to-one superiority over the Luftwaffe in Tunisia. His job is to cover the Allied Forces on the invasion.

Spaatz, an experienced warrior, made a notable record in World War I when as a pursuit pilot he won the Distinguished Service Cross for heroism in action. He was an intimate friend of Billy Mitchell and is one of the fathers of military aviation. While a major in 1929, he and Ira Eaker won distinction by breaking a world record—they kept the airplane "Question

Mark" in the air one hundred and fifty non-stop hours, for which they received the D.S.C.

At the outbreak of World War II, in 1939, Spaatz was called to Washington and made Assistant Executive Officer to General "Hap" Arnold, chief of the Air Forces. Intimate friends of "Tooey" Spaatz state that he is friendly, blunt, fearless, and predict that he will blast Hitler's fortresses until it breaks the heart of the Nazis.

The genial, smiling countenance we now look upon is a "devil on wings"—Major General James H. Doolittle, age forty-eight, born in California, in command of the United States Eighth Air Force. The first to raid Tokyo, he gained world fame. He was widely known as a racing pilot and stunt flier before we entered the war, also as an aeronautic engineer. He crossed the American continent in twenty-one hours in 1922 and won the D.F.C. For high-speed test flights, he won the Oak Leaf Cluster. He flew over the Andes with both legs in casts in 1926. First to fly "blind" in 1929, he won the coveted racing trophies. And in 1940 he was President of the Institute of Aeronautical Sciences.

Jimmy, when only three years old, went with his father to the Klondike goldrush in Alaska; here he became the "schoolboy pugilist of Nome." When World War I broke out, he was a college senior in California and joined the Army as a flying cadet.

With the outbreak of World War II, he entered the struggle as a major and in two years became a brigadier general. Under Eisenhower in Africa, he organized and led the Twelfth Air Force, whose exploits are almost legendary. They blasted the way for the ground forces with their raids on Tunisia, Sicily, Italy, and were the first to bomb Rome.

His courage and daring set an example for the fliers who work with him. Their affection for Jimmy is like that of a brother. One of them so describes him: "Jimmy is one of the grandest fellows on earth. He is always friendly and courteous. He is tough only when absolutely necessary and he has got a heart of gold, but he gets what he goes after."

Now meet the man who says, "I'm from Missouri, show me!" Lieutenant-General Omar N. Bradley, fifty-one years old, leading the American ground forces under Eisenhower. This "Missouri mule" in determination is one of Ike's old friends and classmates at West Point. He came out of Missouri at the same time that Ike came out of Kansas, and they graduated together from the United States Military Academy in 1915. Tall, lanky, he was a star athlete at West Point.

He, too, had a long road to travel and had done duty at thirty-three Army posts when the United States entered World War II. While Ike got to the Philippines, Omar got to Hawaii. An accomplished master of ground warfare and infantry tactics, he was Eisenhower's field aide in North Africa and then commander of the American Second Corps. Bradley and his men captured Bizerte, which was the key that unlocked the gates to the conquest of Tunisia. It was to this Missourian that 25,000 Nazi troops unconditionally surrendered.

A quiet thinker with terrific driving power, he is also a family man. His wife and daughter say that he never forgets to send them flowers on Easter and Mother's Day. They state that he has another habit: he reads *Ivanhoe* at least once every year. He also is a fisherman and hunter, skeet-shooter, and plays golf. Bradley admits that he has but one ambition: "To lead my soldiers straight to Berlin."

We need no introduction to the wiry little man, wearing a beret jauntily on his head. He is "Monty," General Sir Bernard L. Montgomery, loved by every man who ever fought under him. He commands the British Invasion Armies under Eisenhower. "Monty of El Alamein" is fifty-six years old, a minister's son. His military fame was established when, in command of the

British Eighth Army, he outfoxed Rommel and chased him with his Afrika Korps across the North African deserts, 1400 miles, from Egypt to Italy.

"Monty" fought in World War I when he was twenty-one years old and won the D.S.O.; he has seen service on the Rhine, in Italy, Palestine, England, and Ireland. At the outbreak of World War II he was in command of a British division in France, led his men through the hell of Dunkirk and became commander of the epic Eighth Army in 1942.

This genial, two-fisted warrior is deeply religious and can be found between battles reading his Bible. He is a widower, devoting his life to his country. His men describe him as, "a Spartan leader who knows no fear. The toughest man you ever saw in a fight, but devoted to his men. We all love 'Monty'; he's got the spirit of the old crusaders. He's a military wizard and we'd follow him into hellfire."

The next man we meet looks like the executive of a great corporation, the banker-business man—lawyer type, Sir Trafford L. Leigh-Mallory, fifty-five years old, Commander in Chief of the Allied Air Forces. He, like "Monty," is the son of a clergyman. When World War I broke out he was a student at Cambridge, entered his country's service and quickly won a D.S.O. He gave up the study of law to join and help build the British Air Force and won his way to Air Chief Marshal.

Known as a "brains officer," he carefully organizes his invasion plans as if they were law cases. Thoroughness, scientific calculation, careful planning and then "attack" are his watchwords. These qualities made him an instructor at various army colleges. He served as an air officer in Iraq and later commanded RAF fighter groups. He helped organize the Polish Air Force in England, and is considered a genius in the coordination of air power with ground forces. His legalistic ability is used in ascertaining all advanced data before he sends his men out on raids.

The ceaseless air invasions over Europe, preceding the land invasions, were directed by Sir Trafford. He gained mastery of the air over the Luftwaffe and struck deadly blows in preparation for the Second Front.

The last man we meet on Eisenhower's "Invasion Team" is a typical Englishman in appearance, Sir Arthur T. Harris, fifty-two years old, father of four children, and known as "Ginger" Harris. He commands the British Strategic Air Forces. While he serves under Air Chief Marshal Leigh-Mallory, as does General Spaatz, his job is the destruction of Hitler's war-production centers. The bombing raids under Harris testify to his tenacity. He first took charge of the RAF Bomber Command in March, 1942, and began to blast more than fifty German key cities, crippling the power of the Nazis. The gigantic raids, day and night, have terrified the German populace.

This is "Ginger's" second war. He first saw action in World War I with the Royal Flying Corps. After the end of that conflict, he went to the Northwestern Frontier of India to pacify belligerent tribes. Serving later in Iraq and the Middle East, he returned to London to become Air Minister.

Men under Harris say, "He may look like an English shopkeeper, but when he gets into action he is a British lion. Some people call him 'bloody,' but we find him one of the most human men in the world if you are doing your job. He demands results and gives you credit for them. He's got no use for a second-rater."

What "Ginger" Harris has accomplished in blasting the road for the Second Front proves him to be not only a British lion, roaring over the Axis strongholds, but also an English bulldog tearing at the seat of the pants of Hitler.

We have now met General Eisenhower's "Invasion Team." Under these eight men are great organizations of fighting men—battlefront generals, admirals of fleets, leaders of the air forces in action. And under these are the mighty forces on the invasion of Europe—millions of men offering their lives to human freedom—the soldiers on the ground, the men fighting in the skies and on the seas.

The full power of the Allied Forces is a well-kept secret. Behind them is Eisenhower, with the greatest headquarters staff ever assembled, numbering thousands of officers who plan strategy and conduct the organization which is the "brains" of modern warfare.

The air battles and bombing raids over Europe developed into the most gigantic war in the air the world has ever known. Relentless assaults brought ruin to Nazi strongholds. Thousands of planes thundered with titanic might over the invasion routes from dawn to dusk, followed from dusk to dawn by never-ending armadas of bombers, pouring terror and destruction on vital targets.

Hitler, who had brought this inferno upon himself by his own wanton bombings of London and the capitals of Europe during his first blitzkriegs, whined and whimpered when he witnessed the ruins of his own fatherland. He was getting the answer to what he, himself, started; the inexorable result of his own conduct. The man who had proudly boasted, "Yes, we are barbarians," hypocritically raved against aerial warfare when he was on the receiving end of retributive justice.

The headlines in the American press told the story: "Half Million Fire Bombs Rake Nazis . . . Allied Bombers Rip Five Countries . . . Bombers Smash Reich . . . Continuous Air Blitz Lays Germany in Ruins . . . 3,000 Planes Blast Hitler's Strongholds . . . 65,000 Tons of Bombs Dropped on Europe in Ten Days . . . Raids Stagger Nazis . . . Luftwaffe Blasted from the Skies . . . Liberation Day Not Far Away."

Huge aerial armadas of more than three thousand bombers and fighting planes reigned death and devastation day and night over Germany and the three thousand miles of heavily fortified coastline from France to Norway. Eisenhower blasted the roads for his Second Front invasion of Europe.

As hours and days passed, with ceaseless bombing rising to a crescendo in its terrifying might, the "invasion jitters" seized Europe. Germans fled in terror from their homes. Their largest cities were laid in ruins. The Allies had won mastery of the air.

Huge Nazi armies were rushed to the fortified coast and stood behind their embattlements, waiting for Eisenhower. The people of France, Belgium, Holland, Denmark, Norway, with their underground leaders ready for uprisings, counted the hours, waiting for liberation.

Back in America one hundred and thirty million home folk were anxiously waiting for the news from the Second Front. The whole world was under severest tension. Our American boys in Ike's mighty army in England strained under the leash. Huge British and American fleets waited to convoy them across the channel, to meet Hitler's armies in decisive combat.

Zero hour was approaching. "It is now about five minutes to twelve o'clock," the announcement came from Allied Head-quarters. General Eisenhower inspected his stupendous forces and issued the final warnings. He was ready, waiting only for the psychological moment to strike.

"I have complete confidence in the final result," he said. "It will be a hard and bloody struggle, but victory will eventually be ours. The power of the United Nations under the flag of freedom shall triumph."

The mightiest struggle in the world's history was hanging in the balance.

NEMCO 293